Multiculturalism and Integration
A Harmonious Relationship

Multiculturalism and Integration
A Harmonious Relationship

Edited by the late Professor Michael Clyne and Dr James Jupp,
for the Academy of the Social Sciences in Australia.

ANU
THE AUSTRALIAN NATIONAL UNIVERSITY

E PRESS

ANU

E PRESS

Published by ANU E Press
The Australian National University
Canberra ACT 0200, Australia
Email: anuepress@anu.edu.au
This title is also available online at: http://epress.anu.edu.au

National Library of Australia
Cataloguing-in-Publication entry

Author: Michael Clyne and Dr James Jupp

Title: Multiculturalism and integration : a harmonious relationship / edited by
               Michael Clyne and James Jupp, for the Academy of the Social Sciences in
               Australia.

ISBN: 9781921862144 (pbk.) 9781921862151 (eBook)

Notes: Includes bibliographical references and index.

Subjects: Multiculturalism--Australia.

Other Authors/Contributors:
               Clyne, Michael, 1939-2010.
               Jupp, James, 1932-
               Academy of the Social Sciences in Australia.

Dewey Number: 305.8

Cover design and layout by ANU E Press

Contents

Contributors

Emeritus Professor Reg Appleyard AM, FASSA, Senior Research Fellow in Economic History, University of Western Australia.

(The Late) Professor Michael Clyne AM, FASSA, FAHA was a Professorial Fellow in the Research Unit for Multilingualism at the University of Melbourne. Professor Clyne died during 2010 after his work on this book was completed. The book was largely his idea and it is dedicated to him as an outstanding and internationally renowned scholar.

Professor Graeme Hugo, FASSA, ARC Australian Professorial Fellow, Professor of Geography, University of Adelaide.

Dr Christine Inglis, Honorary Associate Professor and Director of the Multicultural and Migration Research Centre, University of Sydney.

Dr James Jupp AM, FASSA, Centre for Immigration and Multicultural Studies, Australian National University.

Dr Siew-Ean Khoo, Senior Fellow, Australian Demographic and Social Research Institute, Australian National University.

Professor Kim Kirsner FASSA, Centre for Experimental and Regenerative Neuroscience, University of Western Australia.

Dr Geoffrey Levey, Senior Lecturer in Politics, University of New South Wales.

Professor Andrew Markus FASSA, Director of the Australian Centre for the Study of Jewish Civilisation, Monash University.

Acknowledgements

This volume is dedicated to the memory of three distinguished pioneers in the study of ethnic diversity in Australia:

Professor *Michael Clyne* (1939 – 2010) (Monash University)

Professor *Jerzy Zubrzycki* (1920 – 2009) (Australian National University)

Dr *Charles Price* (1920 – 2009) (Australian National University)

And to the founder of Australian demographic studies:

Professor *Mick Borrie* OBE, CBE (1913 – 2000) (Australian National University).

This research was funded by the Australian Research Council through the Learned Academies Special Projects scheme (LASP).

Abstract

Multiculturalism is a public policy adopted by all Australian governments, with varying enthusiasm, since 1978. It has always been controversial and is currently facing new challenges, especially in the growth of a Muslim community in Australia. However, it has been defined and refined over more than thirty years as a method of settling a wide variety of immigrants from non-English speaking backgrounds and has been relatively successful.

Multiculturalism has always been seen as a function of the Commonwealth and has not concerned itself with Indigenous affairs. It has normally been seen as a concern of the Immigration Department and has been less interested in second and subsequent generations of immigrant parentage, who now form a substantial part of the population. Together with the overseas-born, they constitute 40 per cent of the population, although a substantial number are of English-speaking descent.

This study draws on a variety of academic disciplines and results from an ARC Learned Academies grant awarded to the Academy of the Social Sciences in Australia, which has managed the business side. The disciplines represented here are Linguistics, Political Science, Sociology, Political Philosophy and Demography, rather than the central concern with economic factors which dominates official thinking.

The object is to inquire into precisely what is meant in practice by such terms as multiculturalism, integration, national identity and assimilation. The focus is not simply on the migrant generation in its early years but on long-standing social attributes such as language and religion. Academic studies of the long-term impacts of a diverse migration policy have been neglected in Australia compared with the situation in Europe and North America. While this may be due to the less acute problems here, it remains true that much more needs to be done to illuminate the ongoing issues. This work is intended to start a debate within the formal disciplines but also to suggest directions and issues which have so far been inadequately surveyed by academics and policy makers. To this end a group of academics known to each other for some time has come together to discuss the importance and impact of their disciplines on this important area of public concern.

JJ

MGC

Introduction

James Jupp and Michael Clyne

It is often argued that Australian multiculturalism as a public policy has never been explained. This is quite untrue, but it remains true that changes of emphasis between governments of different persuasions have created a confusing impression. Different usages of the term in various European and North American democracies have added to this confusion. However, Australia has good claims, along with Canada, of having developed and implemented a coherent set of policies over a period of almost forty years. A range of public and private institutions has taken part in this process. What is still lacking is a widespread understanding of the ethnic, cultural and linguistic changes which have occurred in Australia during this period. Partly this reflects the fact that multicultural interactions are largely confined to metropolitan areas (in which the majority of Australians live), a few provincial cities, and irrigation and mining districts. They have only marginally impacted on the provincial and rural districts on which so much of the 'myths' of Australia continue to rest. They have also been resisted by many established politicians, bureaucrats, academics and business leaders who still conceptualise Australia as an homogenous and uniform society, as it largely was in the era in which they grew up.

A diverse world

Multiculturalism is a term which has been used and disputed for four decades in various democracies in Europe, North America and Australasia. It refers essentially to political systems based on liberal democratic principles. There have been many other systems in many parts of the world which recognize ethnic variety – the Russian Federation, India and former Yugoslavia being examples. However these have usually dealt with ethnic variety by federation, where each ethnic community has its own political institutions and geographical boundaries. Multiculturalism as practised in Australia, Canada or Sweden, is essentially intended for mixed populations created by international migration. These are typically found in major cities living together but having different origins, religions, languages and other aspects of distinct cultures.

The typical multicultural situation is one where there is a dominant ethnicity, usually based on early settlers, although these might also contain Indigenous or earlier communities such as Roma, Welsh, Aborigines or Maori. The dominant ethnicity has typically seen itself as a 'founding nation' even when others have been established in the modern territory for much longer but in smaller numbers. This is obviously the situation in Australia, where 'Europeans' (in effect from the British Isles) have only formed the majority since the 1830s, or over most of North America below the Arctic Circle.

The 'founding nation' through its control of the instruments of government, education and the economy, has historically defined the characteristics of the nation as a whole, including its language, its religion, its 'way of life' and its sense of superiority. However mass immigration by others may well challenge this status or, alternatively, be expected to conform to its values, institutions and practices. In liberal democracies, of course, the domination of the 'founding nation' is justified in terms of voting majorities. These determine the social institutions, practices and attitudes. Others may be excluded from the franchise, as were many Afro-Americans in the southern US, Jews in Nazi Germany or Africans in South Africa.

The need for multiculturalism was not strongly felt in most liberal democracies until after the Second World War. Prior to that, and especially after the First World War, empires began to break up into component parts based on the Wilsonian notion of self-determination. This was enshrined in the principles of the League of Nations and, after 1945, the United Nations. The result to date has been the creation of two hundred sovereign states, each one with the legal and constitutional status of all other nation states. Yet even these units are not ethnically uniform. On the contrary, there are very few states which do not contain ethnic variety within them. As population migration continues despite borders and legal obstacles, this variety also increases. States which broke away from others in the past now face the danger of lesser ethnic groups breaking away from them. The most obvious recent case has been in Yugoslavia. The alternative to such a breakdown has been to devolve power to ethnic groups on a quasi-federal basis. In recent years once unitary states such as the United Kingdom and Spain have chosen this solution. India is the largest state in the world to devolve authority on a linguistic basis, creating new states where there is a political demand for them. It works well except in the state of Kashmir, where the Muslim religion is more important than language.

Well-established states do not favour total defection and may fight to prevent it, as the UK has done in Northern Ireland. States which are ethnically diverse but do not have distinct concentrations of minorities on which a viable unit could be built, may turn to multiculturalism as a solution. But this is not universal and many liberal democracies, including the United States, Germany, France and Denmark, have specifically rejected this approach, even while adopting some of its practices. In Australia there are no distinctive population concentrations large and developed enough to form the base of a viable state. All component states and territories of the Commonwealth have a mixed population with Anglo-Australians dominant. In the United States and Canada there are states which are ethnically distinct. That is not the basis on which their original boundaries were drawn, except for the newly created Nunavut area of northern Canada. Indigenous North Americans (First Nations) all have claims on territories and exercise some authority within them. But apart from Canada these do not constitute self-government.

The multicultural political solution to ethnic diversity is, then, not universal. But some aspects of multiculturalism are found in many societies which have not adopted it as a national policy; in particular, many cities with large immigrant populations have adopted welfare services, interpreting systems, school curricula, grants to organisations and religions, and festivals. Looking at the policies of cities and provinces in Germany, France or the United States will show close resemblances to those in Australia, Sweden, Canada or Britain. Indeed, while Britain is not officially multicultural at the national level, its local government authorities are legally obliged to foster policies and practices that cater for their multi-ethnic populations. The opposite trend may also be true, where second rank authorities impose restrictions, as with the English-only policy adopted by many American States. In Switzerland, a multicultural society with power largely devolved to cantons, the building of minarets at mosques was forbidden by a majority referendum, and many other issues are also decided this way. Apart from local variety, multiculturalism is usually sustained by legal provisions protecting minorities from discrimination. These are endorsed in detail by the European Union and the government of the United States, mainly in response to the civil rights campaign of the 1960s.

While Australia insists on preserving English as its only official language and rigorously subscribes to the equal treatment of all religions (s.116 of the Constitution) this is no longer very common in the rest of the world. Most nation states recognise or give official status to a variety of languages, with the largest choice being in India and South Africa. Others giving multiple official choices include the majority of recently colonial societies, with English and French a common official or second language throughout Africa, English in the Pacific and Russian in central Asia. Second languages, usually on a regional basis, are recognised legally in the United Kingdom, Switzerland, Finland, Belgium, Spain, Russia, Canada, Peru, Bolivia, Sri Lanka, New Zealand, Singapore and Malaysia, among others. The outstanding exceptions, the United States, Australia, Germany, France, Greece, Turkey and Pakistan, for example, are by no means monolingual. Australian public policy has funded English language classes for immigrants since 1947, has a state owned multilingual broadcasting system and issues public notices in sixteen languages. Even in the United States, in response to court rulings, voting information is published in Chinese and other languages where there is a significant number of voters using a language other than English.

State support for religion is also quite common. It ranges from the official Protestant churches of England, Scotland, Germany and the Scandinavian states, to public funding for religious schools. This has reached a level of catering for one third of pupils in Australia and is not limited to Christian schools, as in many other states.

What is multiculturalism?

The whole world is multicultural and many states – democratic or authoritarian– make some provision for cultural variety and the needs of minorities. Despite this, multiculturalism under that name has been highly controversial and is currently said to be in retreat, even where it has been officially adopted. In Australia national public policy has moved away from 'multiculturalism' to 'integration' while most State and Territory governments continue their programmes unchanged. In Europe there has been a positive 'backlash'[1]. These changes have been reflected in party politics in most liberal democracies.

Multiculturalism as an ideology and a public policy has most enthusiastically been copied by the liberal and social democratic side of party politics – the Canadian Liberals, the Swedish and other Scandinavian social democrats, British Labour, the Australian and New Zealand labour parties, and the Greens. Most of these have recently suffered electoral defeats or a reduction in their support and cohesion. In Europe democratic socialist governments are now confined to Norway, Spain, Portugal and Greece. In Australia, New Zealand, Switzerland, France, Denmark, the Netherlands, Britain and even Sweden, conservative parties critical of multiculturalism have recently been victorious. Even more importantly, extreme parties have made considerable progress although they have usually been excluded from government. This has not been the case in Australia, where One Nation reached its peak in the 1990s and then disappeared. However some of its attitudes were taken over by the Liberal-National Coalition under John Howard (1996-2007).

Partisan and electoral support for multiculturalism has weakened in most liberal democracies and has always been contested in the United States. It has never been officially endorsed in Germany or France. There are several reasons for this resistance:

- the collision between liberal democracy and Islamic fundamentalism as evidenced by terrorist attacks in various cities in the new century;

---

1   Vertovec, S and Wessendorf, S (eds) (2010). *The Multiculturalism Backlash*, Routledge, London.

- resistance to continuing, increasing and frequently uncontrolled immigration from poorer societies, especially from Africa, the Middle East, South Asia and Latin America;
- economic and social problems which social democracy has failed to solve;
- poverty and social dislocation in some concentrations of immigrants and refugees;
- a perception that the distinct civilisations and cultures built on a European basis are losing their pre-eminence;
- rapidly changing social structures and belief systems which creates anxiety.

The significance of these varies from time to time and place to place. Religious objections to Islam are less powerful in secular societies, including Australia, than in the United States where there are strong movements to reassert the 'Judeo-Christian' inheritance. Fears of terrorism are probably less significant where there has been none within the society, as in Australia, New Zealand, Switzerland or Scandinavia. Extreme anti-immigrant parties vary in strength considerably and this is not related to economic conditions; the concept of national culture may be more rigorously adhered to in some societies (such as Denmark or France) than in others (such as Australia or other immigrant societies). However judgement of some of these influences is often subjective and influenced by partisan loyalties. Eruptions of anti-immigrant feeling and attacks on multiculturalism are not always predictable. The sudden rise and equally rapid fall of One Nation in Australia is but one example. The rapid shift to extreme positions in the Netherlands, prompted by individual acts of terror, was even more spectacular and longer lasting.

What, then, is the multiculturalism which has provoked such opposition and led to such major political shifts? The classic Australian definition is contained in the Galbally report of 1978 (*Migrant Services and Programs*). While this was presented to the Prime Minister, Australian multiculturalism has always been concerned with immigrants and has remained within the Immigration portfolio for most of the past thirty years. This is not the case in Canada, where policy rests with the Department of Canadian Heritage, or in most other states which have adopted the term. In Europe it is common for immigration to be allocated to the Department of Justice (or equivalent). In Britain immigration and multiculturalism were the responsibility of the Home Office through the Commission for Racial Equality, but were later transferred to the Local Government Department as the Commission for Integration and Cohesion.

The Australian definition of 1978 stressed the delivery of services to non-English-speaking background migrants (NESB):

- migrants have the right to maintain their culture and racial identity... provided that ethnic identity is not stressed at the expense of society at large;
- the development of a multicultural society will benefit all Australians;
- the most significant and appropriate bodies to be involved in the preservation and fostering of cultures are the ethnic organisations themselves.

Four guiding principles were laid down[2]:

1. all members of our society must have equal opportunity to realise their full potential and must have equal access to programs and services;

2. every person should be able to maintain his or her culture without prejudice or disadvantage

3. needs of migrants should, in general be met by programs and services available to the whole community but special services and programs are necessary at present;

4. services and programs should be designed and operated in full consultation with clients, and self-help should be encouraged as much as possible with a view to helping migrants to become self-reliant quickly.

The *Canadian Multiculturalism Act* of 1988[3] concentrated on four areas:

1. combating racism and discrimination;

2. ensuring that the Government of Canada represents the country's diverse population;

3. promoting shared citizenship –making sure that all Canadians feel part of Canada;

4. cross-cultural understanding.

These two classic definitions of multiculturalism start from different premises and move in different directions. Canada has been a bicultural (Anglophone/ Francophone) society for three centuries. Australia had just ended an immigration policy (White Australia) which preserved its monocultural character. Most of its NESB migrants had come as Displaced Persons in need of welfare and language services. The new intake from southern Europe was starting to organise and demand greater services from a more sympathetic state. While this was also happening in Canada, the long-term perspective there was that cultural differences would endure. The Australian expectation was that they

---

2   Galbally, F (chair) (1978). *Migrant Services and Programs*, AGPS, Canberra: 4.
3   *Annual Report on the Operation of the Canadian Multiculturalism Act*; Ottawa, 2002 Cat no. Ci95-1/2002.

would fade but should be endorsed while they lasted. Both agreed that their societies were moving from a monocultural (Australia) or bicultural (Canada) form to a multicultural one. At this pioneering stage Canadians were more willing to accept this than were many Australians. But in both societies political leadership on these issues was bipartisan. Neither had much experience with non-Europeans or with non-Christians until the 1980s.

Aims and content of the volume

Against this background, this volume represents the first substantial results of an interdisciplinary project conducted by the Academy of the Social Sciences in Australia, with funding from the Australian Research Council under its learned Academies Special Projects scheme (LASP)[4]. The Academy took a leading role in the early days of multicultural studies in the 1970s, but this has not been evenly developed by the appropriate academic disciplines. This project, entitled *Multiculturalism and Integration – a Harmonious Relationship*, brings together scholars from the disciplines of demography, geography, history, linguistics, political philosophy, political science, psychology and sociology. They are based at seven universities. It goes beyond the usual descriptive work on immigration to look at issues such as population distribution, language usage and adaptation, public attitudes, integration and incorporation and demographic change.

The background to the project is the current concern with social cohesion and national integration. In most Western democracies there has been an increase in academic work on terrorism, Islam, immigration and refugees. Governments have often sponsored these studies, but they are fragmented and of varying quality. Cultural diversity was once a very important interdisciplinary area in Australia which contributed to policy formation and also to Australia's status in the field. This work has tended to be run down in recent years. The object of the Project is to encourage its revitalisation so that policy is informed by local research and collaborative work. Much research emanates from North America or the European Union and is not always relevant to Australia although it has been consulted. Most chapters are supported by substantial statistical and diagrammatic information. This study is concerned with Australian multiculturalism, rather than with the many alternative formulations and policies adopted in other democracies.

This volume is dedicated to the memory of two eminent scholars who were pioneers in the field of migrant and multicultural studies. They paved the way for understanding the kind of Australia we have today.

---

4   Project 10 LS0800003.

The ANU demographer Dr Charles Price, AM (1920-2009) is well known for studies of people of different backgrounds. These indicate both a more diverse and a more integrated society. He also wrote many studies on Germans, Italians, Greeks, Maltese, 'Slavs', Jews, Chinese and other groups at a time when such studies were rare. For several years in the 1950s and 1960s he published bibliographies and digests on Australian immigration, keeping a tab on the state of a small but growing field. He was often the first port of call for graduate students, new scholars and visiting academics, providing excellent advice and networking nationally and internationally.

The ANU sociologist and demographer, Professor Jerzy (George) Zubrzycki, AM (1920-2009), is often credited with being the 'father' of Australian multiculturalism. His rejection of the assimilationist and monocultural attitudes, which greeted those arriving in the post-war migration boom, reflected his own experiences as a new arrival from Poland by way of Britain and the London School of Economics. He embodied and demonstrated the importance of the link between research and policy. His role on the Australian Ethnic Affairs Council, the Immigration Advisory Council, and especially the National Multicultural Affairs Council was essential, as most of these were still dominated by native-born Australians. He was a central figure in the research-focused Australian Institute of Multicultural Affairs between 1979 and 1986 and served on the committee which developed the latest multicultural agenda in 1999.

Professor Zubrzycki saw Australia as offering the world a harmonious model for migrant integration, in which cultural and economic rights were respected. His published work included studies of Polish migration to Australia and elsewhere. His two classics were *Settlers of the Latrobe Valley* (1964) and *The Foreign Language Press in Australia* (1967, with Miriam Gilson).

Exact contemporaries, Price and Zubrzycki had quite different backgrounds. But both saw the multicultural future of Australia more clearly than many of their colleagues at the time. Both left a major legacy of academic work without parallel in the early post-war decades.

All the contributors focus on the complementarity of multiculturalism and integration in Australia. This needs to be done because of the attempts by the Howard government (1996-2007) to wipe the multicultural slate clean by substituting integration, as though it were opposite and superior. In practice the two go together. The debate centred on 'values' was a transparent attempt to isolate Muslims as 'unAustralian', which was both unfair and not sensible in terms of maintaining social harmony. Certainly Muslims have a longer road to travel than, say, Irish or Dutch migrants. James Jupp examines the religious aspect of multiculturalism, which has become increasingly important in the last decade.

Migrants become 'acculturated' in the sense of learning English (which many from Asia know already), by enjoying the delights of an affluent society, perhaps by calling their children Wayne and Kylie. But they speak their own language in the home, attend their own churches, mosques and temples, prefer soccer to rugby league or Australian rules, and keep an 'ethnic' kitchen. They can also maintain links with the original homeland much more easily than in the past, through frequent and relatively cheap flights and mobile phones. Many even maintain a resting place for visits to their home villages and relatives. In a major study of locations, Graeme Hugo sets the scene.

The book follows with an overview by James Jupp of Australian policies on assimilation, integration and multiculturalism. This opens the section devoted to political ideology and public attitudes.

Immigration and ethnic relationships are highly politicised and have led to major wars and revolutions over the past century. While these are unlikely in Australia, social tensions can arise which need amelioration, and individual problems need some assistance from public agencies. The Australian immigration system depends very heavily on selection by government agencies and on settlement through public intervention. Both of these centre on a distinct department of immigration. The whole process is political and determined by ideological views on the nature of the nation state. This is explored from the viewpoint of political philosophy by Geoffrey Brahm Levey.

The complex and sometimes contradictory world of public opinion, which is so important in a democracy, is analysed by Andrew Markus, who has already completed a major opinion study in Melbourne on which his analysis is based. His study of social cohesion among people of differing ethnic origins in suburbs with different demographic backgrounds is rare among Australian social scientists.

The relationship between multiculturalism and integration is followed through from the viewpoints of demography, language and religion. Siew-ean Khoo looks at the often neglected area of intermarriage and the second generation. It is usually assumed that 'problems' arise in the migrant generation or because of marriage within an ethnic or religious community. Her studies show that, as elsewhere, the processes of family building frequently involve the crossing of cultural boundaries. Nor is it self-evident that this creates serious tensions in the resulting children.

Christine Inglis examines the problems and successes of youth in a multicultural world, most of whom have a strong sense of Australian identity but may not be fully accepted by their peers.

Kim Kirsner offers a model for testing the relationship between fluency in language and integration. So many 'New Australians' in the post-war period only acquired a limited proficiency in English. While the state provided English teaching from 1947, this did not solve the problem because of shortage of resources or limited teaching skills. It was not that migrants did not want to learn, as critics often claimed, but that they could not do so and make a living at the same time.

Michael Clyne focuses on the relationship between English and migrant language in Australia. This includes integration of English elements into migrant languages, the differential shift from those languages to English, the geographical distribution of these languages, bilingualism and English proficiency and the changing fate of language policy in Australia.

Reg Appleyard draws on his four-decades-long longitudinal study of a group of imported brides from Greece and their descendants, describing how the families have participated both in multiculturalism and integration. The women arrived in Australia as part of an official plan to avoid the 'un-Australian' practice of proxy brides. Young Greek women were brought to Australia so they could marry single Greek men but this, of course, created families dedicated to maintaining Greek culture – one of the many contradictions in the official attempts to mould others to Australian ways. In their own time and in their own way, these families adopted those aspects of the affluent suburban life which suited them. Links with Greece and the Greek community are maintained, although the narrow village-based clubs have declined. Very high numbers of the children proceed to university, despite the rural and often illiterate backgrounds of their recent ancestors – integrated but not assimilated in the crude sense so popular in the 1950s.

Multicultural policy has passed through several stages, corresponding to differing waves of migration The earliest emphasis was on language in three senses – learning English, maintaining the community language and access to translating and interpreting. Migrants were classified into Non-English-Speaking Background (NESB) and Main English Speakers (MES), until the new division of Culturally and Linguistically Diverse (CALD) was coined by the Howard government in 1996 and slowly adopted. With the final ending of the White Australia Policy in 1973, migrants could no longer aim at being 'like everybody else' as they were urged to do throughout the 1950s and 1960s. Not only did they not look like everybody else, but they had different religions, (including different varieties of Christianity) spoke non-European languages and came from societies which were often much poorer and oppressive than Australia.

Prejudice was revealed by One Nation in 1996, and the Cronulla rioters in 2005 when thousands waving Australian flags attacked a small number of people 'of Middle Eastern Appearance' at a Sydney beach. Despite this, 'CALD' newcomers fitted comfortably into the structures, practices and attitudes created by past generations. They joined actively in multicultural organisations as well as enjoying suburban affluence, just like their European predecessors. The monument to multiculturalism is simply that much of this would have been much more difficult if the changes of the 1970s and 1980s had not happened, or had been repudiated by national and state governments.

The world is multicultural and so are the great majority of 'nation states' that make up the international community. As each state differs in some respects from others this naturally means that multicultural policies and practices will differ. Even with considerable interchange of ideas within the English-speaking world there is no identical model of multiculturalism. In some respects the European social democracies such as Sweden or The Netherlands have been closer in policy terms than the United States. The factors which have recently impacted on harmonious social relations are particularly varied. They include controlled immigration programmes (Australia, Canada, New Zealand); regionally based minorities (Canada, Spain, Switzerland); religious variety (Germany, Switzerland, Netherlands); unplanned migrant arrivals (United States, Italy, United Kingdom); large scale Islamic migration (France, Germany) and so on. Each set of circumstances creates different responses.

Yet there are some similarities that are relevant to Australia. These include a growing Muslim population; the unplanned arrival of refugees; the existence of socially disadvantaged Indigenous peoples; politically focused criticism of changing populations; and a concept of the nation state which privileges some cultural groups and individuals above others. Even quite small changes in the 'ethnic balance' may provoke strong reactions in a society which has been sheltered from foreign occupation or warfare on its own territory and authoritarian or revolutionary politics.

In this context multiculturalism is a manifestation of liberal democracy based on mutual tolerance and co-operation. It does not validate cultural attitudes which are incompatible with these objectives but neither does it glorify Australian culture above all others. Indeed it argues that Australian culture is in a constant state of flux, as befits a society built on successive waves of immigration. Within those changes it has always been liberal-democratic and based on elected responsible government. This implies a high degree of freedom of expression, belief, worship and political competition.

Chapter 1: Changing Spatial Patterns of Immigrant Settlement

Graeme Hugo

Introduction

While the major lineaments of post-war immigrant settlement remain, there have been some small, but nevertheless significant, changes in settlement patterns since 2001. While there are a number of causes of these shifts, undoubtedly one has been the paradigmatic shift which has occurred in Australian immigration policy since the mid 1990s[1]. It has involved a number of elements. Since 1996 Australia has had an increasing substantial skilled temporary labour migration program as well as large student and working holiday-maker migration programs[2]. There has been an increase in the proportion of settlers each year who are 'onshore' migrants who are already present in Australia as temporary residents but successfully apply for permanent residence. In 2007-08 onshore migrants made up 27.5 per cent of permanent additions to the population through migration[3]. The proportion of permanent arrivals in the skilled entry group has increased from 33.3 per cent in 2000-01 to 43.8 per cent in 2007-08. The introduction of the State Specific and Regional Migration Scheme (SSRM) effectively creates two classes of immigrants – one that can settle anywhere and another that is limited (at least initially) in where they settle. Each of these developments has had implications for the distribution of migrants in Australia.

Some data considerations

Australia has some of the most comprehensive stock information relating to immigrants, largely because of the comprehensive set of questions asked at five-yearly census enumerations. The variables collected include:

- Country of birth

---

1   Hugo, G J (1999a). A New Paradigm of International Migration in Australia', *New Zealand Population Review*, 25, 1-2: 1-39.
2   Khoo, S E, Voigt-Graf, C, Hugo, G and McDonald, P (2003). 'Temporary Skilled Migration to Australia: The 457 Visa Sub-Class, *People and Place*, 11, 4: 27-40.
3   Department of Immigration and Citizenship (2008). *Population Flows: Immigration Aspects*.

- Country of birth of parents
- Ancestry
- Length of residence in Australia
- Aboriginality
- Religion
- Nationality
- Language spoken at home
- Ability to speak English.

This allows first- and second-generation immigrants to be identified and later generations to also be partially detected.

These census data are available for the full hierarchy of spatial units with the basic building block being the Collection District (CD), which, for the 2006 census, has an average of about 225 dwellings[4]. After 2011 the building block will be even smaller: the mesh block will have a minimum number of dwellings of between 20 and 50 except where a mesh block is deliberately designed to have a zero population. As a result it is possible to analyse the migrant populations of most formal and functional regions within Australia, although there is some difficulty in matching small areas across time. The Australian census is a complete count for all questions asked (other than for religion), which means that it is possible to identify the location of even relatively small immigrant groups.

A critical question, however, is who among the foreign-born present in Australia on the night of the population census actually get included in census immigrant data? Prior to the 1990s most of the foreign-born in Australia on census night would have been permanent settlers, but international population movement has subsequently undergone massive change. Non-permanent movement has increased in scale and complexity. Figure 1 shows how, since the 1990s, there has been an exponential increase in the number of temporary migrants arriving in Australia with the right to work as students, working holiday-makers and temporary business migrants on 457 visas. Non-settler migration has increased much more quickly than permanent migration as is evident in Table 1.

---

4   Australian Bureau of Statistics (2006). *Census Dictionary: Australia 2006(Reissue)*, Catalogue No. 2901.0, ABS, Canberra.

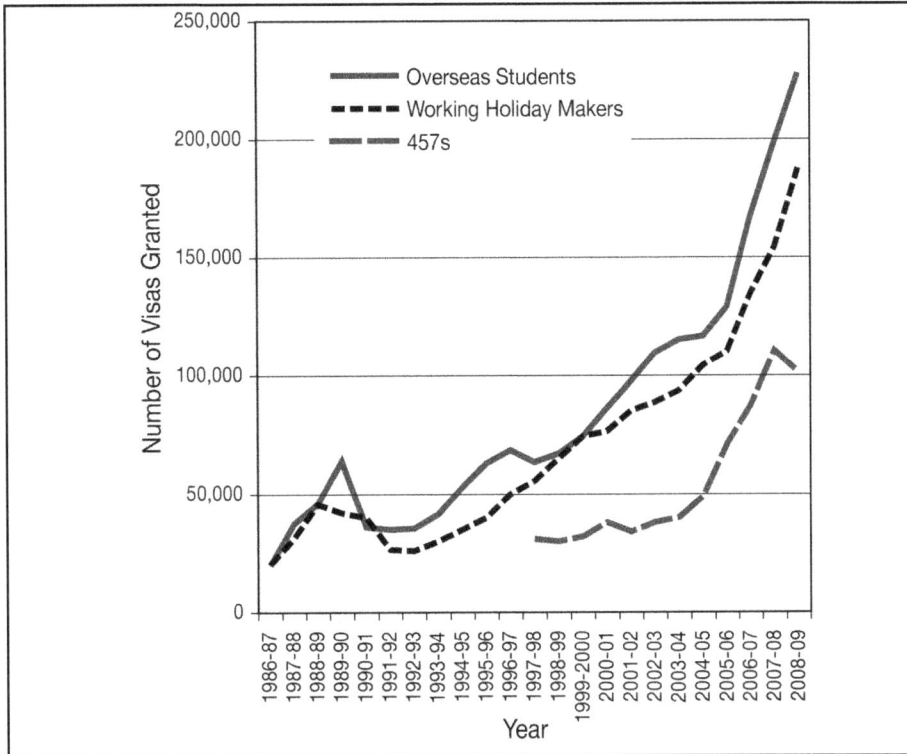

Figure 1 Australia: Temporary Migration, 1986-87 to 2008-09

Source: DIAC, *Population Flows: Immigration Aspects*[5]

To what extent are these people, who are in Australia on some form of temporary visa, included in the census? The Australian census seeks to identify 'visitors to Australia' in order to exclude them from the usually resident population and from the tabulations of key characteristics of the population like birthplace, ancestry etc. Question 8 in the census form asks 'Where does the person usually live?' in order to exclude persons who are usually resident in another country. Prior to the 1996 census, overseas visitors were included in standard census data tabulations, but subsequently they have been excluded. However, the definition of 'visitor' has changed. In the 1996 census, overseas visitors were those people who indicated they would be usually resident in Australia for less than six months. For the 2001 and 2006 censuses this has been increased to less than one year.

---

5   *Department of Immigration and Citizenship (2009a). 'Community Information Summary: Hong Kong-born Community'. http://www.immi.gov.au/media/publications/statistics/comm-summ/summary.htm.*

Table 1 Australia: Permanent, long and short term arrivals and departures, 1996-2001 and 2001-06

	1996-2001	2001-2006
Settler Arrivals	446,860	549,421
Permanent Departures	184,622	288,241
Net Permanent	262,238	261,180
LT Arrivals	1,005,218	1,463,394
LT Departures	754,467	894,799
Net Long Term	250,751	568,595
ST Arrivals	38,284,493	37,060,165
ST Departures	38,352,870	37,454,263
Net Short Term	-68,377	-394,098
Net Total	444,612	435,677

Note: ST Arrivals and Departures not available for 2001-02.

Source: DIAC unpublished data

Table 2 Overseas persons temporarily present in Australia on the night of the census

	Number
1996	139,594
2001	203,101
2006	206,358

Source: ABS

The number of visitors identified in the 1996, 2001 and 2006 census enumerations is shown in Table 2. These numbers differ quite significantly from estimates made by the Department of Immigration and Citizenship (DIAC) of the numbers of foreign citizens 'temporarily present' on 30 June of each year presented in Table 3, which are around three times greater than those identified as visitors by the census. With each new census the numbers of temporary residents who are captured in the census has increased. The distribution of temporary residents is quite different from that of permanent settlers.

Table 3 Australia: Number of persons temporarily present, 30 June 1999-2008

Year (30 June)	Number	Annual Percent Increase
2008	809,628	
2007	687,292	17.8
2006	630,513	14.5
2005	599,629	8.5
2004	590,566	1.7
2003	584,862	1.0
2002	555,569	5.0
2001	554,200	2.4
2000	513,900	8.0
1999	462,510	10.0

Source: DIAC, *Population Flows: Immigration Aspects*, various issues

The significance of place and space

Where people live is important. It exerts important influences on their social and economic lives. The characteristics of places which exert an influence on behaviour include[6]:

- The physical characteristics of the place.
- The characteristics of other people living in that place.
- The level and nature of service provision in that place.
- The place's relationship with other places, especially its accessibility to other places.

For some groups location can be an especially important factor influencing their behaviour. This is certainly the case for recently arrived migrants. Location can influence access to work opportunities and the ability to interact with people who speak the same language and have similar cultural and religious backgrounds. It will influence the extent they are able to draw on the social capital embodied in networks with fellow settlers from the same background, including those who have been in Australia longer who are able to cushion their adjustment to life in a new land. It is a significant factor influencing their access to goods and services, including those provided by different levels of government, which will also impinge on the speed and level of their adjustment.

Immigrants' ability to adjust to, and participate in, Australian housing and labour markets will be influenced by where they live. This influences the extent to which they mix on a day-to-day basis with second, third and later generation

---

6   Hugo, G J (2007). 'Space, Place, Population and Census Analysis in Australia'.*Australian Geographer*. 38, 3: 335.

Australians. It will have an impact on the extent of cultural and language maintenance they are able to achieve. It affects what schools their children can attend and the level of mixing they will have with non-immigrant children. The local community can be a crucial factor in the adjustment of new migrants to life in Australia, since it is the arena in which many of their day-to-day interactions take place.

Australian communities have differed greatly in the extent of their cultural diversity and the spatial patterning of diversity is changing. These changes are profoundly altering the nature of Australian places. In post-war Australia immigrant settlement has increasingly concentrated in Australia's large cities. Waves of new immigrants have reshaped suburbs, transforming their populations from being relatively Anglo-Celtic into diverse mixes of groups from Europe, the Middle East, Asia and more recently Africa. We are now also seeing such transformations outside of large cities.

In pre-war Australia, immigrants were a significant part of non-metropolitan populations, especially in areas of intensive agriculture like market gardening, sugar cane farming and irrigated agriculture[7]. Immigrants did not, however, settle in the extensive dry farming areas of the wheat-sheep belt or the pastoral interior. There was some settlement in mining and fishing communities and large regional industrial centres like Newcastle, Wollongong, Geelong and Whyalla. However, recent years have seen a small but significant settlement of immigrants in dry farming areas hitherto little influenced by immigrants.

Since net migration has contributed around a half of Australia's post-war population growth, where migrants have settled has had a substantial influence on the national population distribution[8]. That migrants do not settle in Australia in the same pattern as the existing population distribution has had a major impact on the national population distribution. Moreover, recent migrants are more mobile within the country than non-migrants, although there is a convergence with increases in their length of residence.

Changing patterns of immigrant settlement in Australia

Australia has a distinctive pattern of population distribution[9] characterised by:

- A high proportion of the population (88.0 per cent in 2006) living in urban areas.

---

7   Borrie, W D (1954). *Italians and Germans in Australia: A Study of Assimilation*, F W Cheshire, Melbourne.
8   Hugo, G J (2003). Changing Patterns of Population Distribution. In S-E Khoo and P McDonald (eds), *The Transformation of Australia's Population 1970-2030*, University of New South Wales Press, Sydney: 200-201.
9   *Ibid.*

- A strong coastal orientation with 85.3 per cent of the population living within 50km of the coast in 2006.

- A high level of population mobility with 16.8 per cent of Australians changing their permanent place of residence in 2006.

- A high proportion of the population (63.7 per cent in 2006) living in the capital cities of the states and territories.

- A concentration of the population in the south-eastern quarter of the continent.

Immigrant settlement during the post-war period has made an important contribution to this distinctive pattern.

A spatial shift has occurred in Australia's post-war population away from the south-eastern states to the northern and western parts of the country. In 1947 the states of New South Wales, Victoria, South Australia and Tasmania accounted for 78.4 per cent of the national population. By 2006 they had 67.9 per cent of the total. On the other hand, Queensland increased its share from 14.6 per cent to 19.7 per cent and Western Australia from 6.6 per cent to 9.9 per cent. This has been a function of structural change in the Australian economy in the last 30 years, with the south-eastern states being heavily reliant on manufacturing and suffering due to the loss of jobs in this sector.

While much of the shift in interstate distribution has been due to interstate population movements, it is also due to a propensity for immigrants to settle in particular states. Table 4 indicates that immigrants have settled disproportionately in New South Wales, Victoria and Western Australia. New South Wales shows an interesting pattern with the state accounting for 41.1 and 40.7 per cent of the nation's migrants who arrived in the last five years at the 1996 and 2001 censuses, compared with 33.2 and 32.6 per cent respectively of the national Australia-born population. However, at the 2006 census it had only 34.1 per cent of the recent migrants, revealing a sharp reduction in the proportion of new migrants settling in New South Wales. Victoria, on the other hand, has increased its share of new arrivals, as have Queensland, Western Australia and South Australia. The former is an interesting case. After a long period of getting less than its proportionate share of immigrants, it is now a significant magnet for migrants.

Table 4 Australian states and territories: Percentage distribution of the population by birthplace and overseas-born arriving in the last five years, 2001 and 2006

State/Territory	Australia-Born			Overseas-Born			Persons Arriving in Last 5 Yrs		
	1996	2001	2006	1996	2001	2006	1996	2001	2006
New South Wales	33.2	32.6	32.1	33.5	35.9	35.1	41.1	40.7	34.1
Victoria	24.0	24.0	24.4	26.6	26.3	25.9	24.2	23.6	26.1
Queensland	20.0	20.4	20.9	14.2	15.0	16.8	15.3	17.5	18.5
South Australia	8.2	8.1	8.0	7.7	7.2	6.8	4.5	4.1	5.7
Western Australia	8.9	9.1	9.1	12.2	12.6	11.8	11.6	11.3	12.5
Tasmania	3.0	2.8	2.8	1.2	1.1	1.4	0.8	0.7	0.9
Northern Territory	1.1	1.2	1.1	0.8	0.7	0.8	0.8	0.7	0.7
Australian Capital Territory	1.7	1.7	1.7	1.7	1.6	1.5	1.7	1.5	1.5
Total	100.0	100.0	100.0	100.0	100.0	100.0	100.0	100.0	100.0

Source: ABS, 2001 and 2006 censuses

The relative contributions of net international migration as well as net interstate migration and national increase to population change in the states and territories are shown in Table 5. In New South Wales, the largest state, there was a net international migration gain of almost 200,000, which accounted for 79.6 per cent of the state's population growth between 2001 and 2006. Moreover, the state experienced a significant net loss due to interstate migration – a longstanding pattern[10]. In the past this has been the pattern in Victoria as well, but a turnaround in the state's economy saw a small net interstate migration gain between 1996 and 2001, although there was a small net loss in 2001-06. Conversely Queensland's net international migration gain was not as large as the net gain by interstate migration. Clearly there are wide differences between the states in the significance of immigrant settlement and this is undergoing substantial change.

---

10 *Ibid.*

Table 5 Australian states and territories: Natural increase, net overseas migration, net interstate migration and total population growth, financial years, 2001-06

State/ Territory	Natural Increase		Net International Migration		Net Interstate Migration		Total Population Growth
	No.	% of Growth	No.	% of Growth	No	% of Growth	
New South Wales	191,089	79.0	192,586	79.6	-136,330	-56.3	241,965
Victoria	143,880	44.5	142,892	44.2	-2,197	-0.7	323,584
Queensland	132,050	28.5	129,944	28.1	164,362	35.5	462,600
South Australia	28,179	49.9	27,522	48.7	-12,639	-22.4	56,476
Western Australia	68,668	43.5	82,832	52.5	-1,399	-0.9	157,886
Tasmania	10,026	58.5	3,758	21.9	3,105	18.1	17,137
Northern Territory	13,862	107.4	3,475	26.9	-8,474	-65.7	12,906
Australian Capital Territory	13,531	90.8	2,412	16.2	-6,428	-43.1	14,908
Australia*	601,389	46.7	585,421	45.4	-	-	1,288,248

* Includes other territories.

Source: ABS, 2007

One of the characteristics of international migration to Australia has been variations in the spatial patterns of settlement of different birthplace groups. This is illustrated in Table 6 which indicates that in 2001 and 2006 the Language Other Than English (LOTE) origin immigrants are disproportionately represented in New South Wales and Victoria, which in 2006 had 73.8 per cent of the group compared with 56.5 per cent of the nation's Australia-born. On the other hand, Mainly English-Speaking (MES) origin settlers are under-represented with 46.2 per cent. This presents a stark contrast to Queensland which has a fifth of the Australia-born population but less than a tenth of the LOTE group and almost a quarter of the MES. Migration to both South and Western Australia is also strongly focused on groups coming from countries which are MES. Queensland now attracts more MES origin migrants than Victoria and about as many as New South Wales.

Table 6 Distribution of LOTE (Language Other Than English Spoken at Home) and MES overseas-born population between states and territories, 2001-2006

State/Territory	LOTE		MES	
	2001	2006	2001	2006
	%	%	%	%
New South Wales	41.9*	41.8*	28.4	27.1
Victoria	32.3*	32.0*	19.0	19.1
Queensland	8.9	9.6	21.8*	23.4*
South Australia	6.0	5.9	9.1*	8.7*
Western Australia	7.3	7.2	17.5*	17.8*
Tasmania	0.5	0.5	1.7	1.8
Northern Territory	1.6*	1.4*	0.9	0.7
Australian Capital Territory	1.5	1.5	1.6	1.5
Total	100.0	100.0	100.0	100.0
Total Number (million)	2.9	3.1	1.6	1.7

*Over-represented compared with Australia-born.

Source: ABS 2001 and 2006 censuses

Within states and territories the Australian Bureau of Statistics (ABS) divides settlements for census purposes into the following 'Section of State'[11] categories:

• Major urban (population clusters of 100,000 or more);

• Other urban (population clusters of 1,000 to 99,999);

• Bounded locality (200 to 999);

• Rural balance (remainder of state/territory); and

• Migratory.

---

11   Hugo, G J (2007). *op cit.*

Table 7 Distribution of Australia-born and overseas-born population between major urban, other urban and rural areas, 1947-2006

	Australia-born						Percent Change 1947-2006
	1947		1996		2006		
	No.	%	No.	%	No	%	
Major urban	3,390,591	49.7	7,627,197	57.7	8,579,875	61.0	153.0
Other urban	1,263,724	18.5	3,485,125	26.3	3,530,407	25.1	179.4
Rural	2,173,068	31.8	2,108,242	16.0	1,958,711	13.9	-9.9
Total	6,827,383	100.0	13,220,564	100.0	14,068,993	100.0	106.1
	Overseas-Born						Percent Change 1947-2006
	1947		1996		2006		
	No.	%	No.	%	No	%	
Major urban	453,368	61.8	3,126,260	80.0	3,654,920	82.8	706.2
Other urban	98,824	13.5	489,550	12.5	494,752	11.2	400.6
Rural	181,180	24.7	290,269	7.5	264,905	6.0	46.2
Total*	733,372	100.0	3,906,079	100.0	4,414,577	100.0	502.0

* Excludes people of no permanent residence.

Note: Overseas-born does not include Birthplace Not Stated.

Table 7 shows the distribution of the Australian- and overseas-born between sections of state over the post-war period. The dominant trend over the post-war period has been an increasing concentration of population in urban areas. However, the pattern has been most marked among the migrant population. While in 1947 only one in eight people living in Australia's major cities was overseas-born, by 2006 it was three out of every ten. The proportion of immigrants living in major cities increased from 61.8 to 82.8 per cent in 2006 while for the Australia-born it grew from 49.7 to 61 per cent. While there was a decline in the numbers of Australia-born living in rural areas there was a small increase in the overseas-born. In 1947, 31.8 per cent of Australians lived in rural areas but, in 2006, it was only 13.9 per cent, while for the overseas-born the population fell from 24.7 to 6 per cent.

This strong pattern of increasing urbanisation of the overseas-born population was especially evident for recently arrived migrants. Table 8 shows that the pattern of concentration in capital cities is especially strong for immigrants who arrive from LOTE origin countries. By 2001, 90.1 per cent of new arrivals settled in capital cities compared with 86.2 per cent of those who had been in Australia longer than five years. The pattern is present but less marked among those from MES countries with 77.0 per cent and 70.2 per cent respectively.

Table 8 Number and percentage of overseas-born persons resident in capital cities by origin and length of residence, 1986, 2001 and 2006

	1986				2001				2006			
	0-4 Years		5+ Years		0-4 Years		5+ Years		0-4 Years		5+ Years	
	No.	%	No.	%	No.	%	No.	%	No.	%	No.	%
MES Origin	142,722	76.9	890,809	73.2	145,936	77.0	936,796	70.2	173,293	74.2	943,568	69.4
LOTE Origin	240,864	88.6	1,245,254	83.8	307,781	90.1	1,762,488	86.2	416,389	88.8	1,857,957	86.8
Total Overseas-born	383,586	83.9	2,136,063	79.0	453,717	85.4	2,699,284	79.9	589,681	83.9	2,801,524	80.0

Source: ABS, 1986, 2001 and 2006 censuses

There were increases in the percentages of new arrivals settling in capital cities with each new post-war census until the 2006 enumeration. While 83.9 per cent of migrants settled in these cities, the proportion fell for the first time during the post war period. The change is relatively small but it may be significant since in Europe and North America the last decade has also seen some decentralisation of migrant settlement away from major centres[12].

At the 2006 census, 63.1 per cent of the Australia-born lived in major cities compared with 93.0 per cent of the LOTE and 76.4 per cent of the MES-born population. For recent arrivals of LOTE and MES migrants the proportions are 92.2 per cent and 83.3 per cent respectively compared with 93.3 per cent and 75.3 per cent of those who had stayed in Australia longer than five years. There is some evidence then of a slight lessening of the dominance of the capital cities in the initial settlement of migrants. Nevertheless, cities are still the dominant settlement choice of migrants. There are then two long established elements in Australian post-war immigrant settlement patterns:

1. Immigrants from MES countries, especially New Zealand and the United Kingdom, although more concentrated in major cities compared with the Australia-born, are more like the Australia-born in their settlement patterns than is the case for those from LOTE origin countries.

2. For both groups, especially the MES group, there is a strong tendency over time, with increasing length of residence in Australia, for settlement patterns to converge toward those of the Australia-born.

These patterns are evident when we examine the pattern of immigrant settlement according to the degree of remoteness/accessibility of the places where they settle. The ABS has adopted the following classification of localities in Australia according to their remoteness:

Highly Accessible Major Cities – Locations with relatively unrestricted accessibility to a wide range of goods and services and opportunities for social interaction.

Accessible Inner Regional Areas – Locations with some restrictions to accessibility of some goods, services and opportunities for social interaction.

Moderately Accessible Outer Regional Areas – Locations with significantly restricted accessibility of goods, services and opportunities for social interaction.

Remote Areas – Locations with very restricted accessibility of goods, services and opportunities for social interaction.

Very Remote Areas – Locationally disadvantaged – very little accessibility of goods, services and opportunities for social interaction.

---

12   Hugo, G J and Moren, R (2008). Immigrant Settlement in non-Metropolitan Areas of OECD Countries; Editorial Introduction, *Population, Space and Place*, 14, 6: 473-477.

Table 9 shows that it is only in the most accessible major urban areas that migrants are over-represented in the Australian population, with 84.8 per cent living in those areas compared with 63.2 per cent of the Australia-born. The proportion of the Australia-born in all other remoteness categories is more than twice that for migrants. However, longstanding migrants are more strongly represented in the two middle level accessibility settled agriculture categories than are recent arrivals. In more remote areas there is little difference between recent and longstanding migrants, although both have only a third the representation of the Australia-born. Table 10 shows that the degree of concentration in the most accessible areas is especially strong among immigrants from countries where languages other than English are dominant. In Australian major cities three out of every 10 residents is a migrant, almost two of them from a LOTE country. In the rest of the country it is close to only one in 10 residents who are migrants.

One way of showing the difference between different groups in their spatial distribution is to calculate the population centroid. This has been defined by Plane and Rogerson as:

> ... also called the mean centre, mean point, the centre of gravity, or sometimes the centre of population. Conceptually, if the mythological Atlas were to hold up the entire area for which the centre is being computed ... (in this case Australia) ... assuming that people were the only objects contributing to the weight ... the point where he would have to stand to balance the country would be the centroid[13].

Figure 2 shows the centroids at the 2006 census for particular subgroups of the Australian population. For the total population the centroid is located in central NSW near Cowra and in fact has changed little over the last century[14]. However, it will be noted that there are some interesting deviations for particular migrant groups:

- The overall centroid has moved northwest over time, indicating the shift of population away from New South Wales and Victoria toward Queensland and Western Australia.
- Centres of MES birthplace groups are located to the northwest, indicating the disproportionate concentration in Queensland and Western Australia.
- Centres of NES groups are located in the southeast reflecting the disproportionate concentration in Sydney and Melbourne.

---

13 Plane, D A and Rogerson, P A (1994). *The Geographical Analysis of Population: with Applications to Planning and Business*, John Wiley, New York: 31.

14 Hugo, G J (2004). *Australia's most recent immigrants*, Australian Census Analytic Program, Cat. No. 2053.0, Australian Bureau of Statistics, Canberra: 58.

Table 9 Remoteness area categories: Breakdown according to birthplace, 2006

	Australia-Born		Overseas-Born		Recent Migrants		Longstanding Migrants		Year of Arrival Not Stated		Total	
	No.	%	No.	%	No.	%	No.	%	No.	%	No.	%
Major Cities	8,889,384	63.2	3,734,914	84.8	622,144	88.5	2,946,814	84.2	175,287	82.6	12,624,298	68.3
Inner Regional	3,250,439	23.1	421,788	9.6	45,620	6.5	354,807	10.1	22,194	10.5	3,672,227	19.9
Outer Regional	1,536,366	10.9	199,394	4.5	24,398	3.5	163,999	4.7	11,475	5.4	1,735,760	9.4
Remote	237,673	1.7	28,332	0.6	5,156	0.7	21,634	0.6	1,644	0.8	266,005	1.4
Very Remote	130,992	0.9	9,636	0.2	1,698	0.2	7,344	0.2	631	0.3	140,628	0.8
Total *	14,071,676	100.0	4,404,546	100.0	702,695	100.0	3,500,507	100.0	212,153	100.0	18,476,222	100.0

Source: ABS CDATA 2006

Table 10 Remoteness area categories: Percentage of population born overseas, 2006

	Australia-born		Recent Migrants				Longstanding Migrants				Year of Arrival Not Stated				Total
			LOTE		MES		LOTE		MES		LOTE		MES		
	No.	%	No.	%	No.	%	No.	%	No.	%	No.	%	No.	%	No.
Major Cities	8,889,384	70.4	395,722	3.1	192,921	1.5	1,517,608	12.0	1,021,193	8.1	90,579	0.7	61,030	0.5	12,624,298
Inner Regional	3,250,439	88.5	19,564	0.5	23,251	0.6	65,747	1.8	222,411	6.1	4,420	0.1	13,098	0.4	3,672,227
Outer Regional	1,536,366	88.5	11,060	0.6	11,722	0.7	38,208	2.2	94,706	5.5	3,343	0.2	6,059	0.3	1,735,760
Remote	237,673	89.3	2,221	0.8	2,846	1.1	3,959	1.5	13,571	5.1	441	0.2	968	0.4	266,005
Very Remote	130,992	93.1	710	0.5	946	0.7	1,434	1.0	4,534	3.2	204	0.1	347	0.2	140,628
Total *	14,071,676	76.2	429,276	2.3	231,686	1.3	1,626,955	8.8	1,356,415	7.3	98,987	0.5	81,502	0.4	18,476,222

Source: ABS CDATA 2006

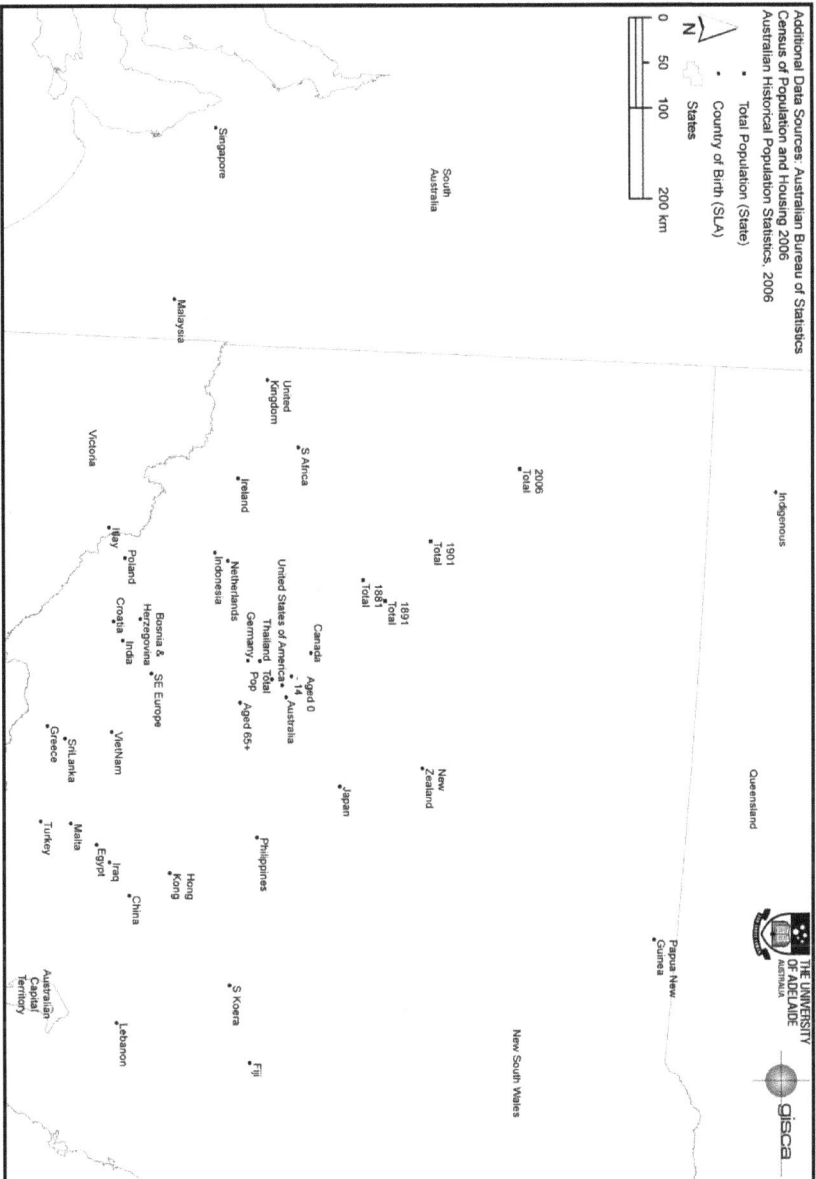

Figure 2 Australia: Population centroids of the Australian population and sub groups in 2006

Source: Calculated using 2006 Australian census data and Australian historical population statistics, 2006

Migrants in Australia's major cities

Not only have post-war migrants tended to settle in Australia's larger urban areas but also they have concentrated especially in two cities – Sydney (2006 population 4.1 million) and Melbourne (2006 population 3.6 million). While their populations have more than doubled, Sydney and Melbourne's share of the nation's overseas-born population has increased from 42.5 per cent in 1947 to 53.2 per cent in 2001, falling slightly to 53.1 per cent in 2006. Their share of the Australia-born has fallen from 38.7 per cent to 34.1 per cent. Of immigrants who have been in Australia less than five years, 56.0 per cent live in major urban areas in New South Wales and Victoria.

Table 11 Sydney and Melbourne statistical divisions: Proportion of population overseas-born, 1947-2006

	Sydney Statistical Division		Melbourne Statistical Division		All Australia
	No. of Overseas-born	% of all Overseas-born	No. of Overseas-born	% of all Overseas-born	No. of Overseas-born
1947	191,107	25.7	125,258	16.8	744,187
1954	308,778	24.0	261,470	20.3	1,286,466
1961	434,663	24.4	444,479	25.0	1,778,780
1966	558,236	26.2	568,365	26.7	2,130,920
1971	681,313	26.4	687,266	26.6	2,579,318
1976	736,754	27.1	706,331	26.0	2,718,855
1981	834,280	27.8	754,117	25.1	3,003,833
1986	912,578	28.1	788,266	24.3	3,247,381
1991	1,070,627	28.5	893,445	23.8	3,755,554
1996	1,148,869	29.4	915,449	23.4	3,908,213
2001	1,233,487	30.0	954,037	23.2	4,105,444
2006	1,307,455	29.6	1,038,430	23.5	4,416,037

Source: ABS 1947, 1954, 1966, 1971, 1976, 1981, 1986, 1991, 1996, 2001 and 2006 censuses

Table 12 Australia: Percentage of immigrants arriving in five years prior to the census settling in capital cities, rest of state and Sydney, 1991-2006

Years		Capital Cities	Rest of State	Sydney
1991-96		86.3	13.7	37.5
1996-2001		85.5	14.5	37.3
2001-06	Total	83.9	16.1	30.6
	MES	74.2	25.8	22.2
	LOTE	88.8	11.2	34.8

Source: ABS population censuses of 1966, 2001 and 2006

In the 1990s Sydney accounted for over 37 per cent of new migrants settling in Australia, while for LOTE groups it was even higher. However, for 2001-06 the proportion fell dramatically to 30.6 per cent. The drop in the proportion settling in capital cities was not nearly so great, indicating that the dispersal away from Sydney was partly to other capitals. The increasing proportion settling outside capitals indicates a wider dispersal of settlement beyond capital cities.

Table 13 Australia: Birthplace groups with the highest concentration in major cities, 2006

Birthplace	Percentage
Vietnam	97.2
Lebanon	97.2
China	96.2
Bosnia-Herzegovina	96.1
Hong Kong	96.0
Iraq	96.0
Former Yugoslavia	95.6
S. Korea	95.2
Sri Lanka	94.5
Egypt	94.1
Turkey	93.5
Greece	93.4
India	92.4

Source: ABS 2006 census

There are significant variations between different birthplace groups in their propensity to settle in major cities. Table 13 shows the groups which have the highest concentrations in Australia's major cities and it is immediately noticeable that all are countries which mainly speak languages other than English. Moreover, several of these groups are among those who have most recently arrived in Australia in substantial numbers, including the Chinese and Indians. However, it also includes several longer standing groups with limited recent flows such as the Vietnamese, Turks and Greeks. If we look at those birthplace groups which have the lowest concentrations in major cities shown in Table 14, the MES origin countries are dominant, together with European countries whose peak of immigration was in the early post-war years and who have mature age structures (Netherlands, Germany and Malta). Papua New Guinea may appear an outlier but many in this group were born to Australians or Europeans working in Papua New Guinea during colonial and early post-colonial days.

Table 14 Australia: Birthplace groups with the lowest concentration in major cities, 2006

Birthplace	Percentage
Australia	61.0
Netherlands	61.0
UK	69.8
Germany	69.1
Papua New Guinea	72.6
USA	75.5
New Zealand	75.1
Canada	76.1
Ireland	79.1
Malta	80.9

Source: ABS 2006 census

Post-war immigration to Australia has occurred in a series of waves, each of which is characterised by a different mix of birthplace groups as Australia's immigration policy and the national and global economic, political and demographic situation has changed. The UK-Ireland-born have been the largest single birthplace group in the immigration intake most years. They have remained a constant element in the post-war immigration streams, although their share of the total intake has declined significantly (from 78.7 per cent in 1947 to 17.4 per cent in 2007-08). However, the mix of other (mainly non-English-speaking) birthplace groups in the incoming stream has undergone significant change with different groups dominating successive waves over the post-war period. Eastern European refugees formed the first of these waves in the late 1940s and early 1950s and were followed by a substantial influx of Dutch and German origin settlers in the early 1950s, who, in turn, were followed in the mid and late 1950s by Italians, Greeks and Yugoslavs. In the 1960s, Lebanese and Turks came and in the 1970s the arrival of refugees from Vietnam was the beginning of a period which saw Asian-origin groups dominate for several decades. First, Southeast Asian groups, then those from East Asia, and finally South Asia, with groups from India and China forming the largest flows into Australia in recent years apart from those from the UK and New Zealand. Finally, in the last decade, African migrants have been significant.

Accordingly there has been a substantial shift in the ethnic structure of Australian cities with those changes. In Sydney, for example, Figure 3 shows changes in the proportions of the overseas-born population at various post-war censuses who originated from various regions of the world. It is clear that the shifts have been substantial.

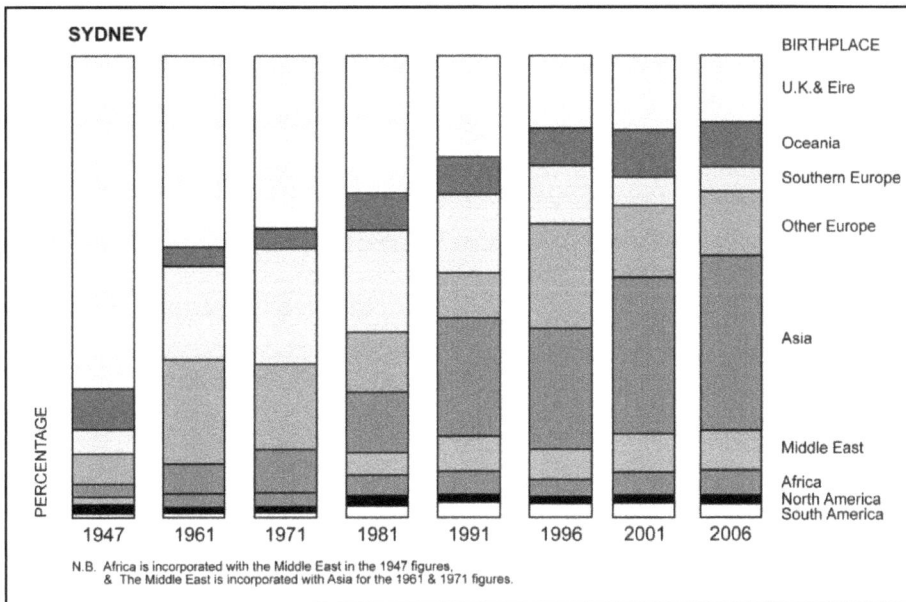

Figure 3 Sydney: Birthplace composition of the overseas-born population, 1947-2006

Source: ABS censuses 1947-2006

Most striking is the consistent pattern of decline in the proportion from the UK and Ireland over the period (from 78.7 to 14.4 per cent) The proportion from Oceania (mainly New Zealand) declined over the first quarter century but subsequently increased. The pattern for Southern Europeans is one of a rapid increase up to 1971 but a subsequent attenuation as the flow of immigrants from Greece and Italy dried up over the last two decades. A similar pattern is apparent for migrants from other Continental European nations for which the trajectory of post-war migration has tended to follow the Southern Europeans.

The spectacular increase of Asian origin immigrants since 1971 is especially apparent, increasing from 3.2 to 33.8 per cent of overseas-born Sydneysiders. In 2006 some 13.0 per cent of Sydney's population was born in Asia. Other origin groups have a much smaller representation but a general pattern of increased significance in the last two decades. In the 2001-06 period there was a small but significant increase in the African origin population. Overall then the rapid increase in the overseas-born population in Sydney has been accompanied by an equally striking increase in ethnic diversity among them.

Figure 3 shows the changing ethnic mix of Sydney in terms of the major origins of migrants but the reality is much more complex, with a myriad of different nations being represented by significant communities. In 2006 there are many more than 20 separate birthplace groups with more than 1,000 representatives in Sydney and there are many other smaller but viable communities[15]. Recent changes in the sizes of the largest overseas-born groups are shown in Table 15. This shows the substantial change which occurred during the 1980s, with the increasing Asian presence being especially pronounced. In Sydney the 10 largest overseas-born groups in 1981 did not include a single Asian origin group, but by 2006 the Chinese, Vietnamese, Indians, Filipinos, Hong Kong-born and South Koreans were in the 10 largest groups. The Asia-born groups all have more than doubled in numbers, while most of the European origin groups actually declined as death and return migration reduced their numbers.

---

15   For example, see Burnley, I H (1996). *Atlas of the Australian People-1991 Census of New South Wales*, AGPS, Canberra; Burnley, I H (1999). 'Levels of Immigrant Residential Concentration in Sydney and their Relationship with Disadvantage, *Urban Studies*, 36, 8: 1295-1315; Burnley, I H (2004). Migration Processes and Geographies of Population Diversity in Sydney, Australia: A 2001 Census Evaluation. Presentation to Conference of New Zealand Geographical Society, Auckland.

Table 15 Representation and growth of major overseas birthplace groups, 1981, 1991, 2001 and 2006 in Sydney

Country	1981	1991	2001	2006	Percent of National Total	Percent Change 1981-2006
United Kingdom	234,598	208,605	183,991	175,166	16.9	-25.3
China	13,162	41,741	82,029	109,142	52.8	729.2
New Zealand	53,025	62,529	81,963	81,064	20.8	52.9
Vietnam	15,385	47,492	61,423	62,144	38.9	303.9
Lebanon	36,010	49,937	52,008	54,502	72.8	51.4
India	10,182	17,851	34,503	52,975	36.0	420.3
Philippines	7,734	33,410	47,090	52,087	43.2	573.5
Italy	62,682	56,887	48,900	44,563	22.4	-28.9
Hong Kong	7,964	29,673	36,039	36,866	51.3	362.9
Korea, Republic of	3,099	15,044	26,928	32,124	60.9	936.6
Greece	43,628	40,531	33,688	32,022	29.1	-26.6
South Africa	9,012	16,112	25,190	28,427	27.3	215.4
Fiji	5,022	16,972	25,368	26,928	55.9	436.2
Malaysia	8,076	17,501	18,996	21,211	23.0	162.6
Indonesia	4,973	13,174	19,719	20,562	40.3	313.5
Germany	24,097	21,418	19,711	19,364	18.2	-19.6
Sri Lanka	3,261	9,595	15,744	17,917	28.8	449.4
Egypt	14,862	16,194	16,506	16,238	48.5	9.3
Malta	21,265	19,355	16,124	14,680	33.6	-31.0

Source: ABS censuses, 1981, 1991, 2001 and 2006

The distribution of immigrants in Australian cities, especially the degree of spatial concentration, and its implications has been an issue of considerable debate among social scientists in Australia. On the one hand are commentators[16] who argue that the development of immigrant concentrations in particular suburbs jeopardises social harmony and cohesiveness in Australian society. On the other hand there are those[17] who stress the positive roles played by ethnic concentrations in assisting immigrant economic and social adjustment.

---

16   Blainey, G (1993). 'A Critique of Indo-Chinese in Australia: The Issues of Unemployment and Residential Concentration', *BIPR Bulletin*: 9, July: 42-45; Blainey, G (1994). 'Melting Pot on the Boil', *The Bulletin*, 30 August: 22-27; Healy, E and Birrell, B (2003). 'Metropolis Divided: The Political Dynamic of Spatial Inequality and Migrant Settlement in Sydney', *People and Place*, 11,2: 65-87.
17   Viviani, N, Coughlan, J and Rowland, T (1993). *Indo-Chinese in Australia: The Issues of Unemployment and Residential Concentration*, AGPS, Canberra; Jupp, J (1993). 'Ethnic Concentrations: A Reply to Bob Birrell, *People and Place*, 4, 4: 51-52.

A distinctive characteristic of Australia's largest cities compared with some other world cities, however, is that while there are suburbs with high proportions of foreign-born residents, these concentrations are not dominated by a single birthplace group. This is partly a function of the fact that no single birthplace, language or religious group has been dominant in post-war migration to Australia.

Burnley[18] has made a detailed analysis of ethnic diversity at the district level in Sydney. He found that even among the most 'segregated' population, the Vietnam-born, there was only one district in which there was more than half the population born in Vietnam and nine in which 40-49 per cent were. Moreover, 56 per cent of the Vietnam-born lived in districts where they made up less than five per cent of the resident population. For other concentrated groups the relevant percentages were 61 per cent for the Lebanon-born and 86 per cent for the China-born. Indeed, Burnley [19]demonstrates that birthplace diversity is more evident in areas of immigrant concentration than elsewhere in the city.

Recent immigrant arrivals to Australian cities have a greater degree of spatial dispersal than earlier generations of arrivals. This is partly a function of the increasing bifurcation in both global and Australian immigration between high skilled migration (both permanent and temporary) and low skilled migration. Australia has increasingly targeted its immigration program at highly educated, highly skilled, higher income groups[20]. The share of lower skilled migrants through the refugee-humanitarian and family reunion components of the Australian immigration program has decreased substantially. Accordingly, the proportion of newcomers to Australian cities made up of more skilled, English-speaking, better-off migrants has increased compared with early post-war years. Such groups are more likely to select areas to live based on socioeconomic rather than ethnic factors.

There are clearly differences between the two groups in their capacity to exercise choice about where to live upon arrival in Australian cities and the constellation of forces which shape where they settle. Those coming as family or refugee-humanitarian migrants are more constrained in where they can live, both economically in terms of what housing markets they can afford to buy into, and because they rely upon the support of friends, family and compatriots to support them in adjusting to life in Australia. The balance between the numbers in the skilled and family-refugee groups settling in major cities has moved in favour of skilled migrants since the mid-1990s, although it has been argued that the unskilled group are more likely to settle in Sydney and Melbourne than in other parts of the nation.

---

18   Burnley, I H (2004). *op cit.*
19   *Ibid.*
20   Hugo, G J (1999b). *Regional Development through Immigration? The Reality behind the Rhetoric,* Department of the Parliamentary Library Research Paper No.9 1999-2000, Department of the Parliamentary Library, Canberra; Hawthorne, L (2005). 'Picking Winners': The Recent Transformation of Australia's Skilled Migration Policy, *International Migration Review,* XXXIX, 3: 663-696.

The differing patterns of settlement of birthplace groups in Australia's major cities can be examined through the extent to which they are spatially concentrated. In order to do this we have calculated the Index of Dissimilarity for the major birthplace groups in Australia's major cities and these are depicted in Table 16.

Table 16 Australia's major capital cities: Index of Dissimilarity, 2006

Birthplace	2006 Census
Bosnia and Herzegovina	50.9
Canada	26.7
China (excl. SARs and Taiwan Province)	50.9
Croatia	38.5
Egypt	42.0
Fiji	48.6
Macedonia (FYROM)	66.9
Germany	14.7
Greece	50.9
Hong Kong (SAR of China)	50.9
India	38.5
Indonesia	45.5
Iraq	72.4
Ireland	22.0
Italy	40.7
Japan	44.7
Korea, Republic of (South)	58.4
Lebanon	64.0
Malaysia	42.6
Malta	51.2
Netherlands	21.6
New Zealand	23.0
Papua New Guinea	38.0
Philippines	39.3
Poland	29.0
Singapore	42.8
South Africa	35.0
Sri Lanka	47.3
Thailand	34.8
Turkey	58.7
United Kingdom(d)	21.6
United States of America	28.2
Vietnam	60.7

Source: ABS CDATA 2006

The Index of Dissimilarity can be interpreted as the percentage of a particular sub-population which would have to change their place of residence if the distribution of that group between sub-areas of the region under study is to be made exactly the same as that of the other sub-group. An index of 0 would mean that the two sub-populations had exactly the same relative distribution while an index value of 100 represents a complete 'apartheid' situation, with no person of one sub-group living in the same sub-area as people of the other sub-group.

These two extremes rarely occur. If the index is less than 20 there is little spatial separation of the two sub-populations, if it exceeds 30 there is some significant separation and if it exceeds 50 there is very significant separation.

There are wide differences between birthplace groups in their propensity to concentrate, with the highest being mainly for those groups that have come to Australia as refugee-humanitarian settlers, such as those from Iraq (72.4), Macedonia (66.9), Lebanon (64.0) and Vietnam (60.7). The lowest are for the MES groups such as those born in the UK (21.6), Ireland (22.0), New Zealand (23), Canada (26.7) and the USA (28.2). The figures are also low for longstanding Western European groups like those born in the Netherlands (21.6), Germany (14.7) and Poland (29). The Greece- and Italy-born are still quite concentrated (50.9 and 40.7 respectively) but their second generations have dispersed more widely throughout Australian cities, especially the Italians.

A spatial concentration among some Asian, African and Middle Eastern birthplace groups is evident. For the Vietnamese, for example, 39.7 per cent of the group in Sydney live in a single local government area, Fairfield, which has 4.5 per cent of the total population of Sydney. There have been two major interpretations of those spatial patterns. Firstly Healy and Birrell[21] argue that '… not only is the city's population growing it is also bifurcating … there are now two Sydneys – one increasingly dominated by low to moderate income non English-speaking migrant communities in the west and south-west and the other comprised of established, inner, affluent areas and predominantly English-speaking 'aspirational' areas in the metropolitan periphery'.

Other commentators[22] argue that Sydney is *not* characterised by ghettos or polarised ethnic enclaves but is rather an example of ethnic mix. They argue that it is inappropriate to regard all non-English-speaking groups as a single group because it ignores the differences between individual groups; also that it is necessary to separate more recent and longer standing migrants as well as including consideration of not just the first-generation migrants included

---

21   Healy, E and Birrell, B (2003). *op cit*: 65.
22   Poulsen, M, Johnston, R and Forrest, J (2002). 'Is Sydney a Divided City Ethnically?' *Australian GeographicalReview*, 41, 3: 356-377.

in birthplace data but the second generation as well. A more nuanced analysis of changing patterns of ethnic distribution in Sydney, which considers these issues, concludes that:

> The primary feature of Sydney's ethnic population to emerge from this study is one of residential mixing not of segregation or bifurcation ... Sydney appears to be moving towards being a city in which most of the population will live in areas that are classified as either non-isolated host communities, associated assimilation – pluralism communities or mixed enclaves – a hybrid city (to use a term popular with post modern theorists) in which the ongoing process of hybridisation [is] clearly reflected in the city's geography[23].

There has been a substantial increase in Sydney's foreign-born population, not an expansion of areas which are polarised ethnic enclaves but areas which are characterised by ethnic mix – in both high and low socio-economic areas. This is not to say that there are not significant divisions within Sydney, rather, as Burnley[24] has written:

> Overall, the experience of major immigrant concentrations in Sydney is different from that in American and European cities. While there are serious societal issues in these concentrations, notably low incomes and unemployment, the ethnic composition of disadvantaged communities is not the central issue ... the issue now is not the distributional aspect of ethnically or racially distinct 'subgroups' but the conditions of life of racialized minorities, and more importantly, the dominant cultural forms which result in racialization.'

An increasing role for government in influencing where migrants settle

Immigrants have concentrated in New South Wales and especially Sydney in recent years. But it has been demonstrated here that the 2001-06 intercensal period saw for the first time in several decades a reversal of the trend of increasing concentration. It is apparent that government policy is playing a role in this change. While, during the post-war period, Australian immigration policy has been overwhelmingly concerned with shaping the scale and composition of the immigration intake, there have been some attempts by government to

---

23 Poulsen, M, Johnston, R and Forrest, J (2004). 'Plural Cities and Ethnic Enclaves: Introducing a Measurement Procedure for Comparative Study', *International Journal of Urban and Regional Research,* 2: 375):
24 Burnley, I H (1999). *op cit*: 1313.

influence where immigrants settle after their arrival in Australia[25]. The federal government had a two-year bonding scheme for persons accepted as displaced persons in the early post-war years[26]. These allocated settlers to areas suffering labour shortages, often in remote non-metropolitan areas such as large-scale construction projects like the Snowy Mountains Hydro Electric Scheme. At the end of the bond period many made their way to capital cities, but substantial communities remained.

It was not until the mid 1990s that the Australian government considered trying to shape on a large scale where immigrants settle. The sustainability of rural and regional communities became an important item on the national agenda with the establishment of a federal government department on regional development and the initiation of a rash of programs to facilitate regional development. Similarly, states which were lagging economically, like South Australia, were pressing for immigration to assist their economic development.

In May 1996 the annual meeting of Commonwealth, State and Territory Ministers for Immigration and Multicultural Affairs established a working party to examine ways in which a higher proportion of migrants might settle in regional Australia and in states which were lagging economically. Accordingly, a number of initiatives were taken to attract immigrants to areas which were receiving small intakes. Labour shortages began to be reported in regional areas and in the states receiving smaller numbers of migrants. Accordingly the State Specific and Regional Migration Scheme (SSRM) was initiated in May 1996 to attract immigrants to areas which were receiving small intakes. Several visa categories have been added to the scheme and a range of modifications has been made. A mechanism has been set up for the states, territories and the Department of Immigration and Citizenship to regularly assess and modify the scheme. The essence of this program was to enable employers, state and local governments and families in designated lagging economic regions to sponsor immigrants without the immigrants having to fully meet the stringent requirements of the Australian Points Assessment Scheme. There is an array of visa categories available under the scheme and some of their characteristics are summarised below.

The scheme focused on skill, restricting most SSRM visa categories to people who narrowly miss reaching the high pass threshold of the Points Assessment Scheme.

---

25 Hugo, G J (1993). The Changing Spatial Distribution of Major Ethnic Groups in Australia 1961-1986. (revised version of a report prepared for the Office of Multicultural Affairs, April; Hugo, G J (1999a). *op cit.*
26 Kunz, E F (1988). *Displaced Persons: Calwell's New Australians*, Australian National University Press, Sydney.

Some categories require the settler to live in a designated area as a temporary resident for three years, after which their degree of adjustment is assessed and they are given permanent residence. Thereafter they are free to settle anywhere in Australia.

Foreign students who study in an institution in a designated area get five bonus points in the Points Assessment Test.

In addition a 'Regional 457' (Long Term Business Migrants) visa was developed whereby concessions were granted which gave regional certifying bodies a greater role in supporting sponsorships in regional Australia. It allows them to grant exceptions from the gazetted minimum skill and salary requirements for positions nominated under temporary business visas, which are located in regional and low population growth areas and have been certified by a Regional Certifying Body.

This makes a fundamental distinction between types of migrants – settlers and provisional settlers. The precedent was established by the Australian government's action in 1999 of introducing a three-year Temporary Protection Visa for persons who entered Australia as asylum seekers and were assessed as having a valid claim for refugee status. This compared to other refugees accepted offshore who were granted full settler status[27]. In the case of the SSRM, however, a distinction is made between those settlers who can live anywhere in Australia and those who are restricted, in their initial years at least, to live in designated areas.

The success of the SSRM programs is evident in Table 17 which shows that the SSRM Scheme increased its share of the total non-humanitarian intake from 2.3 per cent in 1997-98 to over a fifth in 2008-09. While South Australia has only 7.5 per cent of the national population and averaged only 4.9 per cent of the national immigrant intake between 1997 and 2009, the table shows that it has made disproportionate use of the SSRM Scheme. The locational requirements of the various SSRM visa categories vary, but *all* of South Australia has been eligible for all SSRM categories. This has meant that the major city of Adelaide (2006 population 1,105,839) has been eligible for settlement of SSRM immigrants, whereas other mainland state capital cities have not. The SSRM Scheme is targeted at 'contributing to the economic, demographic and social development of regional Australia and low population growth areas'[28]. Adelaide is the only major metropolitan centre that has had access to the full suite of SSRM programs. This has undoubtedly given South Australia an advantage in its ability to attract migrants under the SSRM scheme.

---

27   Hugo, G J (2002). From Compassion to Compliance? Trends in Refugee and Humanitarian Migration in Australia, *GeoJournal*, 56: 27-37.

28   Deparment of Immigration and Citizenship (2007). *Population Flows*: 41.

Table 17 Number of immigrants with visas granted under the state specific regional migration mechanisms and their proportion of the total non-humanitarian intake, 1997-98 to 2005-06

Year	Number	Percent of Total Non-Humanitarian Intake	Percent in South Australia
1997-98	1,753	2.3	34.5
1998-99	2,804	3.3	36.9
1999-2000	3,309	3.6	21.2
2000-01	3,846	3.6	19.5
2001-02	4,136	4.6	17.5
2002-03	7,941	8.5	16.7
2003-04	12,725	11.4	16.6
2004-05	18,700	15.6	26.5
2005-06	27,488	19.2	29.8
2006-07	25,845	17.4	27.7
2007-08	26,162	17.5	26.9
2008-09	33,470	21.2	22.9

Source: DIAC *Population Flows: Immigration Aspects,* various issues; DIAC *Immigration Update,* various issues; DIAC unpublished data

The bulk of the SSRM Scheme visa categories relate only to skilled migrants and those eligible are potential immigrants who have narrowly failed the stringent Points Assessment Test. However, there have also been SSRM family-based initiatives and initiatives to attract business migrants to designated areas[29]. There have been some elements in the Humanitarian part of the program which direct settlers to particular areas; South Australia in recent years. This has been a deliberate strategy of the South Australian government that has been active in providing support for refugee-humanitarian migrants and has lobbied DIAC to take a substantial number of refugee-humanitarian migrants.

The differential impact of different types of migration on the Australian states and territories can be measured using an Index of Dissimilarity. In Table 18, for example, there is little difference between settler arrivals and onshore migrants in the way in which they distribute themselves between states and territories. Only 8.9 per cent of onshore migrants would have to change their state of residence to duplicate the distribution of settler arrivals. There is a slightly greater difference between humanitarian settlers and non-humanitarian settlers with one in eight humanitarian settlers having to change states to duplicate the distribution of other settlers. However, nearly a half of SSRM migrants would

---

29   *Ibid:* 43.

need to change their state of residence to duplicate the distribution of those settling in Australia under the regular migration program. This is of course to be expected given the targeting of the SSRM program to lagging parts of Australia.

Table 18 Australia: Indexes of dissimilarity between different types of international migration between states and territories, 2004-05 and 2008-09

Comparison	Index of Dissimilarity	
	2004-05	2008-09
SSRM vs Regular Migration	45.3	34.2
Onshore vs Offshore Migration	8.9	6.3
Humanitarian vs Non-Humanitarian	12.6	14.1

Source: Calculated from data in DIMA, 2006

South Australia is clearly the biggest proportionate user of the SSRM scheme. In 2004 it was the first state to introduce a population policy[30], which, among other things, sought to increase the state's share of immigrants to around 7.5 per cent by 2014. International migration has been a key element in the Population Policy and in the State's Strategic Plan[31]. The state government initiated a number of strategies in order to achieve an increase in international migration. It set up a state government agency *Immigration SA* within the Department of Trade and Economic Development to drive the achievement of the immigration objectives. It set up an agency *Education Adelaide* to increase the state's share of foreign students. It set up offices in key origin countries of immigrants to facilitate the recruitment and emigration of settlers for South Australia.

It appointed a number of Migration Officers to be affiliated with Regional Development Boards in South Australia to assist local governments and employers to bring in migrants.

---

30 Government of South Australia (2004a). *Prosperity through People: a Population Policy for South Australia*, Government of South Australia, Adelaide.
31 Government of South Australia (2004b). *South Australia's Strategic Plan*, Government of South Australia, Adelaide.

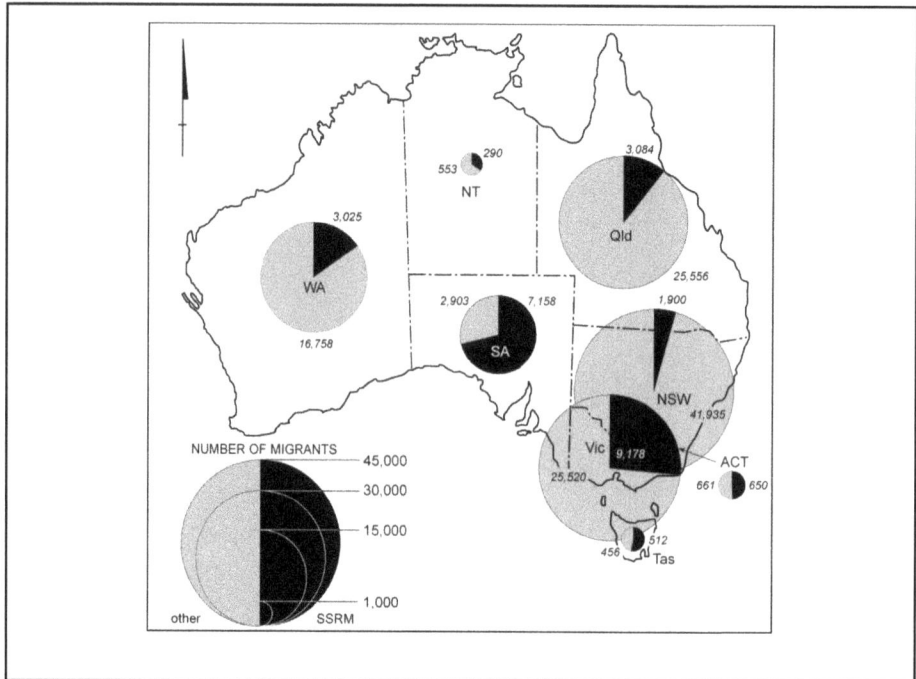

Figure 4 Australia: Settler arrivals by state according to whether they are state specific and regional migration scheme migrants or other migrants, 2006-07

Source: DIAC *Population Flows: Immigration Aspects*, various issues; DIAC *Immigration Update*, various issues

At no time since Federation have state governments been more heavily involved in the immigration policy and operations. Victoria has had the largest number of SSRM migrants since that state too introduced a population policy[32]. New South Wales has not been very active in this program.

Migrants in Australia's non-metropolitan areas

Until 2006 there had been successive increases in the proportion of immigrants living in Australia's major cities. However, 2006 saw the percentage of immigrants living outside of Australia's cities increased, albeit marginally, as is indicated by Table 19.

---

32   Government of Victoria (2004). *Beyond Five Million: The Victorian Government's Population Policy*, State of Victoria, Melbourne.

Table 19 Australia: Distribution of overseas-born between major urban, other urban and rural areas, 2001 and 2006

	2001		2006	
	Number	%	Number	%
Major Urban	3,363,323	82.5	3,654,920	82.8
Other Urban	442,723	10.9	494,752	11.2
Rural	271,690	6.7	264,905	6.0
Total	4,077,736	100.0	4,414,577	100.0

Source: ABS 2001 and 2006 censuses

Immigrants outside the capital cities, especially those from a LOTE background, tended to settle in particular areas, such as:

- Intensive agricultural areas such as sugar farming in Queensland, irrigated agriculture along the Murray and Murrumbidgee Rivers and in intensive horticultural areas close to major cities[33].
- Major provincial centres where many were involved in small businesses.
- Mining and industrial centres like Wollongong, Newcastle, Whyalla, Geelong.
- Some fishing communities.

They avoided the dry farming, extensive agricultural areas of the Australian wheat-sheep belt. Accordingly, the non-metropolitan overseas-born population in Australia has been even more concentrated than those settling in major cities. Table 20 shows that the Indices of Dissimilarity calculated for non-metropolitan areas are quite a big higher than those for the same birthplace groups in major urban areas (Table 16). Again, however, it is the LOTE groups which are most concentrated.

---

33   Borrie, W D (1954). *op cit*; Price, C A (1963). *Southern Europeans in Australia*, Oxford University Press, Melbourne.

Table 20 Australia non-metropolitan areas: Index of Dissimilarity, 2006

Birthplace	ID
Bosnia and Herzegovina	67.4
Canada	29.1
China (excl. SARs and Taiwan Province)(b)	44.1
Croatia	50.5
Egypt	44.1
Fiji	35.1
Former Yugoslav Republic of Macedonia (FYROM)	80.8
Germany	23.3
Greece	44.8
Hong Kong (SAR of China)(b)	43.5
India	34.5
Indonesia	38.8
Iraq	71.3
Ireland	25.1
Italy	44.9
Japan	59.2
Korea, Republic of (South)	56.5
Lebanon	58.7
Malaysia	33.4
Malta	44.9
Netherlands	22.2
New Zealand	36.5
Papua New Guinea	44.5
Philippines	27.5
Poland	36.9
Singapore	43.7
South Africa	35.8
Sri Lanka	38.2
Thailand	36.2
Turkey	68.4
United Kingdom(d)	24.4
United States of America	27.1
Vietnam	48.0

Source: ABS CDATA, 2006

For the first time there has been some settlement in areas previously eschewed by immigrants, especially those from a LOTE background, partly because of severe labour shortages in many such areas where low fertility and ageing have been exacerbated by youth out-migration[34].

Immigrants add an element of diversity to what, in many regional areas, have been strongly Anglo-Celtic dominant societies. Regional communities lack both formal post-arrival services as well as established communities of similar ethnic backgrounds that can provide informal support during initial settlement. A particular problem relates to the lack of interpreter services which can be a barrier to non-English-speaking groups accessing health, education and other services. The dearth of formal and informal support services has in some areas been countered by the mobilisation of local community groups, organisations and local government. The enthusiasm with which some communities have welcomed migrants has been at odds with conventional stereotypes of regional populations having conservative and even racist attitudes[35]. Indeed in many cases the newcomers are seen as valuable additions to communities which have been struggling to maintain services, losing young populations and have not been able to fill job vacancies, while the cultural diversity they add has been embraced with enthusiasm. There have however also been instances of backlash.

Issues remain about the injection of new elements of diversity into regional communities which have not previously been multicultural. Undoubtedly the adjustment of new migrants in regional communities and of the communities to the migrant is a topic of needed research.

There are a number of work related concerns. Birrell, Hawthorne and Richardson[36] show that regional skilled migrants experience more problems in entering the Australian labour market than any other category of skilled settlers. Satisfactory entry into regional labour and housing markets will be a critical factor in attracting and retaining immigrant families in regional communities.

One issue that will need to be faced is that in many regional communities the labour shortages which are emerging require unskilled or semi-skilled labour, whereas the bulk of available immigration visa categories relate to skilled migrants. The focus has been strongly on regional employers in this lobbying[37]. Thus far the government has resisted pointing to the 4.5 per cent unemployment level within Australia and arguing that it would work against the integrity of

---

34   Hugo, G J (2008a). 'Immigrant Settlement Outside of Australia's Capital Cities' In *Population, Space and Place*, 14,6: 553-571.

35   *Ibid*.

36   Birrell, R, Hawthorne, L and Richardson, S (2006). *Evaluation of the General Skilled Migration Categories*, AGPS, Canberra.

37   Senate Standing Committee on Employment, Workforce Relations and Workforce Participation, 2006. *Perspectives on theFuture of the Harvest Labour Force*, Department of the Senate, Canberra.

the Australian immigration program[38]. However, these pressures seem likely to increase and it could be advisable for the Australian government to develop a pilot program to assess the efficacy of a temporary labour migration strategy. This could perhaps be focused on particular industries (e.g. harvesting, aged care) and focus on particular countries of origin (eg, some Pacific nations). New Zealand has begun such a program.

A major issue relates to the question of retention of immigrants in regional areas once they are free to settle wherever they wish. There is likely to be significant leakage out of regional areas. Tomas Hammar[39] shows that in Sweden in the 1970s there was a policy of dispersal of immigrants and most 'leaked' back to Stockholm. Also studies in the UK[40] and Australia[41] showed that Vietnamese refugees settled in dispersed locations later gravitated to major metropolitan centres. This is a challenge which many regional communities are taking up and it will be interesting to see how successful their efforts turn out to be.

Temporary migration

One of the most profound changes in Australia's immigration system since the mid 1990s has been an increase in non-permanent migration. On 30 June 2008 there were 809,628 persons temporarily present in Australia[42] and, until the onset of the Global Financial Crisis, the numbers were increasing by 15 per cent per year. Where these groups go when they arrive in Australia has an impact on population distribution. Moreover, DIAC[43] reports that 64 per cent of groups stay in Australia longer than three months and not all are detected in the census.

One of the major categories of temporary migrants is the Long Stay Temporary Business Entrants (Visa Category 457) which numbered a record 110,570 in 2007-08. Although the numbers declined a little in 2008-09 (101,280), these migrants are restricted to the top three skill categories and are able to stay in Australia for up to four years. They need to be nominated by an employer and the numbers are not capped. They are more concentrated in Australia's major cities than are permanent migrants. Some 51 per cent of all 457s coming in 2001-

---

38   Hugo, G J (2005). 'Migration Policies in Australia and their Impact on Development in Countries of Origin'. In *International Migration and the Millenium Development Goals*, UNFPA Expert Group Meeting, United Nations Population Fund, New York.

39   Hammar, T (1993). 'The 'Sweden-wide Strategy' of Refugee Dispersal'. In R Black and V Robinson (eds), *Geographyand Refugees*, Belhaven, London.

40   Robinson, V and Hale, S (1989). *The Geography of Vietnamese Secondary Migration in the UK*, Warwick University Centre for Research in Ethnic Relations, Coventry (UK); Robinson, V (1993). 'North and South: Resettling Vietnamese Refugees in Australia and the UK'. In Black, R and Robinson, V (eds), *Geography and Refugees*, Belhaven, London.

41   Burnley, I H (1989). *op cit*.

42   Department of Immigration and Citizenship (2009b). 'Community Information Summary: Malaysia-born Community'. http://www.immi.gov.au/media/publications/statistics/comm-summ/summary.htm.

43   *Ibid*.

03 went to Sydney and 83.6 per cent went to Australia's five largest cities[44]. In 2002 a regional version of the 457 visa was introduced with a number of 'concessional arrangements ... to reflect the skill needs of regional Australia[45]'. These concessions included a lower minimum level of skill and salary than was the case for the regular 457 program. They needed to be endorsed by relevant state, territory or regional certifying bodies, be at locally relevant wage levels and it had to be shown that no locals were available to fill the job. The numbers of regional 457s grew quite rapidly but they became the subject of controversy because of accusations that employers have used the visa to undercut the wages and conditions of Australian workers in regional areas – especially in the abattoir industry. Accordingly, there was a tightening of regulations. Although 457s are disproportionately concentrated in major cities, they are increasingly important in filling job vacancies in regional areas, especially regional cities. One group of temporary skilled migrants of great significance in regional areas is doctors and other health personnel.

The largest category of temporary residents is overseas students who numbered 317,897 in 2008. There is a strong concentration in major mainland cities which is to be expected since most universities are located in such centres (Figure 5). It is interesting to note, however, that there are more students in Melbourne than in Sydney, which is different to the pattern for permanent settlers and 457s. Regional centres with universities like Ballarat are making a substantial effort to attract students both to contribute to the local economy as students but also in the hope that they will later become permanent residents locally when they finish their studies.

One of the categories of temporary migration which has increased in scale over the last decade and which has impinged on non-metropolitan Australia is Working Holiday Makers (WHM). This program involves '... the temporary entry and stay of young people wanting to combine a holiday in Australia with the opportunity to supplement travel funds through incidental employment[46]'.

They can stay for a period of a year and work in a single job for up to three months. They are especially involved in the hospitality, horticultural and rural industries and many of the jobs are located outside of Australia's major cities. Hugo[47] shows, for example, how this group has become fundamentally important in providing seasonal harvest labour in horticultural, irrigated fruit growing and grape harvesting activities. Indeed they have been so significant

---

44 Khoo *et al*, (2003). *op cit.*
45 Department of Immigration and Multicultural Affairs (2007). *Population Flows: Immigration Aspects*: 46.
46 *Ibid*: 64.
47 Hugo, G J (2001). International Migration and Agricultural Labour in Australia. Paper presented at Changing Face Workshop, Imperial Valley, California, 16-18 January.

that since late 2005 WHM 'who have undertaken seasonal work in regional Australia for a minimum of three months[48]' are eligible to apply for a second 12 month WHM visa.

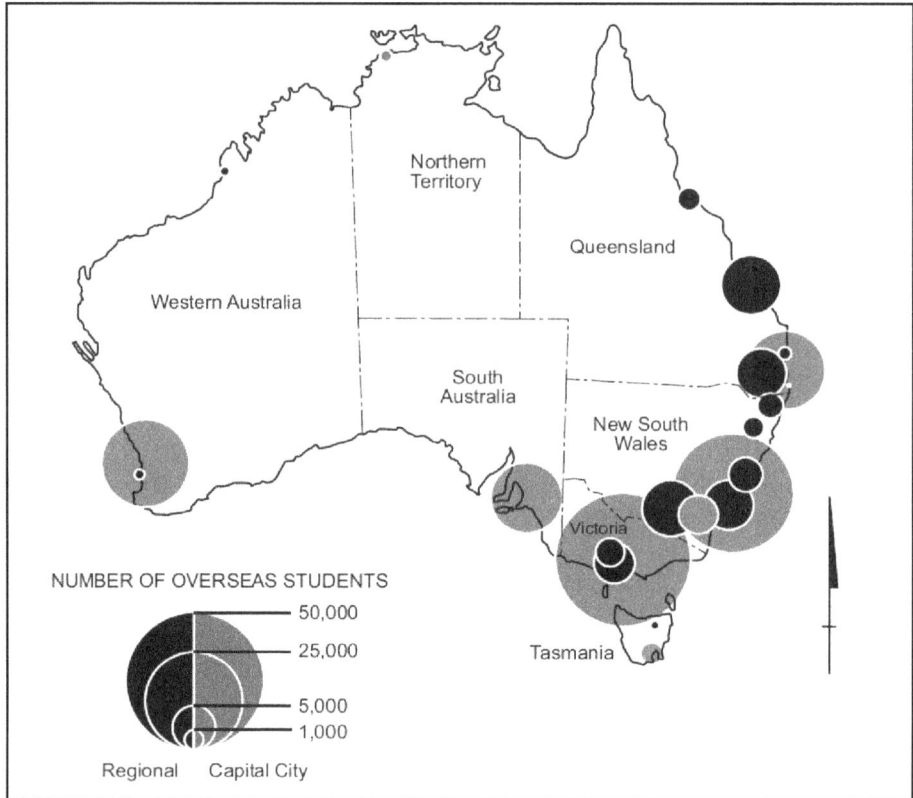

Figure 5 Location of overseas fee-paying students, 2002

Source: Department of Education, Science and Training

In 2008-09 there were 187,696 WHM visas granted, an increase of 21.8 per cent on the previous year and a doubling since 2003-04. Hence they have become an important element in the population of particular communities on a seasonal basis. The harvesting industry in Australia has been very active in lobbying the federal government for permission to bring in unskilled agricultural workers from Asia and the Pacific, but has not been successful. The WHM are filling a niche in regional seasonal labour markets which in countries like the US, New Zealand, Canada and in Europe are filled by seasonal agricultural workers migrations[49]. However, Figure 6 depicts the location of places visited by a sample of WHMs in a 2008 study and it is immediately apparent that there is less concentration in the

---

48   Department of Immigration and Multicultural Affairs (2007). *Op cit*: 64.
49   Hugo, G J (2001). *op cit*.

major cities than is the case for other immigrant groups. There is a particularly strong geographical concentration in coastal areas. However, the large cities are significant for WHMs since, in an earlier survey of WHMs, 42 per cent reported spending some time working in Sydney[50].

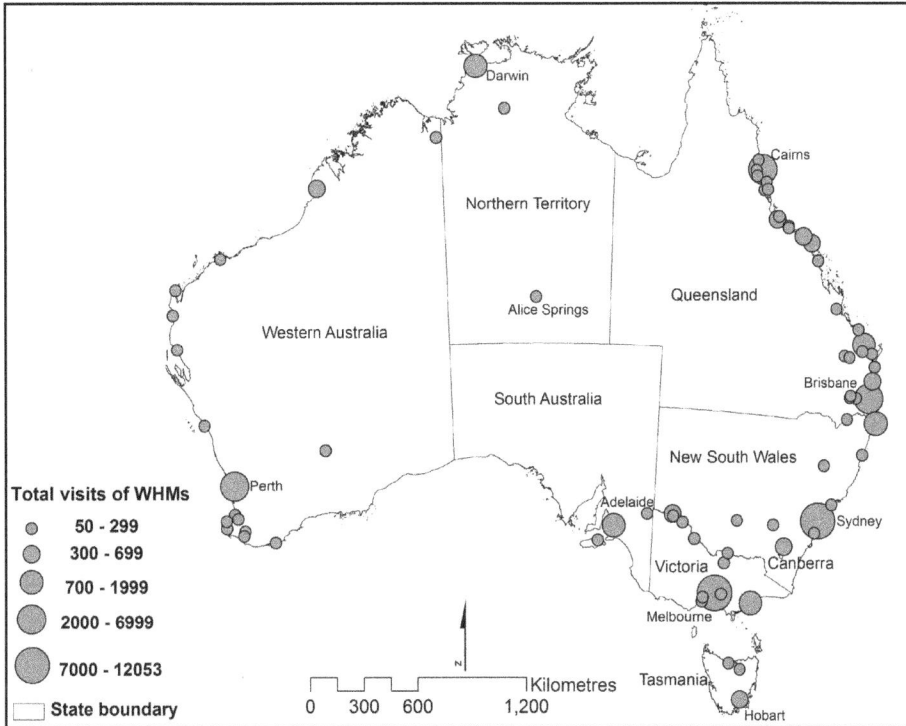

Figure 6 Major localities which WHMs visited, 2008

Source: Tan *et al*, 2009: 70

While temporary migration is playing an important role in some non-metropolitan communities, in total they are more concentrated in major cities than are permanent settlers. They are more directed to Australia's largest cities, especially Sydney. Census data significantly understates the impact of non-permanent international migration on world cities like Sydney. Sydney has a crucial gateway function not only for permanent settlers but large numbers of temporary migrants who circulate between it and other world cities. Moreover this group includes many transnationals who move from one world city to another on job transfer or as they change jobs within global labour markets. With high-level skills and income they represent a significant presence in the world city and play an important role in its economic growth and labour market.

---

50   Harding, G and Webster, E (2002). *The Working Holiday Maker Scheme and the Australian Labour Market*, Melbourne Institute of Applied Economic and Social Research, University of Melbourne.

Conclusion

Australia's population distribution has changed little over the last century[51]. Figure 2 shows the nation's population centroid has shifted little since 1901. However, it is a deceptive stability since there is a great deal of dynamism and international migration is an important element of this dynamism. International migration has been of crucial significance in the urbanisation of Australia and in dramatically changing the composition of Australia's urban populations. Immigration is the key demographic process in the development of Australia's major cities, especially the 'Gateway City' of Sydney[52]. It is not only the major demographic growth engine, it also has an important role in economic and social change. Immigrants are crucial to several sectors of the urban economy and they shape much of the social and cultural life of Australian cities. Immigrants are increasingly developing and strengthening transnational networks that link Australian cities with the rest of the world. Yet our understanding of the dynamics of immigration in shaping Australian cities and its impacts remains limited. This, especially, applies to the scale and impact of temporary international migration.

This study has also identified a significant, albeit small, shift in the settlement patterns of immigrants in recent years; a shift away from New South Wales as the predominant destination of immigrants and a reduction in the significance of Sydney as the initial settlement of immigrants. Immigration is playing an increasingly significant role in regional and state development in Australia. It is being increasingly factored into economic planning at state, regional and local levels. However, our understanding of settlement in these areas remains limited and it is likely that immigration to peripheral states and to regional areas will grow in importance in the future.

---

51 Hugo, G J (2003). *op cit*.
52 Hugo, G J (2008b). 'Sydney: The Globalization of an Established Immigrant Gateway', in M Price and L Benton-Short (eds), *Migrants in the Metropolis - the Rise of Immigrants Gateway Cities*, Syracuse University Press: 68-96.

Chapter 2: Politics, Public Policy and Multiculturalism

James Jupp

A major problem in discussing multiculturalism rationally is that it means many different things to many different people in many different situations[1]. This is quite normal for all terms ending in 'ism', which suggests some sort of ideological basis relevant to political and organisational outcomes, such as 'socialism'. The difference is that socialism has been around for nearly two centuries, while multiculturalism was only coined forty years ago. Within a single generation states and individuals have moved from assimilative nationalism and open racism towards the concepts of human equality and cultural variety. Still, many are yet to adopt these novel approaches, or they find them incompatible, and, it remains the case that they are not acceptable to all citizens or political parties. In short, multiculturalism is normally a contested term. In recent years the topic has been further confused by the adoption of alternative terms like integration, which may simply describe a preferred situation very like multiculturalism or alternatives very close to assimilation.

One way of avoiding this dilemma, and analysing Australian multiculturalism in practice, is to concentrate on policy formulation and application within the local political system. The development of multicultural policies has been well documented in official Australian sources, though it is still surprising how few critics seem aware of this and persist in arguing that multiculturalism 'has never been defined'. The basic Australian definition, which has never been significantly altered, was contained in the 1978 report of Frank Galbally's Committee, *Migrant Servicesand Programs*[2]. Significantly this report was delivered to Prime Minister Malcolm Fraser rather than to the Minister for Immigration, within whose responsibilities most of it lay. Unusually it was produced in ten languages, which was a symbolic gesture rather than an attempt to reach a mass readership. Multiculturalism as a public policy area, has rested uncertainly between two Commonwealth departments ever since, being transferred from Prime Minister and Cabinet to Immigration by John Howard in 1996[3]. It was eventually taken up at state level, mostly by the 1980s.

---

1 Parekh, Lord B (2006). *Rethinking Multiculturalism*, Palgrave Macmillan, Basingstoke (UK); Castles, S, Kalantzis, M, Cope, B and Morrissey, M (1992). *Mistaken Identity: Multiculturalism and the Demise of Nationalism in Australia,* Pluto Press, Sydney.
2 *Galbally, F (chair) (1978). Migrant Services and Programs, AGPS, Canberra.*
3 Jupp, J (2002). *From White Australia to Woomera*, Cambridge University Press, Melbourne: chapter 5.

The Galbally report placed its emphasis on language ability, moving away from the previous concern with physical appearance. Assistance was needed for 'those who arrive here with little understanding of the English language'[4]. The responsibility for advising government of immigrant needs was to pass from existing mainstream welfare organisations to ethnic communities. The costs of ethnic welfare services were to fall largely on the budget of the Immigration Department, with the teaching of English to adults to become the largest single cost. Thus policy was centrally concerned with settlement. However it went well beyond that into potentially more controversial areas. The basic principles, which have never been officially abandoned, were summarised as:

- All members of our society must have equal opportunity to realise their full potential and must have equal access to programs and services.

- Every person should be able to maintain his or her own culture without prejudice or disadvantage and should be encouraged to understand and embrace other cultures.

- [The] needs of migrants should, in general, be met by programs and services available to the whole community. But special programs and services are necessary at present to ensure equality of access and provision.

- Services and programs should be designed and operated in full consultation with clients, and self-help should be encouraged a much as possible with a view to helping migrants to become self-reliant quickly [5].

Thus from its origins, multicultural policy was seen as a national responsibility but a special concern of immigrants of 'non-English-speaking background' - a term not officially changed until replaced with 'culturally and linguistically diverse' by the Howard government in 2002. The report stated firmly that 'migrants have the right to maintain their cultural and racial identity'[6]. Australian multiculturalism differs from the original Canadian approach in being aimed in practice at immigrants, an approach eventually defined by the Immigration Department to embrace those who have arrived within the past two years. However, in practice, and at the state and territory level, multicultural activities extend much more broadly and many engage in multicultural organisations that are Australian-born. The term 'ethnic' more effectively describes the reality, if it is taken to include those not of British and Irish descent. It excludes Australian Aborigines and Torres Strait Islanders, even though the first *National Agenda*

---

4   Galbally, F (chair) (1978). *op cit:* 1.9.

5   *Ibid*: 1.7.

6   *Ibid*: 9.6.

for a Multicultural Australia of 1989 specifically included them[7]. Indigenous policies and programs have continued to be distinct from those included under 'multiculturalism'.

These ambiguities reflect the fact that multiculturalism is not just an administrative approach but also incorporates certain values and attitudes. Some of these move away from long-standing Australian traditions, such as building a new British nation on the basis of racial purity. To a younger generation these traditions might seem antiquarian. But they were consensual as recently as the 1960s and had lasted for over a century. Many were revived by the One Nation movement of Pauline Hanson, which gained one million votes in the 1998 Commonwealth election, mainly in Queensland and monocultural rural districts of New South Wales and Western Australia. One Nation, in effect, rejected all forms of ethnic variety, favouring assimilation of immigrants and Aborigines, calling on multiculturalism to be 'abolished', for mass immigration to be abandoned and for the ending of welfare services allocated on the basis of Aboriginality or ethnicity. The temporary support for One Nation suggests that it represented a lingering but still widespread adherence to attitudes which the introduction of multiculturalism in the early 1970s was designed to abandon. The rapid collapse of the movement, while largely due to internal indiscipline, marked the end of an era rather than the start of a consistent reaction. However the adoption of some One Nation proposals relating to asylum seekers by the Howard government suggests that resentment against ethnic minorities continues in the background.[8]

The stages of policy development

To better understand the ambiguities and compromises involved in multicultural policy development, it is necessary to look briefly at the various stages through which national policy towards ethnic variety has moved since the start of the post-war mass migration program in 1947 [9]. Prior to that the state had strongly favoured British immigration and discouraged or even prevented settlement from other sources [10]. Thus there was little ambiguity and the only major controversy surrounded the opposition to migration based on a presumed threat to the wages and conditions of organised labour. There had, in any case, been very little immigration between 1930 and 1945. A refugee intake of Jews fleeing Nazi

---

7   Office of Multicultural Affairs (1989). *National Agenda for a Multicultural Australia*, Australian Government Publishing Service, Canberra.

8   Leach, M, Stokes, G, and Ward, I (2000). *The Rise and Fall of One Nation*, University of Queensland Press, St Lucia (Qld).

9   Castles, S, et al (1992). *Op cit*.

10   Tavan, G (2005). *The Long, Slow Death of White Australia*, Scribe, Melbourne.

Germany, Austria and Czechoslovakia had not been met with much enthusiasm among the general public and had been strongly criticised by some of the more reactionary media commentators and conservative politicians. The settlement of the Jewish refugees was left to the Jewish community and the expectation that they would not place a burden on the taxpayer was regularly stated [11]. However the post-war situation was very different. For the first time since 1901 the assisted passage schemes were extended to non-British aliens from Europe, of whom 171,000 were Displaced Persons. Most of these came from places which had sent few if any migrants to Australia in the past [12].

The assimilation phase 1947-1966

The arrival of Displaced Persons in a short period between 1947 and 1954 presented a challenge almost as disturbing as the mass arrival of Chinese gold seekers in the 1850s. However, as they were all of European origin and mostly of Christian religion, the assumption was made that they would not present such a major challenge nor breach the expectation of social cohesion and rapid assimilation on which the White Australia policy was still based. Policy was not determined by any real knowledge of social science analyses of immigration, which at this stage was mainly confined to the experience of the United States. There was considerable confusion in public debate about the American experience, with the descendants of African slaves being lumped together with southern and eastern European 19th century immigrants and blamed for producing 'ghettoes' and 'race riots'. Commonwealth migration to Britain did not take off until the mid-1950s. When it did, Australians concluded that rioting and discrimination in Britain fully justified the retention of White Australia [13].

The academic study of ethnicity (other than the anthropological study of Aborigines) and of immigration scarcely existed, apart from the work of Jens Lyng in the 1920s and Lodewyckx in the 1930s. It took off in Australia in the 1960s, with the work of Price, Zubrzycki, Borrie, Jean Martin, Taft and Appleyard. By then the Displaced Persons had been settled for a decade and were being replaced as immigrants by Italians, Greeks, Maltese, Dutch and Germans. Alongside them were still a substantial majority from the United Kingdom, who were of academic interest only to Appleyard and Alan Richardson[14]. While the Immigration Department created a research section, this was inhibited by the public policies of racial exclusion and assimilation. Attitude surveys were in

---

11   Benjamin, R (1998). *'A Serious Influx of Jews'*, Allen and Unwin, Sydney.

12   Kunz, E F (1988). *Displaced Persons: Calwell's New Australians*, Australian National University Press, Sydney.

13   Tavan, G (2005). *op cit.*

14   Appleyard, R T (1964) *British Emigration to Australia*, ANU Press, Canberra; Richardson, A (1974). *British Immigrants and Australia*, ANU Press, Canberra.

their early stages, with the most relevant being developed in the Psychology Department of Melbourne University by Oscar Oeser. These showed that assimilation and racial categories strongly affected public opinion. The most popular migrants were British, Dutch and Germans – the least popular 'Negroes', Chinese and Jews.

Public policy was largely determined by the hope and expectation that Europeans who 'looked like' Australians would rapidly become 'Australians', grateful for the freedom and prosperity of Australia and willing to forget the languages, behaviour and 'ancient quarrels' of their original homelands. Of course many of the 'ancient quarrels' were the very recent suppression of nations by Nazi Germany and Soviet Russia. Fierce and lasting opposition to that was fully approved by Australian authorities as the Cold War developed. The Liberal and Democratic Labor Parties both recruited among Displaced Persons, while the ALP found more sympathy among the Greeks, Maltese and Italians. But as a general rule the formation of ethnic organisations with political objectives was not welcomed. Some were of interest to the newly formed ASIO (and to the Soviet embassy until its expulsion in 1956).

Had there been more experience of ethnic variety or more study of American ethnic scholarship, some of the assimilationist policies might have been modified or abandoned earlier than was eventually the case. The crude expectation that individuals would somehow change their personality, language, behaviour and beliefs to become 'real Australians' was not only silly but created a great deal of resentment, and was a barrier to effective integration into Australian society. Change was seen as a one-way process whereby the 'old ways' were abandoned for the much more progressive, democratic and liberal 'new ways'. Many otherwise tolerant Australians subscribed to this view, which was by no means confined to conservatives.

Yet in many respect the migrants quickly adopted traditional attitudes based on class solidarity, trade unionism, support for Labor and a sceptical attitude to Australian patriotism, and especially to British imperial pride. The most conservative elements in the post-war migration came from the refugees from Communism. But the Greek, Italian and Maltese arrivals soon formed the backbone of the Labor vote in the major cities[15]. Eventually this seeped through into the ranks of the ALP which began to respond to this new constituency, if only slowly. Even the much sought after north Europeans sometimes proved to be very militant, especially the large contingent of Finns in the mining industry.

---

15   Jupp, J (1998). *Immigration*, Oxford University Press, Sydney.

Integration 1966-1972

By the late 1960s it was becoming obvious that ethnic variety was not about to disappear and that crude assimilationism was antagonising many Europeans who were acquiring citizenship and the vote. There was a growing movement back to (non-Communist) homelands, frustrating the objective of nation building. The persistence of White Australia was also causing concern within the bureaucracy in the light of independence for most of Australia's neighbours. Thus the agitation to end White Australia, which in 1960 was mainly limited to students and clergy, had gained political support by the change of national leadership in 1966 and 1967 created by the retirement of Sir Robert Menzies and Arthur Calwell. Political leaders such as Gough Whitlam, Don Dunstan and Harold Holt were sympathetic to change, as were influential public servants in the Immigration and Foreign Affairs departments[16].

Within the Commonwealth bureaucracy the Immigration Department changed its Assimilation division into the Integration division in 1964. This was more than symbolic and created an obligation to redefine social and political objectives. Essentially 'integration' (which has recently been revived), accepted that ethnic variety and organised ethnic interests would continue and were entitled to some consideration in policy making. This recognised the reality that foreign language media was growing and that ethnic clubs and distinct religions were becoming firmly established rather than withering away as previously expected. Indeed such manifestations still exist, based on the first and subsequent generation of immigrants in many cases.

Strong influences continued to resist the argument that Australia was changing its monocultural character. Among these were the Good Neighbour Councils, set up in 1950 and subsidised through the Immigration Department. These were based on affiliated 'mainstream' welfare, charitable and religious organisations which defined their role in charitable terms but refused to accept affiliation from overtly ethnic counterparts. Politically they were close to the conservative side of Australian politics and continued in a tradition created by similar bodies in the 1920s which had organised a welcome for British migrants. Good Neighbour, in fact, did a reasonable job of welcoming British migrants and had some support among the Displaced Persons and the Dutch. However the Displaced Persons were also actively organising their own structures, which was not quite what Good Neighbour had in mind[17].

More important was the indifference and even hostility of the large numbers of southern Europeans who poured into Australia, and especially Victoria

---

16   Tavan, G (2005). *op cit*.
17   Martin, J (1965). *Refugee Settlers*, ANU Press, Canberra; Jupp, J (1966). *Arrivals and Departures*, Cheshire-Lansdowne, Melbourne.

and South Australia, between 1955 and 1970. Strong organisations like Greek Welfare or the Italian FILEF and Co-As-It were not given the recognition they deserved. Moreover some trade unions began to cater for their newly enrolled migrant members, encouraging the slow abandoning of traditional suspicion within the labour movement. These trends were enhanced by the radical reform of the ALP in Victoria in 1971 under the influence of the new national leader, Gough Whitlam. He, among others, recognised that the new intake of industrial workers from Italy, Greece, Malta and Yugoslavia were potential Labor voters and outnumbered the strongly anti-Communist DPs, who had previously been the core of the 'New Australian' population. From then onwards those electorates, in which such migrant workers were concentrated, became Labor strongholds, as they still are today.

Integration was a transitional phase in which the continuing reality of organised diversity was accepted by policy makers. However the acceptance of Australian loyalties, the English language and eventual citizenship remained central. The Immigration Department was resistant to some aspects of policy as it developed within the Labor Party context. Indeed the department was abolished altogether during the Whitlam government of 1972 to 1975[18]. Whitlam publicly claimed that it was 'racist' because of its continuing commitment to White Australia and in this he was supported by his new Minister for Immigration, Al Grassby.

Integration, then, was quietly buried, a victim of political necessity. In the process a rift was created between the mainstream charities making up Good Neighbour and the rising welfare and cultural agencies created within the ethnic communities. Integration was never effectively defined in public policy, although academics such as Charles Price, Jean Martin and Jerzy Zubrzycki were working in various ways to give the policy a sound rationale. The model was one of toleration and acceptance of new elements in society, but certainly more of dramatic changes to Australian society as a whole. Integration was transformed into multiculturalism fairly painlessly in the early 1970s, just at the point when immigration from continental Europe began its inexorable decline.

Multiculturalism 1972-1996

Assimilation and multiculturalism were essentially opposite concepts. Integration and multiculturalism were much more compatible. The movement from one to the other in public policy was both smooth and bipartisan. It was politically viable because two Prime Ministers, Whitlam and Fraser, were both committed to it. State leaders like Don Dunstan in South Australia and Neville

---

18   Whitlam, E G (1985). *The Whitlam Government 1972-1975*, Penguin Books, Victoria: 503.

Wran in New South Wales also recognised what was happening in their own jurisdictions in terms of a steadily rising 'ethnic vote'. The main resistance came from the conservative leadership of Queensland under Joh Bjelke-Petersen.

It has been argued by Mark Lopez in his definitive study of the origins of multiculturalism, that a small and dedicated group of Labor activists in Melbourne ran a highly focused lobbying campaign to influence Whitlam and the Victorian ALP[19]. This is undoubtedly true, but many of the conclusions drawn from this analysis by later opponents of the policy are illegitimate. The same processes were developing in New South Wales and South Australia, where there had been large intakes of southern Europeans into factory labour. Lopez rightly traces the central role of Victorian Labor supporters but gives inadequate attention to their alliance with ethnic organisational leaders drawn especially from among Greeks, but also including Jews, Italians and Maltese. The notion that multiculturalism was dreamed up by a small clique and was not really wanted by those to whom it appealed is quite inadequate as a description of what was happening in Melbourne in the 1970s. Nor does it give any credit to the parallel developments in Sydney and Adelaide and the work of Migrant Education Action or the Migrant Workers Conference[20].

As already indicated, the founding document of multiculturalism was the Galbally report of 1978. It withdrew funding from the Good Neighbour Councils and transferred this to ethnic welfare organisations; it argued for regular consultation with the 'ethnic' population about their social needs; it argued that language and cultural variety were not damaging to national unity and that all Australians should give their first allegiance to Australia and become citizens; it favoured the modest encouragement of languages other than English when responding to a Senate inquiry, although it was to be another ten years before Jo Lo Bianco developed a detailed policy of implementation[21]; it began the creation of the Special Broadcasting Service, which became the icon of multiculturalism until eroded by its acceptance of commercial advertising and increased ratings; it supported Migrant Resource Centres in major areas as a focal point for services to the non-English-speaking (NESB) population which was starting to be concentrated in certain suburbs; it began the process of funding local ethnic community councils within a national body FECCA (the Federation of Ethnic Communities' Councils of Australia), formalised in 1979. All of this drew NESB Australians into political and organisational activities conducted in English and oriented towards public institutions and public policy formation. Lopez notwithstanding, most of this program was designed by the Liberal Party

---

19   Lopez, M (2000). *The Origins of Multiculturalism in Australian Politics 1945–75*, Melbourne University Press, Melbourne.
20   *Australian Mosaic* (2009). Issue 23, 23 October.
21   Lo Bianco, J (1987). *National Policy on Languages*, Australian Government Publishing Service, Canberra.

activist, Petro Georgiou. It was developed at the State level in 1978 by the New South Wales report *Participation* followed by the Victorian report *Access and Equity* in 1983. *The National Agenda for a Multicultural Australia* was published in 1989[22].

All major political parties gave this program their support for the next decade, with the consensus being broken by John Howard in debates about the 1988 bicentenary of British settlement. The argument that 'billions of dollars' were sloshing about uncontrolled to the benefit of migrants was launched by a handful of vocal conservatives. It eventually found its rightful nesting place in the One Nation movement created by Pauline Hanson after her election victory in 1996. This was, of course, an excellent example of the oft-repeated lie which eventually becomes the accepted fact. The largest element in public expenditure at this stage was in the teaching of English to adults and children under two distinct programs which predated the adoption of official multiculturalism. One of the first acts of the Howard government in 1996 was to abolish the modestly funded research and advocacy agencies, the Office of Multicultural Affairs and the Bureau of Immigration Research. This saved very little money but seriously impaired the ability of the new government to conduct wide-ranging research. Neither agency, or its equivalent, has ever been restored and the Immigration Departmental library was also later abolished.

'Post-multiculturalism'

After eleven years of conservative national government (1996-2007) multiculturalism seemed to have lost its appeal. In 1988 the most influential report on immigration policy had already been very critical of multiculturalism[23]. The word was used sparingly by the national government and was specifically rejected by some of its ministers. Other terms began to be modified, including 'non-English-speaking background' and 'ethnic'. The New South Wales Labor government tried to prohibit the term 'ethnic' from public use and this was generally the attitude of Liberal state and national governments as well. The emphasis on language ability became less relevant as immigration requirements moved towards English ability and higher levels of overall education. Apart from some relatives in the family reunion stream, very few immigrants were as ignorant of English as the intake between 1947 and 1980. The main, if fairly limited, exceptions were in the humanitarian stream. Increasingly language and welfare provision moved towards this element, which was drawn largely from Asia and Africa, with Yugoslavia providing a major exception in the mid-1990s under a program which the Howard government immediately abolished

---

22   Office of Multicultural Affairs (1989). *op cit.*
23   FitzGerald, S (chair) (1988). *Immigration: A Commitment to Australia*, AGPS, Canberra.

in 1996. The main users of translating and interpreting services shifted towards this new constituency and its organisations began to influence the national and local ethnic organisational structures.

It was a tribute to the success of multiculturalism among immigrants that this transition was accomplished with little friction. The structures and services remained, although many were subject to competitive tendering. Because 'access and equity' had been adopted by the main service delivery departments, they were able to adapt to new clients as well as continuing to deal with the ageing Europeans. However some of these did present problems, coming from very underdeveloped areas such as Afghanistan, Sudan and the Congo, or from war-torn societies such as Bosnia and Iraq. Under the internment policy of the Howard government towards asylum seekers, the numbers with severe traumatic experiences were also a serious and ongoing problem. This policy was pursued by the same agency – the Immigration Department – which funded many of the services for immigrants. By the late 1990s the emphasis had not only shifted from multiculturalism to integration, but also from welfare to compliance and even repression[24].

Multiculturalism was subject to a concerted onslaught by conservatives from the mid-1980s through to the 21st century. It was actively defended by the Hawke and Keating Labor governments and by most of the Labor-controlled states. The Immigration Department shifted its emphasis, staffing and budget away from welfare and education and towards compliance and border protection[25]. Vast sums were spent on specially built detention centres in Woomera, Baxter and Christmas Island, the first and second now closed and the third replacing the distant island of Nauru as the major off-shore detention centre for those arriving by boat. The detention centre in Nauru was another grossly expensive deterrent, especially as the great majority of its inmates were judged to be genuine refugees and are now settled in Australia.

At the same time Migrant Resource Centres were instructed not to assist asylum seekers and to restrict their clientele to recent 'legal' immigrants. Grant recipient organisations were punished for criticising these wasteful policies by having grants removed with consequent loss of staff. The national body representing the 'ethnic constituency', FECCA, was faced with the dilemma of remaining silent or risking almost its entire income being removed by the Immigration Department. State Ethnic Affairs Commissions fared better as most operated in Labor-controlled states and were not subject to the Commonwealth. Multiculturalism retained a momentum of its own. But with eleven years of consistent discouragement much of the enthusiasm of the past was drained

---

24 Jupp, J (2002). *op cit.*
25 Mares, P (2001). *Borderline*, University of NSW Press, Sydney.

away. Those organisations which prospered were often financially independent, like some of the Adult Migrant Education agencies, the Queensland ECC, or MRCs like St George (Sydney), which had varied their sources of income.

In some respects the multicultural movement needed a shock to shift it out of the welfare focus of the 1980s and to cater for new realities. One of these was the shift away from southern European industrial workers and towards educated Asian professionals, enforced to a large degree by changes in immigration policy[26]. The corollary of this was the ageing of the previous European generation and the reluctance of many of their Australian-born children to participate in organisations looking to the past. This compounded the overall decline of social and industrial organisations throughout Australia as in many other developed countries. Those agencies which have prospered have been remarkably successful in bringing together activists from Asia to replace the ageing European pioneers. Particularly favoured have been those from societies where English is widely spoken, such as India, Sri Lanka, Singapore and Malaysia. They in turn have extended a much-needed welcome to the new refugee arrivals from Africa. The dilemma still remains that there is always a pull of loyalties between 'multicultural' and 'ethnic' organisations. Clubs and churches based on a specific nationality often triumph in this competition for sparse organisational talent.

In a sense multiculturalism has to be restructured and revived. This can best be done with positive encouragement from governments and especially from the Commonwealth. State governments, which have given strong support in the past, have been vital in maintaining momentum in trying times. Current attitudes towards the immigrant minorities are still strongly influenced by the expectation that they will 'integrate', even 'assimilate'. With conservatives gaining dominance in the federal parliamentary Liberal Party at the end of 2009 this approach is likely to gain political influence. Yet the fact is that 'assimilation' has not proceeded to the extent wished upon migrants by 'mainstream' policy makers and political advocates. In a democracy people assimilate at their own pace and in accordance with their own traditions and values, regardless of what governments expect[27].

This reluctance to give up and disappear into the multitude is the basis on which Australia will remain as a multicultural society catering equitably for all those it has encouraged to come to its shores. Acculturation will occur as it does everywhere and minority languages will probably suffer most from this process. But the history of policy development over the past sixty years suggests that

26   Markus, A, Jupp, J and McDonald, P (2009). *Australia's Immigration Revolution*, Allen and Unwin, Sydney.
27   Jupp, J, Nieuwenhuysen, J and Dawson, E (eds) (2007). *Social Cohesion in Australia*, Cambridge University Press, Melbourne.

working with ethnic diversity is more fruitful in maintaining social harmony and individual wellbeing than is working in favour of uniformity. A monocultural Australia will not return and public policy must adjust to that reality as it has spasmodically over the past six decades. It must also seek to gain the active involvement of elements which now appear to be alienated or remote, such as many Muslims, African refugees or new arrivals such as Pacific Islanders. Australia has built an excellent if under-funded strategy for sustaining social harmony and it would be a pity to waste it.

Chapter 3: Multilingualism, Multiculturalism and Integration

Michael Clyne

As nearly a quarter of the Australian population were born in non-English-speaking countries or are children of such people, multilingualism and multiculturalism are allied issues. In order to assess the role of language in integration and multiculturalism, we should begin by listing the main functions of language[1]. Language is:

- the most important medium of human communication;
- a symbol of identity;
- an expression of culture;
- a medium of cognitive and conceptual development;
- an instrument of action (Language is, for instance, sufficient to perform acts such as promise, complaint, invitation, and reprimand).

These functions are the arena in which the relationship between English and community languages[2] and expression of multiple identities are played out. Plurilingualism enables us to consider diversity, dynamism and hybridity[3]. Linguistic indicators of integration and multiculturalism and also of assimilation and segregation are:

- changes in the structure of the community language as a result of living in Australia and the use of the English language;
- shift from the use of the first language to that of English in general or in specific domains and institutions within a plurilingualism;
- geographical concentration or dispersion of the users of specific languages, including of monolingual English speakers;
- level of bilingualism and level of proficiency in English;
- discourse about multilingualism and monolingualism;
- community-based, governmental and other language maintenance institutions;
- Australian policies towards the public use of English and other languages.

---

1 Clyne, M (1991). *Community Languages: The Australian Experience*, Cambridge University Press, Cambridge: 3-4.
2 Usually defined as non-Indigenous languages other than English used in the Australian community. The term emphasises the reality that these languages are not 'foreign' in Australia.
3 Levey, G B (chapter 4), this volume.

As all community languages are in contact with the national language, English, in Australia, changes in the structure of various community languages and the use and maintenance of such languages can be explored differentially. Also, policies on languages can be examined over time. These topics will form the basis of this chapter.

Historical background

Prior to the first European settlement, Australia was a multilingual continent in which most people needed several languages to communicate. Some of the communities in Australia practised compulsory exogamy, where the men of one community had to marry women from another and the children learned a different language from their father and mother. Today many Australian children from different backgrounds are acquiring their bilingualism in the same way.

The First Fleet and subsequent British settlers introduced monolingualism as the norm to the Australian continent, though sizeable numbers of them spoke Irish, Gaelic or Welsh. Political and economic conditions in the homeland and the lure of gold brought many languages other than English to Australia from Europe and Asia as is reflected in the numerous community language newspapers published in the Australian colonies in the 19th century. At that time, rural enclaves using a dominant language other than English existed in various parts of Australia: the German settlements in the Barossa Valley and the Adelaide Hills, the Wimmera and Western Victoria and parts of south-eastern Queensland were best known. Bilingual education was more prevalent in Australia in the 19th century than in the 20th or so far in the 21st. But the First World War and the period immediately before and after it created an environment for the next seven decades, including the period of post-Second World War mass immigration, in which the use of languages other than English (especially in public) was considered undesirable. Then came an era of pluralistic policy. Australia's self-concept as a multicultural society was reflected in new opportunities in education, the media and public services, which will be discussed below. The history of non-indigenous Australia has been one of tension between monolingualism and multilingualism.

Today's Australia is a multilingual nation, in a multilingual world in which there are far more plurilinguals (those using two or more languages) than monolinguals. Among the almost 400 languages used in the homes of Australia's residents are Indigenous languages, Auslan, and community languages from all corners of the earth.

Table 1 Top 20 LOTEs spoken at home in Australia in 2006

	Top 20 LOTEs in 2006	Speakers in 1991	Speakers in 2001	Speakers in 2006	% Change since1991	% Change since 2001
1	Italian	418801	353605	316893	-24.3	-10.4
2	Greek	285702	263717	252222	-11.7	-4.4
3	Cantonese	163266	225307	244554	+49.8	+8.5
4	Arabic	162855	209372	243662	+49.6	+16.4
5	Mandarin	54430	139288	220596	+305.3	+58.4
6	Vietnamese	110185	174236	194858	+76.8	+11.8
7	Spanish	90477	93593	97998	+8.3	+4.7
8	Tagalog/ Filipino	59109	78878	92330	+56.2	+17.1
9	German	113335	76443	75634	-33.3	-1.1
10	Hindi	22727	47817	70013	+208.1	+46.4
11	Macedonian	64428	71994	67831	+5.3	-5.8
12	Croatian	63081	69851	63615	+0.8	-8.9
13	Korean	19756	39529	54619	+176.5	+38.2
14	Turkish	41966	50693	53858	+28.3	+6.2
15	Polish	66933	59056	53390	-20.2	-9.6
16	Serbian	24336	49203	52534	+115.9	+6.8
17	French	45496	39643	43219	-5.0	+9.0
18	Indonesian	29803	38724	42038	+41.1	+8.6
19	Persian		25238	37155		+47.2
20	Maltese	52997	41393	36517	-31.1	-11.8

According to the 2006 census, 16.8 per cent of the Australian population, including 31.4 per cent of those in Sydney and 27.9 per cent in Melbourne, speak a language other than English (LOTE) at home. This understates the number using a LOTE as it is based entirely on self-reporting of home use and many people employ a community language in the homes of parents or other relatives or in community groups but not in their own homes. Those living on their own will be counted as monolingual English speakers because of the wording of the question 'Does this person speak a language other than English at home?'

Community languages are strongly concentrated in urban areas, especially the suburbs of capital cities. This is illustrated by the examples of New South Wales (4.7 per cent of non-metropolitan residents speaking a LOTE, cf. 31.4 per cent of Sydneysiders) and Victoria (4.9 per cent, cf. 27.9 per cent of Melburnians). If we discount certain urban centres outside capital cities, such as Newcastle and Wollongong, Geelong and Shepparton, there is very little language diversity in the rest of the states, in contrast to the 19th century situation, with rural enclaves of German, Italian, Gaelic and other languages. In Queensland, decentralisation and low language diversity in Brisbane make for smaller metropolitan: non-metropolitan variation (11.3 per cent Brisbane, 5.7 per cent rest of state). The language distribution in rural and most regional areas usually reflects earlier developments in capitals – relatively more use of Italian and German and low incidence of Asian languages than in the cities.

Table 1 shows the top 20 languages in Australia. They include five of the six most widely taught languages in Australian schools, three of the four languages of our main Asian trading partners, and nine of the 20 most widely used first languages in the world. Italian and Greek are the top two community languages, followed by Cantonese, Arabic, Vietnamese and Mandarin. The past fifteen years have seen substantial decreases in the home use of a number of European languages especially German, Maltese, Italian, and Greek but far greater increases in Mandarin (305 per cent), Hindi (206 per cent), Persian, Korean, Filipino, and Vietnamese. If the changes continue, Mandarin will be the most widely used community language at the time of the 2011 census when the number of community languages with more than 100,000 speakers is likely to rise to nine, including Hindi, Filipino and Spanish[4].

Language has been a key issue in all Australian policies towards settlement of migrants and their families. Assimilation policy and public attitudes required them to learn English very quickly and to stop using their first language, especially in the public domain. As English is the national language and lingua franca, better provision for English as a second language instruction has been an essential part of any integration policy in Australia, before and after its proclamation as a multicultural society as an act of inclusive nationalism and part of a social justice agenda. At the same time, multiculturalism celebrated Australia's multilingualism and also propagated the position that at least for a transitional period, services (information, interpreting and translating) need to be available through community languages. The 'ethnic lobby' groups in the early years of the Whitlam government demanded such facilities but also the teaching of community languages for everyone in primary and secondary schools, electronic media in languages other than English, and adequate professional interpreting and translating services. Services in community languages were projected as being an essential for the integration of migrants[5]. Many of these demands were actually met, and multilingual radio, multicultural TV and the telephone interpreter service can be regarded as successes. Multilingualism, alongside a cohesive national language and lingua franca, English, was being presented, according to 'liberal nationalist' principles[6] as a desirable feature of

---

4   Clyne, M, Hajek, J and Kipp, S (2008). 'Tale of two multilingual cities in a multilingual continent', *People and Place*, vol. 6, 3: 1-8.

5   Clyne, M (2005). 'The use of exclusionary language to manipulate opinion: John Howard, asylum seekers and the reemergence of political incorrectness in Australia'. *Journal of Language and Politics*, vol. 4: 145-153.

6   (Cf. Levey, G B (chapter 4), this volume.

diversity within unity which entailed recognising plurilinguals as every bit as Australian as monolingual English speakers. In fact, some Australians employ different varieties of English for different people (eg, Greek Australian English or Jewish Australian English) within an ethnic in-group and mainstream Australian English in the wider community[7].

Language policy

For most of the 20th century, Australia's language policy was implicit, negative and ad hoc. That is, there was no codified policy, and it was mainly a policy in which languages other than English played no role. For instance, until 1973, broadcasting in 'foreign languages' was limited to 2.5 per cent of total transmission time (with limited dispensation to one Sydney and one Melbourne station). Very few languages were taught within the education system. Ethnic schools were private community organisations which received no financial aid from the Australian government and were regarded (by teachers) as disrupting children's sporting and recreational activities and possibly harming their English.

It was not until the mid-1970s that linguists and language teachers, and subsequently ethnic, Indigenous and deaf groups started agitating for a comprehensive and explicit national languages policy. This built on the pluralist policies noted above accompanying multiculturalism. In 1982, the Fraser Government responded with a senate committee to investigate the need for a national languages policy. Over more than 12 months, the committee heard evidence from 94 witnesses and received 241 submissions, from government departments, statutory bodies, ethnic, teacher and other professional organisations, and individuals. The most substantial submission was received from ten professional language associations. The comprehensive nature of the enquiry ensured that linguists could provide much input[8].

The scope of the inquiry was broad, including English, Indigenous, community and sign languages, thereby emphasising the complementary role of English and the other languages and thus of both integration and multiculturalism. The report of the Senate inquiry set the guiding principles for the subsequent national policy:

- English for all;
- maintenance and development of Indigenous and community languages;

---

7 Clyne, M, Eisikovits, E and Tollfree, L (2002). 'Ethnolects as in-group markers', in A Duszak (ed), *Us and Others*, Benjamin, Amsterdam: 133-157.
8 Ozolins, U (1993). *The Politics of Language in Australia*, Cambridge University Press, Cambridge.

- service provision in Indigenous and community languages for those requiring them;
- opportunities for the learning of second and additional languages.

After the Senate inquiry, responsibility for language policy was vested in the Minister for Education[9]. The actual National Policy on Languages[10] was preceded by recently developed pluralist state languages-in-education policies from Victoria (1985) and South Australia (1985). The explicit national policy used Australian and international research to argue motivations for multilingualism in Australia – economic, social and cultural – and to justify the complementary roles of English and other languages. The policy encompassed implementation strategies to achieve the guiding principles and budgetary recommendations which were all passed by Parliament. However, the public agenda swiftly changed from social justice to economic rationalism, and a new Australian Language and Literacy Policy was developed[11], with an emphasis on English literacy and languages of Australia's major trading partners. However, there was a strong push to increase retention in senior secondary school LOTE programs. This was the last of the coordinated national languages policies. It was followed by a refragmentation of language policy into single issue policies such as literacy, Asian languages, interpreting and translating policies – with each of the states and territories developing their own languages-in-education policies. The Dawkins Report also brought to an end the participatory model of policy making on language and multicultural issues. Donald Horne[12] described the National Policy on Languages as a 'blueprint for change stamped by the voice of ordinary citizens'. By 1991, planning was top-down[13].

LOTE will be the fifth key learning area to be included in the Gillard Government's national curriculum but it is as yet uncertain if and for how long students will have to take a LOTE. The Howard Government's push for a monolingual national core curriculum has been followed by a reinstatement of a new version of the Rudd/Gillard national Asian languages and studies program[14]. This policy marginalises the needs of speakers with a background in these languages as learners in the education system or their value as bilingual

---

9 (Cf. the Galbally Report, which was under the jurisdiction of the Prime Minister, see Jupp, J (chapter 2), this volume.

10 Lo Bianco, J (1987). *National Policy on Languages*, Australian Government Publishing Service, Canberra.

11 Dawkins, J (1991). *Australia's Language: The Australian Language and Literacy Policy*, Australian Government Publishing Service.

12 Horne, D (1994). *The Public Culture: An argument with the future*, Pluto Press, London: 20.

13 Lo Bianco, J (2001). 'Language Policy and Education in Australia', in J Lo Bianco amd R Wickert (eds), *Australian policy activism in language and literacy*, Language Australia, Canberra: 11-44; Moore, H (2005). *Identifying 'The Target Population': A genealogy of policy making for English as a Second Language (ESL) in Australian schools (1947-1997)*, PhD thesis, Ontario Institute for Studies in Education, University of Toronto.

14 Department of Education, Employment and Workplace Relations (2010). *National Asian Languages and Studies in Schools Program – Overview*, DEEWR, Canberra.

resources professionally or to provide input and output for second language learners. Moreover, part of the recent discourse on languages-in-education policy in Australia has been to represent 'background speakers' as people with an 'unfair advantage' who need to be penalised to avoid demotivating 'real learners'[15]. Among other things, this ignores the continuum of levels of plurilingual skills encompassed by the term 'background speakers'[16]. What constitutes a 'background speaker' (those who 'speak Chinese' at home) is also not problematised in Orton's[17] recent report on Chinese language education in Australian schools, which does argue for differentiated classes as well as assessment systems for three groups: first language speakers, background speakers and second language learners. Witchhunts in the interests of discrimination have a negative effect on language maintenance[18]. It appears that despite the commodification of certain languages, the dominant group wishes to be assured of power over those who speak those languages. Just who are the beneficiaries of multiculturalism is an issue that recurs in Ghassan Hage's writings[19]. Yet the commodification of languages could have been represented as an opportunity for speakers of community languages in Australia to make a special contribution to the nation and for second language learners to utilise the potential for interaction in the languages. Research literature demonstrating the cognitive benefits of bilingualism[20] is often cited in favour of second language learning[21] but very rarely presented in relation to enhancing the dynamism, creativity or innovativeness of Australian workplaces.

The return of the term and concept 'foreign languages' to include languages used in Australia concurs with the post-2001 discourse around 'Australian values' which excluded people of 'non-Anglo-Celtic backgrounds' and reversed the policies of the past thirty years. This mono-dimensional position is also consistent with the representation of multiculturalism as being in conflict with integration, which is often confused with assimilation. In the following quote, John Howard is referring to refugees: 'I think assimilation or integration, whichever word you want to use, into the Australian community can from time-to-time be an issue[22]'.

---

15   Clyne, M (2005). *Op cit*: 118-133; Slaughter, Y (2007). *The study of Asian languages in two Australian states: Considerations for language-in-education policy and planning*, PhD thesis, University of Melbourne.

16   Clyne, M (2005). *Op cit*: 129.

17   Orton, J (2008). *Chinese language education in Australian schools*, University of Melbourne, Victoria.

18   Clyne, M, Fernandez, S, Chen, I and Summo-O'Connell, R (1997). *Background Speakers*, Language Australia, Canberra; Clyne, M (2005). *Op cit*: 128.

19   Since Hage, G (1998). *White Nation: Fantasies of White Supremacy in a Multicultural Society*, Pluto, Sydney.

20   Summarised eg, in Clyne, M (2005). *Op cit*.

21   Group of Eight statement (2007).

22   *The Australian*, 3 October, 2007.

While Australia is a multilingual society, it has, paradoxically, also been recaptured by a pervasive monolingual mindset which sees monolingualism as the norm and multilingualism as the exception, even as a problem or a deficit. This is reflected in the inadequate LOTE programs in schools, the low retention rates to VCE in languages, the persistent assessment of children's early development in English only even when it is the weaker language, and, again in recent years, in the frequent failure to see the value of linguistic diversity for the individual and the nation.

Changes in the structure of community languages

A common feature of community languages in Australia is the transference of English lexical items (vocabulary), which adequately refer to the new lifestyle that has been experienced in Australia, including work, school and Australian institutions. The actual items transferred vary as each person's life varies. Among many examples are *beach, gum-tree, paddock, creek, brick-veneer, rates, assembly, locker bell, superannuation, milkbar, chemist, serve* and *fix*. Due to personal preferences and differences in the structure of the community languages, there is variation in the way in which English items are integrated into the phonological, grammatical and semantic systems of the recipient language. But there are general rules of grammatical integration, so that English-derived verbs will tend to be conjugated in a particular way in German or Spanish, English-derived nouns assigned to genders in a particular way in Croatian or Romanian. Existing devices such as suffixes to form professional terms or diminutives in the community language are employed to help express their Australian reality – It. *farmista* (farmer), *bus-ista* (bus driver), Gk. *agentadiko* (agent), *contractodoros* (contractor)[23], Dut. *fensje* (little fence), *flokje* (little flock)[24], Gk. *milkbaraki* (milk bar), *boksaki* (little box)[25]. Italian *fattoria* (Italian small farm) takes on the meaning of the similar sounding *factory*, while Australian farms are referred to by the integrated English transfer, *farma*.

Community languages in Australia also undergo grammatical changes, including ones leading to simplification under English influence, such as the generalisation of 'have' as an auxiliary in most European languages. There is variation between speakers, but also evidence of major typological changes such as in word order, even in the first generation in Dutch, for instance,

---

23   Tamis, A (1986). *The state of Modern Greek as spoken in Victoria*, PhD thesis, University of Melbourne.
24   Clyne, M (1977). ''Nieuw-Hollands' or Double-Dutch?' *Dutch Studies*, vol. 1: 1-30.
25   Tamis, A (1986). *Op cit*.

and some dropping of personal endings in verbs in the second. This is a product of limited use of the community language, convergence between English and the other language and widespread code-switching between the languages among bilinguals. However, in this case there is also evidence of the beginnings of similar grammatical developments in the home country which are greatly accelerated in a diasporic context[26]. The Australian context offers many opportunities to explore how languages of different types are adapted in a situation where multiculturalism finds a place for community languages, and how they are integrated to cope with communication. Code-switching between languages can be either accidental, reflecting reduced use of the community language, and deliberate, reflecting a conscious understanding of domain separation, semantic differences and identity issues. And yet listener tests[27] have demonstrated that heavy 'mixtures' of languages are not valued by at least some immigrant communities.

Among older bilinguals, less disciplined and therefore bi-directional code-switching (ie, not just from English into the other language but also vice versa) is one of the factors that has given credence to the myth that as (healthy) people get older, they lose skills in their second language and revert to their first. Another factor is slower recall where English is employed less due to changes in social networks. However, a longitudinal study of Dutch-English bilinguals[28] suggests a multiplicity of changes in the balance between the languages. The level of proficiency and code-switching patterns earlier in life are also an important factor. Seebus[29] shows that the residents of Dutch old people's villages in Melbourne use and need both languages as part of their identities.

The identity functions of community languages are not necessarily lost within the shift to English. Phonological and lexical features are transferred from the community language to English to form ethnolects of Australian English such as Greek Australian English and Jewish/Yiddish Australian English, employed within the in-group alongside the mainstream Australian English used by the same second and later generation speakers within the wider community. Such ethnolects are strengthened by concentrated settlements and an ethnic

---

26 Clyne, M (2003). *Dynamics of Language Contact*, Cambridge University Press, Cambridge: 133-134.
27 Bettoni, C and Gibbons, J (1988). 'Linguistic purism and language shift: A guise-voiced study of the Italian community in Sydney', *International Journal of the Sociology of Language*, vol. 72: 37-50; Pauwels, A (1990). 'Dutch in Australia: Perception of and attitudes towards transference and other language contact phenomena', in S Romaine (ed), *Language in Australia*, Cambridge University Press, Cambridge: 228-240.
28 de Bot, K and Clyne, M (1989). 'Language reversion revisited', *Studies in Second Language Acquisition*, vol. 9: 167-177; de Bot, K and Clyne, M (1994). 'A 16-Year Longitudinal Study of Language Attrition in Dutch Immigrants in Australia', *Journal of Multilingual and Multicultural Development*, vol. 15, 1: 17-28.
29 Seebus, I (2008). *Dinkum Dutch - Aussies language and identity among elderly Dutch-Australians*, PhD thesis, University of Melbourne.

religious denomination with religious schools, so that the ethnolect serves as an indicator of multiple identity (eg, religion, ethnicity – or in the case of former German rural enclaves, also region)[30].

Language shift

A high degree of language shift from the community language to English is indicative of assimilation. A low degree of shift can reflect multiculturalism or a desire to segregate but does not necessarily indicate a reluctance to integrate, since it is compatible with a high degree of bilingualism (see below). The shift varies between groups - from a 3 per cent shift among Vietnamese-born to 64.4 per cent among Netherlands-born. Post-war northern and central European groups who came to Australia during the assimilation era (eg, Dutch, Germans, Austrians, Lithuanians, Latvians) record the greatest shift while recent communities from Asia, Africa and the Middle East, and also more established communities from the eastern Mediterranean (speakers of Macedonian, Turkish, Arabic, Greek), are maintaining their languages most (Table 2). In between are the other groups, which include Italian, Spanish, Polish, Japanese and Filipino speakers. Among the more retentive groups, intermarriage between first- and second-generation speakers of a language may be a factor.

Space does not permit a discussion of all the factors relating to pre- and post-migration experiences promoting higher or lower language shift. Some relate to the status of the language in the heartland and the multilingualism of the region or the complexity of the language's address system; others to the kind of Australia they came into and lived through, and sometimes there was an element of continuity in the two. Different vintages may behave differently. While later Hungarian-speaking minorities from Romania and Serbia tended to continue their community language, the earlier vintages of displaced persons and refugees from Hungary reacted ambivalently to what they perceived as a xenophobic and culturally unsophisticated host community – often resulting in first generation maintenance and second generation shift[31]. Chinese and Arabic speakers reacted quite differently to racist and xenophobic attitudes in small sections of the Australian mainstream in the late 1980s – with language shift among many Chinese- Australians and stronger maintenance efforts on the part of Arabic speakers.

The earlier vintage of Macedonian speakers from northern Greece were initially reluctant to claim Macedonian use because of past suppression of the language,

---

30   Clyne, M, Eisikovits E and Tollfree, L (2004). 'Ethnic varieties of English', in *English in Australia*.
31   Clyne, M and Fernandez, S (2007). *Community Language Learning in Australia*, Springer, Berlin.

while the later vintage from the Republic of Macedonia, having been educated in the language and having experienced it as a national language, also felt more secure in Australian multiculturalism. The co-settlement of the groups facilitated vigorous language maintenance efforts after 1994 when the Kennett Government required a change in the name of their language to 'Macedonian-Slavonic' in response to the demands of sections of the Greek community. This the Macedonian-speaking community challenged in two successful court appeals, something that strengthened the community's Australian identity[32].

There are perhaps two important factors in language maintenance that stand out. One is cultural (including religious) distance from the mainstream group (often promoting in-group marriage). The other is the role of language among the core values of the culture and the intertwining of language with other core values. This has been the basis of a model developed by Smolicz[33], on the argument that each group has particular values such as language, religion or family cohesion which are fundamental to their existence to the group. While this went some way to explaining differentials in language shift, the model had to be refined on the basis of further research. This, he believed, would facilitate a differentiation between low and high language maintenance groups. But the model had to be subsequently refined by him and his associates[34] on the basis of further research and critiques. Among other factors that have to be taken into account are variation between attitudes and practice, generational, sub-group and contextual factors and the importance of the intertwining of factors[35]. Seebus[36] draws attention to the monolingual first-language basis of the cultural value theory relating to people who are bilinguals.

Gender is a multifaceted factor. The census statistics indicate that for most groups from Europe, Latin America, the Middle East and the Horn of Africa, men maintain community languages more than women, though this tendency is weaker in the second generation than in the first. However, among those born in Japan, Korea and the Philippines, and to a lesser extent those from Cambodia, India, Singapore, Sri Lanka and Taiwan, but not those born in China, the shift is greater among women. With the exception of India, these are the birth countries from which women have married out more than men, the reverse of the tendency among most of the groups from Europe, Latin

---

32   Clyne, M and Kipp, S (2006). *Tiles in a Multilingual Mosaic: Macedonian, Somali and Filipino in Melbourne*, Pacific Linguistics, Canberra: 27-30.

33   Smolicz, J J (1981). 'Core values and ethnic identity', *Ethnic and Racial Studies*, vol. 4: 75-90.

34   Smolicz, J J (2001). in M Secombe (ed) *Education and Culture*, J Nicholas, Melbourne.

35   *Ibid;* Katsikis, M (1993). Language attitudes, ethnicity and language maintenance: The case of second generation Greek-Australians, BA (Hons) thesis, Dept of Linguistics, Monash University; Katsikis, M (1997). The generation gap: Insights into the language and cultural   maintenance of third generation Greek-Australians. MA thesis, Dept of Linguistics, Monash University. Clyne, M (2005). *Op cit*: 73-85; Clyne, M (2006). *Tiles in a multicultural mosaic*, Pacific Linguistics, Melbourne.

36   Seebus, I (2008). *Op cit.*

America, the Middle East and the Horn of Africa[37]. In a comparative study across three groups – German, Greek and Vietnamese-speaking – Pauwels and Winter[38] show the complementarity of domains and gender in language use. It is Greek females and Vietnamese males who use their community languages most and also identify it more with the neighbourhood domain. Greek women employ their community language across all the domains and show the highest community language use of any of the groups.

Table 2 Language shift in the first generation, 2006. Language shift, overseas-born, 2006

Viet Nam	3.0%	Russian Fed	14.2%	Mauritius	28.5%
China	3.8%	Ukraine	14.2%	India	34.4%
Iraq	3.9%	Ethiopia	14.9%	France	35.0%
Eritrea	4.4%	Indonesia	17.3%	Malaysia	35.0%
Somalia	4.5%	Italy	17.3%	Sri Lanka	35.0%
Taiwan	4.8%	Japan	17.4%	Hungary	36.7%
Cambodia	5.3%	Argentina	18.1%	Malta	39.9%
Fmr Yugoslavia	6.5%	Other Sth America	19.3%	Latvia	42.4%
El Salvador	7.0%	Brazil	20.0%	Lithuania	44.6%
Lebanon	7.4%	Portugal	20.5%	Switzerland	44.9%
Turkey	8.2%	Egypt	22.2%	Singapore	49.1%
Greece	8.6%	Poland	23.6%	Germany	53.9%
Hong Kong	11.2%	Philippines	27.0%	Austria	55.2%
Chile	13.8%	Spain	27.5%	Netherlands	64.4%

37   Clyne, M (2005). *Op cit*: 79; cf. also Khoo, S E (2009). 'Migrant youth and social connectedness', in F Mansouri (ed), *Youth identity and migration: Culture, values and social connectedness*, Common Ground Publishing, Melbourne: 165-177.
38   Pauwels, A (1995). 'Linguistic practices and language maintenance among bilingual women and men in Australia', *Nordlyn*, vol. 11: 21-50; Winter, J and Pauwels, A (2000). 'Gender and Language Contact Research in the Australian Context', *Journal of Multilingual and Multicultural Development*, vol. 21, 6: 508-522.

Table 3 – Language shift, second generation contrasting exogamous and endogamous families, 1996 (English only by birthplace of parents)[39]

Birthplace of parent(s)	Language shift (%)		
	Endogamous	Exogamous	Second generation (aggregated)
Austria	80	91.1	89.7
Chile	12.7	62.3	38
France	46.5	80.4	77.7
Germany	77.6	92	89.7
Greece	16.1	51.9	28
Hong Kong	8.7	48.7	35.7
Hungary	64.2	89.4	82.1
Italy	42.6	79.1	57.9
Japan	5.4	68.9	57.6
Korea	5.4	61.5	18
Lebanon	11.4	43.6	20.1
Macedonia, Republic of	7.4	38.6	14.8
Malta	70	92.9	82.1
Netherlands	91.1	96.5	95
Other South American	15.7	67.1	50.5
Poland	58.4	86.9	75.7
China	17.1	52.8	37.54
Spain	38.3	75	63
Taiwan	5	29.2	21
Turkey	5	46.6	16.1

To estimate the shift to English in the second generation (Australian-born), we have to go back to the 1996 Census since it was the last to elicit responses on the parents' country of birth, which is the nearest we have to language first acquired. The shift to English is much greater in the second generation than in the first. It follows the same rank ordering as in the first but for an exceptionally substantial inter-generational shift in the groups originating in Hong Kong and PR China – increased from 9 per cent to 35.7 per cent and from 4.6 to 37.4 per cent respectively (Table 3). However, it is by no means certain that this is still

---

39   Clyne, M and Kipp, S (1997). *Pluricentric Languages in an Immigrant Context,* Mouton de Gruyter, Berlin: 463.

the trend. The 2006 data for the first generation show an appreciable drop in language shift among the China-born from 4.3 per cent to 3.8 per cent and a rise from 3.8 per cent to 4.8 per cent among the Taiwan-born. The 1996 second generation statistics represent a very much smaller Cantonese and Mandarin population, but one with a much higher level of exogamy. In our table we see that the shift is generally highest in families with exogamous parents. This can be illustrated best among families with a Japanese background (second generation from endogamous family, 5.4 per cent, from exogamous family, 68.9 per cent) and for a Korean one (from endogamous family, 4.4 per cent, from exogamous family, 61.5 per cent). My guess would be that the second-generation shift for Australians of China, Hong Kong and Taiwan backgrounds will have decreased considerably. This is just one reason why data on parents' country of birth badly needs to be elicited in the 2011 Census.

The higher shift in exogamous families is not to say that languages other than English cannot be transmitted by *one* of the parents. Workshops for parents raising, or wishing to raise, children in more than one language are very well attended (400 parents attended a recent one at the University of Melbourne) and overwhelmingly by 'ethnolinguistically mixed' couples opting for the one parent one language strategy.

Language maintenance ought to be an informed choice and so should language shift.

Family communication

As census data does not provide us with a detailed picture, I will employ some recent and earlier indepth studies of language contact in Australia, especially ones relating to German, Dutch, Arabic, Cantonese, Mandarin and Spanish-speaking bilinguals, to explore who speaks what language to whom and when[40], especially in the family setting. There are a considerable number of other facts about that speech situation that impinge on language choice — the participants/interlocutors in interaction, the range of communications in the home, the communicative functions and intentions, the symbolic significance of language choice in the home.

The *participants* in a plurilingual setting tend to be identified according to age/generation. There is variation between the communities in the general pattern of family discourse[41]:

---

40   A question initiated by Fishman, J A (1968). *Readings in the Sociology of Language*, Mouton, The Hague.
41   Clyne, M (2003). *Op cit*: 43.

- parents speak English to each other and to the children;
- parents speak the community language to each other but English to the children;
- parents speak the community language to the children who answer in English;
- parents and children speak to each other in the community language.

Comparing the patterns in German- and Dutch-speaking post-war migrant families from whom linguistic data was recorded in 1962-64 and 1970-71 respectively, the dominant pattern among the Dutch–Australians already appeared to be the use of English to the children. Among the German speakers, either the whole family spoke German or the children spoke to each other and were addressed in English. It seems that the shift to English in German-speaking families was instigated by the children, while the shift in Dutch-speaking families was instigated at least in part by the parents. It is possible that this is due to the Dutch speakers being recorded some years after the German speakers, but my impression that there is a major difference in community language use between the two communities was confirmed by census statistics and similar German responses to other surveys[42].

In exogamous families across communities, English is generally either used throughout or is the language of family discourse and each parent interacts with the child in 'their own language'. The role of participants in language shift is related to the nature of social networks.

A comparative study of Chinese, Spanish and Arabic[43] shows a predominance of English as the medium of communication among the children and the community language as the medium in which the adults communicate. (This concurs with the situation among Greek-Australians reported by Tsokalidou[44].) Thus, strong maintenance among parents does not necessarily translate into a similar pattern among the children. This is the general pattern in the Spanish and Egyptian groups but much less common among the Taiwanese, who are the most recently arrived of the families, in which the parents have the lowest English proficiency.

---

42   For example, Clyne, M (1970). 'Migrant English in Australia', in W S Ransom (ed), *English Transported,* ANU, Canberra.

43   Clyne, M and Kipp, S (1999). *Pluricentric Languages in an Immigrant Context: Spanish, Arabic and Chinese,* Mouton de Gruyter, Berlin.

44   Tsokalidou, R (1994). Cracking the code. An insight into code switching and gender into second generation Greek Australians, unpublished PhD thesis, Monash University: 220.

Table 4 Home language use by birthplace group[45]

Group	Adult to adult	Mother to child	Child to mother	Child to child
Egypt group	CL: 77.8% E: 16.7% CL/E: 5.6%	CL: 40% E: 26.7% CL/E: 33.3%	CL: 37.5% E: 25% CL/E: 31.3%	CL: 7.8% E: 80.8% CL/E: 11.5%
Lebanon group	CL: 83.3% E: 3.3% CL/E: 13.3%	CL: 57.1% E: 5.7% CL/E: 37.1%	C: 54% E: 5% CL/E: 35%	CL: 26.9% E: 53.8% CL/E: 19.2%
Hong Kong group	CL: 76.9% E: 0% CL/E: 23.1%	CL: 55.9% E: 0% CL/E: 44.1%	C: 53% E: - CL/E: 42%	CL: 30% E: 50% CL/E: 20%
Taiwan group	CL: 100% E: 0% CL/E: 0%	CL: 89.2% E: 0% CL/E: 10.8%	C: 90% E: - CL/E: 11%	CL: 33.3% E: 20.8% CL/E: 45.8%
Chile group	CL: 80% E: 8% CL/E: 12%	CL: 25.8% E: 0% CL/E: 74.2%	C: 24% E: - CL/E: 70%	CL: 0% E: 84.6% CL/E: 15.4%
Spain group	CL: 96.9% E: 0% CL/E: 3.1%	CL: 51.4% E: 0% CL/E: 48.6%	C: 49% E: - CL/E: 46%	CL: 0% E: 82% CL/E: 18%

(CL – community language; E- English)

However, none of these more recent groups replicate the tendency for children to respond to their parents in English, as was the case among the earlier Dutch and German-speaking communities. In all groups, except those of Spanish origin, differences between mothers' and fathers' use of CL with the children was small. Fathers of Spanish origin used considerably more CL with their children than did mothers.

The Chinese and Spanish groups[46] showed a marked drop in 'same group' *social networks* between the first and second generation (42 per cent to 5 per cent, Spanish, 70 per cent to 10 per cent, Chilean; 88 per cent to 14 per cent, Hong Kong, 74 per cent to 28 per cent). Spanish-born (55 per cent) and Hong Kong-born informants (52 per cent), who had the highest proportion of social networks with 'others' in the first generation, were the groups in the study whose children exhibited the highest shift.

In other groups or families such as post-war German-speaking, it is the *range of communications*, and therefore the topic and domain that determines language choice, often with much 'code-switching', especially where there is an intermingling of domains (people talking about school or work or 'mainstream' institutions in the context of the home domain). This is subject to change, eg, as

---

45   Clyne, M (2003). *Op cit*: 44, based on Clyne, M and Kipp, S (1999). *Op cit*.
46   Clyne, M and Kipp, S (1999). *Ibid*.

children extend their experience outside the family and proceed through school they will increasingly be unwilling or unable to express their experiences and needs in the community language only.

The symbolic significance of language choice in relation to identity also varies. It may express solidarity with non-English-speaking relatives (eg, in the Taiwan, Chinese and Lebanese communities) but simultaneously exclude others (eg, English-speaking monolinguals). A clear-cut functional differentiation between languages is particularly strong among trilinguals (e., Hungarian with spouse, German with friends, English with their children and work colleagues; Italian to express personal identity, Spanish for family identity, English for everyday wider communication. This also applies to Sicilian–Italian–English and Venetian–Italian–English trilinguals in Sydney[47], where Italian is the inter-regional language employed in the more public and formal domains, dialect is bound to communication with people of the same regional background and especially with the first generation. The choice between dialect and English is often domain-specific (home versus away from home). Pauwels[48], on the other hand, found that Limburgers are less likely to maintain Dutch because the identification of Limburgs as 'their' language and the rigid functional specialisation between the languages separates them from the rest of the Dutch–Australian community.

Concentration

There are a number of reasons why speakers of a particular language may cluster together. Initially limited English is one of these factors[49] but there are many others, including religious and dietary ones and chain migration. Table 5 shows the relative concentration of specific ethnolinguistic groups in the Sydney and Melbourne metropolitan areas. The concentration factor is derived from the formula:

Number of users of the language in LGA	Population of LGA
Number of users of language in metropolitan area	Population of whole metropolitan area

For the purpose of this table, the three LGAs with the highest concentration of the language are included in the average.

Some of the languages with the highest concentration factors are those of recently arrived groups, such as Karen and Khmer in Melbourne and Somali and

---

47   Bettoni, C and Rubino, A (1996). *Emigrazione e compartamento linguistico. Un' indagine sul trilinguismo dei siciliani e dei veneti in Australia,* Congedo.

48   Pauwels, A (1986). *Dialects and Language Maintenance,* Foris, Dordrecht.

49   Winter, J and Pauwels, A (2000). *Op cit.*

Dari in Sydney. However, this does not always follow. Somali speakers arrived in Sydney and Melbourne about the same time and their concentration factor in Sydney is more than twice that in Melbourne. Hindi speakers, a relatively new group, are the most dispersed group in Melbourne – far more so than in Sydney. High concentration is often accompanied by low language shift – Macedonian is an example in both cities. However, Maltese in Melbourne with a high shift has a higher concentration factor than Turkish with a low shift, and Dutch is more concentrated in Melbourne than German, which has a lower shift rate.

Some languages are especially strongly concentrated in one municipality and there is a big drop to the second most concentrated LGA and then to the third most concentrated (the latter does not apply to Bosnian in Melbourne).

In Sydney examples of these are:

Somali	Auburn (21.797)	Botany Bay (10.752)	Canterbury (5.466)
Serbian	Leichhardt (18.519)	Liverpool (6.414)	Fairfield (5.514)
Dari	Auburn (15.293)	Holroyd (8.384)	Parramatta (4.847)
Tamil	Strathfield (15.850)	Holroyd (6.564)	Auburn (5.726)
Turkish	Auburn (15.622)	Botany Bay (4.508)	Holroyd (3.503)

In Melbourne:

Karen*	Wyndham (20.780)	Hobsons Bay (8.058)	Maroondah (3.487)
Khmer	Greater Dandenong (15.018)	Kingston (2.763)	Casey (2.276)
Macedonian	Whittlesea (10.280)	Brimbank (4.282)	Darebin (2.620)
Russian	Glen Eira (10.154)	Port Phillip (4.490)	Bayside (2.292)
Bosnian	Greater Dandenong (7.5)	Casey (1.748)	Melton (1.465)

* In 2006, 96 per cent of Karen speakers in Australia lived in Melbourne. It should be noted that the number of Karen speakers in this country has increased substantially since then.

Table 5 Concentration factors: Sydney and Melbourne, 2006 census

Sydney		Melbourne	
Language	Concentration	Language	Concentration
Somali	12.669	Karen	10.775
Serbian	10.149	Khmer	6.685
Dari	9.508	Vietnamese	5.866
Tamil	9.380	Macedonian	5.727
Turkish	7.877	Russian	5.646
Karen	7.858	Maltese	5.495
Macedonian	7.291	Somali	5.417
Khmer	6.920	Turkish	5.048
Vietnamese	5.562	Arabic	3.607
Russian	5.277	Dari	3.559
Greek	4.792	Mandarin	3.559
Maltese	3.964	Serbian	3.435
Arabic	3.931	Tamil	3.181
Mandarin	3.822	Italian	3.076
Italian	3.516	Dutch	2.655
German	2.397	Greek	2.379
Dutch	2.290	German	1.857

Chapter 4: Multicultural Integration in Political Theory

Geoffrey Brahm Levey

The mass migrations to the United States from the 1880s to 1920 inspired a wealth of influential work by sociologists, historians, and public intellectuals on the integration of people arriving in a new society from the corners of the globe. People such as Israel Zangwill, Randolph Bourne, Horace Kallen, Oscar Handlin, Will Herberg, John Higham, Nathan Glazer and Milton Gordon[1] helped frame the analysis of immigrant absorption in the United States and beyond. In contrast, political theorists have turned their attention to this subject only recently. There had long been debate over the status of *national* minorities, going back to J S Mill's[2] famous warning in 1859 that 'free institutions are next to impossible in a country made up of different nationalities', a position endorsed by T H Green[3]. And this debate became especially energetic among Austro-Marxists (eg, Bauer and others[4]) leading up to and following the imperial disintegrations after the First World War. But the subject of *immigrant* minorities and their integration was largely ignored in political theory for most of the twentieth century.

The English pluralists – J N Figgis, H J Laski and G D H Cole – emphasised the importance of groups such as churches and trade unions as an important check on the state's aggrandisement of power[5]. Similarly, the American pluralists typically had in mind socio-economic interest groups rather than identity groups[6].

---

1   Zangwill, Israel (1909). *The Melting-Pot: Drama in Four Acts*. New York: Macmillan; Bourne, Randolph (1916). 'Trans-National America' *Atlantic Monthly* 118: 86-97; Kallen, Horace M (1924). *Democracy and Culture in the United States*. Boni and Liveright, New York; Handlin, Oscar (1951). *The Uprooted: The Epic Story of the Great Migrations that Made the American People*. Grosset and Dunlap, New York; Herberg, Will (1955). *Protestant–Catholic–Jew: An Essay in American Religious Sociology*. Doubleday, Garden City, N Y; Higham, John (1955). *Strangers in the Land: Patterns of American Nativism, 1860-1925*. Rutgers University Press, New Brunswick, N J; Glazer, Nathan and Moynihan, Daniel Patrick (1963). *Beyond the Melting Pot: The Negroes, Puerto Ricans, Jews, Italians, and Irish of New York City*. MIT Press and Harvard University Press, Cambridge, Mass.; Gordon, Milton M (1964). *Assimilation in American Life: The Role of Race, Religion, and National Origins*. Oxford University Press, New York.

2   Mill, John Stuart 1972 [1859]. *Utilitarianism, On Liberty, and Considerations on Representative Government*, H B Acton (ed). J M Dent and Sons, London: 361.

3   Green, T H (1911). *Lectures on the Principles of Political Obligation*. Longmans, London and New York.

4   Bauer, Otto 2000 [1907]. *The Question of Nationalities and Social Democracy*. University of Minnesota Press, Minneapolis; Zimmern, Alfred E (1918). *Nationality and Government*. Robert M McBride and Co., New York; Barker, Ernest (1927). *National Character and the Factors in its Formation*. Harper and Brothers, New York.

5   Barker, Ernest (1915). *Political Thought in England from Herbert Spencer to the Present Day*. New York: Henry Holt; Burrow, J W (1988). *Whigs and Liberals: Continuity and Change in English Political Thought*. Clarendon Press, Oxford; Hirst, Paul (ed) (1989). *The Pluralist Theory of the State: Selected Writings of G D H. Cole, J N Figgis and H J Laski*. Routledge, London.

6   See, for example, Bentley, Arthur F (1908). *The Process of Government*. Principia Press, Bloomington, Ind.; Truman, David B (1951). *The Governmental Process*. Knopf, New York; Schattschneider, E E (1960). *The Semi-*

And philosophical pluralists such as Isaiah Berlin[7] were concerned with the incommensurability of *values*, and not groups at all. Although multiculturalism as a public philosophy was inaugurated in Canada in 1971, and in various other countries (including Australia) later in the seventies and eighties, there is no entry for it in the corrected edition of the *Blackwell Encyclopedia of Political Thought* two decades later[8]. For the most part, post-war political theorists assumed either that the 'state should treat cultural membership as a purely private matter', or – as in the early work of John Rawls[9] and Ronald Dworkin[10] – that liberal democracies were simplified nation-states, 'where the political community is co-terminous with one and only one cultural community'[11].

This situation began to change in the 1980s with the so-called communitarian challenge. Communitarian critics argued that liberalism concentrated on the relationship between the individual and the state to the exclusion of ethnic groups and other collectivities, and that liberal individualism was fundamentally hostile to constitutive identities[12]. In the 1990s, however, and partly in response to the communitarian critique, the debate over cultural identity and recognition was increasingly conducted *within* the terms of liberal theory. A key impetus, here, was Will Kymlicka's ground-breaking book, *Liberalism, Community and Culture*, published in 1989. Kymlicka supplied an argument showing how respect for individual autonomy and the other terms of Rawls's[13] egalitarian liberal theory of justice could actually mandate the recognition of cultural identity and minority cultural rights. Still, even *Liberalism, Community and Culture* had no index entry for 'multiculturalism'; Kymlicka, a Canadian, was initially concerned with the plight of the Indigenous peoples in his country. However, within a few years, he and other political theorists were addressing the

---

Sovereign People. Holt, Rinehart and Winston, New York; and Dahl, Robert A (1967). *Pluralist Democracy in the United States: Conflict and Consent*. Rand McNally, Chicago. For two contrasting interpretations of American pluralism, see Walzer (1980). 'Pluralism: A Political Perspective'. In *The Harvard Encyclopedia of American Ethnic Groups*, Stephen A (ed) Thernstrom. Harvard University Press, Cambridge, Mass.; and Gunnell, John G (2004). *Imagining the American Polity: Political Science and the Discourses of Democracy*. Pennsylvania State University Press, University Park.

7   Berlin, Isaiah (1969). *Four Essays on Liberty*. Oxford University Press, Oxford and New York.

8   Miller, David, Coleman, J, Connolly, W and Ryan, A (eds) (1991). *Blackwell Encyclopedia of Political Thought*. Basil Blackwell, Oxford.

9   Rawls, John (1971). *A Theory of Justice*. Harvard University Press, Cambridge: Mass.

10   Dworkin, Ronald (1985). *A Matter of Principle*. Harvard University Press, Cambridge, Mass.

11   Kymlicka, Will (1995). *Multicultural Citizenship: A Liberal Theory of Minority Rights*. Oxford: Clarendon Press: 53; Kymlicka, Will (1989). *Liberalism, Community and Culture*. Clarendon Press, Oxford: 177.

12   For example, Van Dyke, Vernon (1977). 'The Individual, the State, and Ethnic Communities in Political Theory'. *World Politics* 29: 343-69; Van Dyke, Vernon (1982). 'Collective Entities and Moral Rights: Problems in Liberal-Democratic Thought'. *Journal of Politics* 44: 21-40; Sandel, Michael J (1982). *Liberalism and the Limits of Justice*. Cambridge: University of Cambridge Press; Svensson, Frances (1979). 'Liberal Democracy and Group Rights: The Legacy of Individualism and its Impact on American Tribes'. *Political Studies* 27: 421-39; Taylor, Charles (1985). 'Atomism'. In *Philosophical Papers Vol. 2:Philosophy and the Human Sciences*. Cambridge University Press, Cambridge.

13   Rawls, John (1971). *Op cit*.

situation of immigrant minorities[14]. By the turn of the century, multiculturalism and ethno-cultural diversity – covering migrant groups as well as national and Indigenous minorities – had become one of the main research areas in the field[15]. The recent *Oxford Handbook of Political Theory*[16], for example, devotes an entire section of four chapters to aspects of cultural identity, including one on multiculturalism.

The point of departure for much multicultural political theory – liberal and anti-liberal alike – is the recognition that the ethno-cultural neutrality of liberal democracies is a fiction. All liberal democracies - including the standard exemplar of state 'benign neglect', the United States - privilege particular cultural practices and traditions. They insist on a particular language or languages as the *lingua franca* of state business and societal intercourse, organise their year in terms of a particular calendar, recognise certain public holidays; prescribe what narratives are taught as history; and draw on particular cultural motifs and stories for the official symbols, insignia, flags and anthems of the state. Some have gone— and do go—much further than this in mandating particular cultures. Many multiculturalists believe that this cultural privileging—typically, of a majority group—warrants some redress for cultural minorities who are also members of the political community, if only to smooth the integration process.

In this paper, I propose to put aside the specific normative arguments in defence of multiculturalism and consider instead its implications for national integration and identity[17]. This issue tends to occasion the most public anxiety and debate over multiculturalism in Australia. Certainly, it is not hard to see why many people think multiculturalism is at odds with national integration. So it is important to analyse whether there is a way of preserving the value of national-cultural identity whilst also accommodating cultural difference. The Australian debate on national identity and cultural diversity has mostly been concerned with the questions of *whether* there is a national culture and identity, and, if so, *what* their content is or should be. I want to argue that there are also important questions of *where*, *when* and *how* national culture, identity and character should apply. Let me begin by teasing out the assumptions of the main contending positions in the Australian debate.

---

14   For example, see Kymlicka, Will (1995). *Op cit*.

15   Another influential work of the time was Charles Taylor's essay on the 'politics of recognition': Taylor, Charles (1992). *Multiculturalism and the 'Politics of Recognition': An Essay*, Amy Gutmann (ed) Princeton, N J, Princeton University Press. Taylor was especially concerned with the status and cultural interests of Quebec.

16   Dryzek, John, Honig, Bonnie and Phillips, Anne (eds) (2006). *The Oxford Handbook of Political Theory*, Oxford University Press, Oxford.

17   For an overview of liberal and anti-liberal arguments for multiculturalism, see Levey (forthcoming).

Multiculturalism and national integration

Three vying approaches frame the public and scholarly discourse on Australian national identity: 'thick' or cultural nationalism, 'thin' or liberal nationalism, and civic or post-nationalism[18].

On the 'thick' or cultural conception, multiculturalism is considered to be, at best, inapt for Australian circumstances[19], and, at worst, destructive of Australian national identity and cohesion[20]. Australia is said to have a distinct Anglo-Australian character and identity, which has great capacity to integrate newcomers. Advocates point to the fact, for example, that intermarriage rates across ethnic and mainstream Australians are high, increasing with each generation[21]. 'Thick' conceptions of Australian national identity have the virtue of recognising the deep and abiding influence of Anglo-Australian culture on the institutions and patterns of life in Australia. However, the accounts are problematic in that they tend to do what they accuse Australian multicultural policy of doing - namely, essentialise ethnic group identity and membership, rather than allowing for their internal diversity, dynamism, and hybridity. As John Hirst[22], historian and chairman of the Commonwealth Government's Civics Education Group (responsible for designing the civics and citizenship program taught in schools), puts the accusation: 'Multicultural policy envisaged a world of distinct ethnic groups. This was more and more make-believe'[23].

There is, of course, some validity to this claim. Attempts to administer resources to cultural groups will perforce invite the problems of group definition and intra-group hierarchy and control[24]. Indeed, Stephen Castles[25] goes so far as to suggest that Clifford Geertz's 'primordialist notions of ethnicity' found their

---

18   Another term – 'ethnic nationalism' – is also common in these discussions. However, strictly speaking, ethnic nationalism prescribes common descent as well as a common culture. While such a position was popular in Australia during the heyday of the White Australia policy, most contemporary advocates of an Anglo-Australian national identity are, as we will see, cultural rather than ethnic nationalists.
19   Galligan, Brian, and Roberts, Winsome (2008). 'Multiculturalism, National Identity and Pluralist Democracy: The Australian Variant'. In *Political Theory and Australian Multiculturalism*, Geoffrey Brahm Levey, ed). Berghahn Books, New York and Oxford.
20   Blainey, Geoffrey (1984). *All for Australia*. North Ryde: Methuen Haynes; Knopfelmacher, Frank (1982). 'The Case Against Multi-culturalism'. In *The New Conservatism in Australia*, Robert Manne, (ed) Oxford: Oxford University Press; Windschuttle, Keith (2004). *The White Australia Policy*. Macleay Press, Sydney: chapter 11.
21   Galligan, Brian, and Roberts, Winsome (2008). *Op cit*; Hirst, John (2001). 'Aborigines and Migrants: Diversity and Unity in Multicultural Australia'. *Australian Book Review* No. 228: 30–35; Windschuttle, Keith (2005). 'It's not a race war, it's a clash of cultures'. *The Australian*, 16 December.
22   Hirst, John (2001). *Op cit*: 30.
23   The same claim is made today by the conservative commentators Janet Albrechtsen, Piers Ackerman and Andrew Bolt—albeit, ironically, with the shrill rider that multiculturalism has succeeded in making 'distinct ethnic groups' a reality.
24   Kukathas, Chandran (1992). 'Are there any Cultural Rights?' *Political Theory* 20, 1: 105–39.
25   Castles, Stephen (2001). 'Multiculturalism in Australia' In *The Australian People: An Encyclopedia of the Nation, Its People and Their Origins*, James Jupp, (ed) Cambridge University Press, Cambridge: 808.

way into early Australian multicultural thinking: 'Australian society could be seen as a collection of relatively homogeneous ethnic communities, each integrated by a distinct set of values and cultural practices, interpreted by 'natural leaders' who were usually male and middle-class.' Yet, this picture of Australian multiculturalism is also misleading.

First, even at its most primordial, Australian multiculturalism has never endorsed the kind of culturally autonomous, self-governing communities evidenced elsewhere around the world or imagined by various thinkers, from libertarians[26] to Austro-Marxists[27]. Nor does it remotely approximate Horace Kallen's[28] original idea of 'cultural pluralism' for the United States as a 'democracy of nationalities'. Kallen's idea involved territorial 'self-government', and was modelled on the cantons of Switzerland and on 'England [as a] union of [four] nationalities'[29]. Even the structural pluralism unsuccessfully promoted by early multiculturalist intellectuals, such as Jean Martin[30], was mild and integrationist compared to worldly conceptions of cultural pluralism[31]. Second, while multicultural policy did turn on some assumption of 'distinct ethnic groups', neither the assumption nor the administration based on it were such as to lock people in or out of ethnic group membership. Third and relatedly, Australian multicultural policy is highly individualistic. The rights to cultural identity and to social justice apply to individual Australians, however they define and practise their cultural identities[32]. So the 'multi' in Australian multiculturalism stands not only for diversity among groups but also *within* groups.

In contrast, Hirst's analysis treats ethnic groups monolithically, yoking the fate of members of ethnic groups to the choices of their co-ethnics. He cites figures to highlight the increasing assimilation of immigrants across the second and third generations and thus the supposed pointlessness of multicultural policy. For example, among Greeks, '[n]inety per cent of the first generation were Orthodox, 82 per cent of the second; 45 per cent of the third'[33]. But these figures also show how large proportions of this community in each generation wish to observe their faith and traditions. They beg the question of why these

---

26 For example, Kukathas, Chandran (2003). *The Liberal Archipelago: A Theory of Diversity and Freedom.* Clarendon Press, Oxford.

27 For example, Bauer, Otto 2000 [1907]. *Op cit.*

28 Kallen, Horace M (1924). *Op cit.*

29 Levey, Geoffrey Brahm (2005). 'National-Cultural Autonomy and Liberal Nationalism'. In *National-Cultural Autonomy and Its Contemporary Critics*, Ephraim Nimni, (ed) Routledge, London: 160–62.

30 Martin, Jean (1981). *The Ethnic Dimension: Papers on Ethnicity and Pluralism by Jean Martin,* Sol Encel, (ed) Sydney: George Allen and Unwin.

31 Lopez, Mark (2000). *The Origins of Multiculturalism in Australian Politics 1945–75.* Melbourne University Press, Melbourne: 54–56.

32 Levey, Geoffrey Brahm (2008). 'Multicultural Political Thought in Australian Perspective'. In *Political Theory and Australian Multiculturalism*, Geoffrey Brahm Levey, (ed) Berghahn Books, New York and Oxford: 1–26.

33 Hirst, John (2001). *Op cit:* 30.

people should not be entitled to cultural consideration where necessary and appropriate. Nor is it clear why the cultural interests of present generations should be answered on the basis of the (anticipated) cultural interests of (some among) future generations. Here and now, many immigrants do seek to observe and retain their ethno-religious heritage. Advocates of a 'thick' conception of Australian identity seem to overlook or dismiss such questions because they tend to assume that multiculturalism necessarily denies the reality or importance of Australian culture. As Hirst puts it,

> The migrants were and are in no doubt that there is an Australian way of doing things, an Australian culture. This is the second way that the multicultural label for Australia is misleading. It suggests that there is simply diversity; that there is no dominant culture. Migrants who want to get on and be accepted know better[34].

Now, it is the civic and post-nationalists who are most concerned to deny the reality or political importance of a distinct Australian culture and identity. In many ways their position is the mirror image of the 'thick' conceptions. Whereas the latter see multiculturalism as undermining Australian national identity, civic and post-nationalists believe that invocations of a national identity are antithetical to Australia's cultural diversity, multiculturalism, and/or universal liberal-democratic values. They believe that Australia's commitment to liberal democratic values together with its cultural diversity requires that the state should be neutral with respect to ethno-cultural matters, although they vary in what this means.

Some argue that Australians should simply dispense with the idea of a national identity altogether. For example, in their well-known book *Mistaken Identity: Multiculturalism and the Demise of Nationalism in Australia*, Stephen Castles and his associates concluded: 'We do not need a new ideology of nationhood... Our aim must be a community without a nation'[35]. On this view, Australian identity should be grounded only in political or civic values, such as toleration, individual liberty, equality, reciprocity, and a commitment to democratic institutions[36]. Others in this camp suggest that Australian identity should be centred rather on the idea or practice of multiculturalism itself[37]. This last idea

---

34   *Ibid*.

35   Castles, S, Kalantzis, M, Cope, B and Morissey, M (1992). *Mistaken Identity: Multiculturalism and the Demise of Nationalism in Australia*, Pluto Press, Sydney: 148.

36   See Horne, Donald (1997). *The Avenue of the Fair Go: A Group Tour of Australian Political Thought*. Pymble, NSW: Harper Collins; Kalantzis, Mary (2000). 'Multicultural Citizenship'. In *Rethinking Australian Citizenship*, Wayne Hudson and John Kane, (eds) Cambridge University Press, Cambridge; Kukathas, Chandran (1993a). 'The Idea of a Multicultural Society'. In *Multicultural Citizens: The Philosophy and Politics of Identity*, Chandran Kukathas, (ed) Centre for Independent Studies, Sydney.

37   Jayasuriya, Laksiri (2005). 'Australian Multiculturalism and the Politics of a New Pluralism'. *Dialogue* 24, 1: 75–84; Theophanous, Andrew (1995). *Understanding Multiculturalism and Australian Identity*. Melbourne: Elikia Books; *Sydney Morning Herald* (2006). 'A glue that keeps Australian society together'. 16 December.

found expression in the National Multicultural Advisory Council report that prepared the ground for the *New Agenda for a Multicultural Australia*: 'Australian multiculturalism will continue to be a defining feature of our evolving national identity'[38]. Former Labor Party leader Mark Latham[39] also picked upon the idea in the 2004 election campaign: 'The challenge is to modernise our multicultural policies, to make them relevant to our multicultural identity'.

Civic and post-nationalist arguments have the virtue of seeking an inclusive definition of Australian identity and culture that acknowledges the cultural diversity of the Australian people. Yet these approaches are flawed and seem destined to fail. First, as Kymlicka[40], among others, has argued, 'civic nationalism' is a misnomer in that it ignores the many ways in which liberal democratic states already and inevitably endorse particular ethno-cultural traditions, from the language spoken to state symbols and the historical narratives taught in schools. Moreover, the putative 'political' or 'civic' values of democracy, toleration, equality and so on have deep cultural imprints and a jagged, if not always a sharp, cultural edge. The reason that stipulated limits of liberal toleration are often so controversial, for example, is precisely because liberal democratic values are anything but culturally neutral: they are friendly to some cultural traditions, not so friendly to others. In short, 'civic nationalism' overlooks the ethno-cultural dimensions of public institutions in liberal democracies and of the stipulated civic values themselves.

Second, national identity can and does play an important role in generating and sustaining social cohesion, a sense of belonging, and a commitment to the commonwealth. Liberal nationalists rightly argue that all these features are legitimate interests of democratic states[41]. They are features, moreover, that would seem to be all the more imperative in culturally diverse democracies. To reject national identity as obsolete, then, or to define it as if it could be ethno-culturally neutral, is to forsake or to ignore one of the most powerful political forces available for bringing people together as a community.

Attempts to fashion a new Australian identity on multiculturalism itself fare little better. On the face of it, this approach seems to be a category mistake: that is, it mistakes political and administrative measures that variously allow, accommodate, and integrate the realm of diverse identities for an identity itself.

---

38   National Multicultural Advisory Council (NMAC) (1999). *Australian Multiculturalism for a New Century: Towards Inclusiveness.* Canberra: AGPS: 13–14. Stephen Castles ((2001) *Op cit*: 811) astutely observes that the NMAC's recommendation that multicultural policy be henceforth called '*Australian* multiculturalism' also seemed to be an attempt to generate nationalist sentiment around multiculturalism.

39   Latham, Mark (2004). 'A Big Country: Australia's National Identity'. ALP press release, 20 April.

40   Kymlicka, Will (1995). *Op cit*; Kymlicka, Will (2001). *Op cit*.

41   For example, Canovan, Margaret (1996). *Nationhood and Political Theory*. Cheltenham: Edward Elgar; Kymlicka, Will (2001). *Op cit*: 20; Miller 1995; Tamir, Yael (1993). *Liberal Nationalism*. Princeton University Press, Princeton, N J.

Yet all national identities are constructed and imagined[42], so why not an identity imagined around multiculturalism? The difficulty is at once semantic and symbolic. The American metaphor of the 'melting pot' helps to illustrate what a national identity focused on multiculturalism is up against. According to Ajume Wingo[43], the image of the melting pot misdescribes American society, since 'the US population is increasingly a collection of distinct subpopulations, with more diversity *between* ethnic, linguistic, or cultural groups than *within* those same groups'. Yet the fact that the 'melting pot' is a myth is irrelevant, he says; what is important is that it offers a powerful symbol of unity that well serves the legitimate interests of American democracy in creating a *sense* of solidarity.

Compare the Australian case. Australian society and culture are highly integrative - or so we are told. Intermarriage rates are high; the title of 'new Australians' is or was eagerly bestowed on immigrants; the nomenclature of hyphenated identities is still uncommon[44]. 'Multiculturalism', the proposed symbol for Australian identity, is also mythic, on this account, in misdescribing Australian society. Yet, unlike the metaphor of the 'melting pot' in the US, the proposed national myth for Australia *semantically* conveys diversity and difference rather than unity and solidarity. 'Multiculturalism' lacks the rhetorical resonance of the 'melting pot' for nation-building purposes.

I stress that the difficulty, here, is more rhetorical than substantive. Multiculturalism is, indeed, concerned with integrating a diverse society based on liberal democratic notions of liberty, equality and justice. Nevertheless, it is the case that many Australians are unable to warm to the term. As the National Multicultural Advisory Council[45] reported, pollster '[Irving] Saulwick's research identified a strong desire for unity in this country. He showed that the concept of multiculturalism raised in many minds an emphasis on separateness rather than togetherness'. By the mid 1990s, even one of the architects of Australian multicultural policy was calling for the term to be dropped, although he continued to support the policies for which it stands[46]. And, of course, the Howard government removed the word from official use in early 2007, a move that has largely been preserved by the Rudd government. For all these reasons, it makes more sense to construe multiculturalism as a set of principles, policies and programs in the service of an Australian national identity than as the locus of that identity itself.

---

42   Anderson, Benedict (1983). *Imagined Communities: Reflections on the Origin and Spread of Nationalism*. Verso, London.

43   Wingo, Ajume (2003). *Veil Politics in Liberal Democratic States*. Cambridge University Press, Cambridge: 126.

44   Hirst, John (2001): 31.

45   National Multicultural Advisory Council (NMAC) (1999). *Op cit*: 96.

46   Zubrzycki, Jerzy (1996), 'Cynics woo the ethnic vote'. *The Australian* 15 October.

This brings us to the intermediate position of 'liberal nationalists'. Their 'thin' account of national identity acknowledges both the legitimate national interests of liberal democracies and the need to make room for cultural minorities. The debate at this level is largely about the precise calibration of the 'thinness'. The Israeli philosopher, and now politician, Yael Tamir[47] includes in 'national identity' virtually all the cultural aspects that 'thick', cultural nationalisms do at the level of nation states. However, unlike these other positions, she insists that national self-determination does not require or presuppose political sovereignty or statehood, cultural attachments are matters of individual choice, and members of cultural minorities are just as entitled to express their 'national identity' as are the members of the majority culture. For Kymlicka, 'nation-building' in liberal democracies is legitimate where it is limited to creating and maintaining what he calls a 'societal culture':

> I call it a societal culture to emphasize that it involves a common language and social institutions, rather than common religious beliefs, family customs, or personal lifestyles... Citizens of a modern liberal state do not share a common culture in such a thick, ethnographic sense...if we want to understand the nature of modern state-building, we need a very different, and thinner, conception of culture, which focuses on a common language and societal institutions[48].

Kymlicka allows that liberal democracies also engage in nation-building by developing a national media, national symbols and holidays, and memorialising majority group heroes and events, a position shared by David Miller[49]. Others draw the legitimate boundaries of national identity more narrowly; for example, around 'a history [and] a set of legal and political institutions'[50].

To my mind, liberal nationalist approaches wrongly dismiss, or lose sight of, two important dimensions of national identity. First, liberal nationalists too quickly dismiss the place of 'national character'[51]. The inclination to do so is understandable enough given the obscene ways in which such notions have been politically exploited or socially expressed in modern history. However, as liberal nationalists know better than most, nationalism itself can serve both illiberal and liberal goals; the task is to distinguish its legitimate roles and uses. The concept of national character is often challenged on the grounds that the attributes highlighted are stereotypical and contradicted by competing images

---

47 Tamir, Yael (1993). *Op cit.*
48 Kymlicka, Will (2001). *Op cit*: 18-19.
49 Miller, David (1995). *On Nationality*. Clarendon Press, Oxford.
50 Kukathas, Chandran (1993b). 'Multiculturalism and the Idea of an Australian Identity'. In *Multicultural Citizens: The Philosophy and Politics of Identity*, Chandran Kukathas, (ed) Centre for Independent Studies, Sydney: 149.
51 A notable exception here is David Miller ((1995). *Op cit*: 25), who includes national character as a component idea of national identity, and equates both with the 'public culture'.

and stereotypes. Consider one of the most celebrated portraits of the Australian character, Russel Ward's *The Australian Legend*: 'According to the myth, the 'typical Australian' is a practical man, rough and ready in his manners and quick to decry any appearance of affectation in others'[52]. Chandran Kukathas cites Ward's portrait and then Jonathan King's opposing assessment to the effect that Australians are 'lazy, arrogant, racist, urban money-grabbers who have surrounded themselves with the myth that they are outback heroes'[53]. Joining many other commentators on the subject, Kukathas notes the 'difficulties in trying to tie down any notion of a 'national character'' and moves on.

And yet, as everyone knows, the French really are different from the Germans. Canadians are different from Americans, and Australians are different from the Brits and even the New Zealanders. Imprinted, as they are, with their national cultures, they tend to exhibit distinctive habits of mind, emotion, and behaving, instantly noticeable to most outsiders. That many nationals do not exhibit their 'national qualities', and that there may be contradictions in the national character or even vying national characters, is neither here nor there; in human affairs, the only surprise should be if it were otherwise. I suspect that liberal nationalists—who tend to travel a lot—might grant this much at a cultural level, but insist that issues of national character should be separated from the state and quarantined from the business of liberal democratic government. However, national character will perforce find expression through a society's governing institutions; how could it not do so? All three schools of thought tend to misunderstand the place of national character. The crucial point about national character is not that it doesn't exist or that it should be quarantined from government or that it should be politically promoted. Rather, the point is that while national character shapes government, government cannot legislate national character; it cannot be the *object* or intention of political administration without doing it violence. This is because national character is constantly evolving and any *deliberate* attempt to represent it will wrench out particular aspects, ensuring that the accounts offered can, at best, bear a passing relation to it. The resultant image is bound to be 'absurdly romanticised and exaggerated'[54], indeed a grotesque.

If national character is not to become national caricature, then it must be left to its own devices. It will find its own expression. Consider, for example, the extraordinary building that is the New Parliament House in Canberra. That ordinary Australians and visitors can walk up grassy banks and literally stand over their political representatives not only exemplifies a characteristic Australian attitude to authority and an egalitarian temper; it emerges from this

---

52   Ward, Russel (1958). *The Australian Legend*. Oxford University Press, Melbourne: 1.
53   Kukathas, Chandran (1993b). *Op cit*: 147-148.
54   Ward, R (1958). *Op cit*.

attitude and temper. Or, still at Parliament House, take the public uproar in 2005 that followed a regulation requiring security guards to cease using the expression 'mate' when addressing politicians and the public. An MP taking umbrage at the informality had prompted the move. The public's sense that acceptable norms had been breached came only when the guards were told to be more formal. National character, because it is character, expresses itself just in and through what we do and find 'natural' or acceptable.

The second dimension of national identity that liberal nationalists tend to underplay concerns what may be called the crucible of civil society. Because they seek to render nationalism compatible with liberal democracy, and thus to make room for cultural minorities, liberal nationalists tend to focus mainly on the legitimate boundaries of state action and on access to the public sphere. National cultures, as we have seen, are 'thinned' out in terms of which ethno-cultural aspects—typically, a shared language, societal and political institutions, the nation's history and national symbols—are deemed to be appropriate for government involvement. Other cultural aspects—regarding food, dress, speech, surnames, leisure activities and family size—some of which were once pursued by states in their more assimilationist days, are deemed to be the prerogative of ethnic groups or their individual members. Thus, we are presented with two domains culture-wise: a national culture embodied in societal institutions and overseen by the state, and ethnocultures that are the province of immigrant groups and individuals[55]. The possibility that a *national* culture might also be constructed and fomented among people's relations in civil society seems to be ignored or denied[56]. Hence Kymlicka's remark: 'The 'melting pot' image was never accurate. Immigrants do indeed integrate into common institutions and learn the dominant language, but they remain, visibly, and proudly, distinctive in their ethnic identities and attachments'[57]. Integration, let alone assimilation, is countenanced only in the restricted terms of the *lingua franca* and societal institutions.

This picture of integration is as unrealistic as the assimilationist model. In Australia, as in other liberal democracies, there are myriads of interactions among immigrant groups and between them and the dominant cultural majority that occur beyond societal institutions, and which result in cultural absorption and integration of one form or another. For obvious reasons, this absorption is mostly in the direction of the patterns of the dominant culture. John Hirst[58]

---

55   Kymlicka ((1995), *Op cit)* allows that states may harbour more than one societal culture where Indigenous and national minorities are present.

56   Again, David Miller ((1995). *Op cit*: chapter 5) is the notable exception: although he frames national identity in terms of a public culture, he emphasises the multiple ways in which a public culture is constructed and shaped.

57   Kymlicka, Will (2001). *Op cit*: 33.

58   Hirst, John (2001). *Op cit*: 30-31.

cites the stories of a Greek husband rejecting his wife's request for the family to acquire a goat as un-Australian, and of a proud Sri Lankan, Bekaboru Kiyanahati Balapan Koyako, coming to the realisation, in meeting other Australians, that he badly needed a shorter name (he chose Kojak). These are great examples of how national cultural integration is mediated also in interpersonal relations in civil society. There are many other examples of the inductive power of Anglo-Australian culture at work in civil society, including the norms governing queue-forming, social space, voice-raising, speech turn-taking, spitting and belching, and the polite reluctance to use the car horn on anything but the most urgent occasions. As Mary Kalantzis observes (albeit critically), although designating a 'set of cultural characteristics' as 'Anglo-Australian', 'Anglo-Celtic Australian' or 'mainstream Australian' is problematic in that it 'masks real internal differences, it alludes to certain ways of speaking, thinking, working and being in the world'[59].

In Australia, 'Anglo-Australian' culture remains dominant, and one cannot begin to make sense of Australian institutions and life without understanding this much[60]. The mistake, of course, is to think that the integration is *always* in the direction of the cultural majority. The impact of Aboriginal culture on Anglo-Australian life—including vocabulary, motifs, art, and even the sense of emplacement and connection to the land—is clear, if too little appreciated[61]. Anglo-Australian culture has also been changed in various ways by successive waves of immigrants, from the rise of soccer to a popular sport, to so-called 'new Australian cuisine' (incorporating Asian and continental influences), to the now national preferment of coffee over tea and wine over beer. Judging by the entries in metropolitan telephone directories, the conventions regarding the complexity of surnames have also been greatly extended. So a national culture is also forged in the hurly burly of civil society, as well as via common societal institutions. In subtle ways, the Anglo-Celtic Australian culture of old is becoming an 'Anglo-meltic' one. That is, Anglo-Australian culture, while still dominant, is being modified at the coalface.

Australian national identity, then, is multifaceted and occupies different domains. There are aspects of national identity having to do with Australian character that will naturally affect the way we govern ourselves, but which we can scarcely do anything about without warping them. There are aspects

---

59 Kalantzis, Mary (2000). *Op cit*: 108.

60 Given the effects today of globalisation and the US hegemony, the American influence on Anglo-Australian culture must also be reckoned with. For a subtle analysis, see Altman, Dennis (2006) *51st State?* Scribe, Carlton.

61 Mulcock, Jane (2002). *Searching for our Indigenous Selves: Belonging and Spirituality in Anglo-Celtic Australia*. PhD Thesis, University of Western Australia; Read, Peter (2000). *Belonging: Australians, Place and Aboriginal Ownership*. Cambridge University Press, Cambridge; Trigger, David (2008). 'Place, Belonging and Nativeness in Australia'. In *Making Sense of Place*, Frank Vanclay, Matthew Higgins and Adam Blackshaw, (eds) National Museum of Australia, Canberra.

of national identity that are duly the province of government, such as the inculcation and transmission of a national language, the teaching of the nation's history, and the establishment of national institutions, holidays and memorials. And there are aspects of national identity that properly belong in the realm of civil society and beyond the business of government, such as how people dress, call themselves, or spend their leisure, what languages they speak to each other, and even in what accent they speak their English. Here, among the myriad relations of Australians, will also be forged the habits and sentiments and character of the Australian people.

I do not mean to suggest that this account of the sites of Australian identity amounts to a radically new model. On the contrary, in differentiating domains of national identity and delimiting those that are and are not the province of government, it is indelibly a version of *liberal* nationalism. It is a version, however, that accepts that Australian character has a place in national identity and an implicit impact on government, and which recognises that Australian national identity and character will be forged in the relations among people in civil society, and not only by state policy and societal institutions. Protagonists of a 'thick' conception of Australian identity like Hirst are right to note that there is more to Australian culture and identity than merely civic values or a multicultural mélange. However, the question is *which* aspects of Australian culture and *which* of its values should define the conditions of membership and govern access to opportunities in the polity. Civic-cum-post-nationalists like Kalantzis[62] are rightly concerned that Anglo-Celtic ways of 'being in the world' are 'explicitly and implicitly valued and rewarded' across the board in Australian society. However, the answer to inappropriate cultural privileging is not to be found in expunging or denying a place for Australian culture and identity, as if this were even possible, and installing a 'new civic compact' in its stead. Rather, the answer lies in delimiting the domains of national culture and checking the privileging.

In terms of Australian policy, the 1989 *National Agenda for a Multicultural Australia* presents a very similar approach to Australian identity. It acknowledges the importance of 'our British heritage' in helping 'to define us as Australian'. It emphasises that 'Multiculturalism does not entail a rejection of Australian values, customs and beliefs'. As part of this 'common core', it highlights the 'basic institutional framework of Australian society', including English as the national language, rule of law, democracy, freedom and tolerance of expression, equality of the sexes, and an 'overriding and unifying commitment to Australia'. It expressly *excludes* from the public definition of Australian identity ethno-cultural aspects such as skin color, style of dress, mode of worship, or other languages spoken. And it recognises that the 'Australian way of life' will evolve

---

62   Kalantzis, Mary (2000). *Op cit*: 108.

and change over time with the 'changing face of the Australian population', among other influences[63]. The *National Agenda* has some weaknesses. For example, it does not explain what is meant by an 'overriding commitment' to Australia's interests 'first and foremost', which seems overreaching[64].

Nevertheless, the *National Agenda* outshines the subsequent national multicultural policies on the matter of national identity. Both the *New Agenda* and *Multicultural Australia*[65] tie multiculturalism to Australian national identity in a much less differentiated fashion. While they also promote the same core civic values, they emphasise the idea of Australians' 'multicultural identity' and treat the country's British heritage and predominant 'Anglo-Australian' culture as if they were of minor significance, if not antiquarian interest. And, of course, prior to the 1970s, government policy was to do the very reverse and emphasise 'thick' conceptions of national identity in the form of Anglo-conformity above all else. It is to the credit of the architects of Australia's first national statement of multiculturalism that they fashioned such a subtle and sophisticated version of liberal-nationalist integration.

Conclusion

Multicultural policy sought to create a space in which cultural identity and difference could be seen as legitimate and a part of one's 'being Australian'. Critics assert that such policies simply gave a green light to cultural separatism, and a shared Australian identity was eroded. Even if there is some truth to this claim, it is also the case that national chauvinism and exclusivity can also spawn minority alienation and separatism. Finding the optimal formula for promoting both national cohesion and cultural liberty is thus a challenge. The debate of this conundrum in Australia has tended to oscillate between two counterproductive approaches: one that construes Australian national identity narrowly in Anglo-Australian terms but is applied widely as the standard of acceptability; and one that, in recent years, has perhaps underemphasised the importance of an Australian national identity, or which has come to define such an identity almost in opposition to Anglo-Australian heritage.

In this essay, I have sought to clarify and defend a particular liberal nationalist conception—or perhaps better, map—of national identity for Australian conditions that avoids these equally problematic alternatives. Understood

---

63   Office of Multicultural Affairs (1989). *National Agenda for a Multicultural Australia*, AGPS, Canberra: 50-52.
64   Kymlicka, W (2001). *Op cit*: 173; Levey, Geoffrey Brahm (2001). 'The Political Theories of Australian Multiculturalism'. *The University of New South Wales Law Journal* 24, 3: 877–878.
65   Commonwealth of Australia (1999). *A New Agenda for Multicultural Australia*. AGPS, Canberra; Commonwealth of Australia (2003). *Multicultural Australia: United in Diversity*, AGPS, Canberra.

multi-dimensionally and as operating across several domains, national identity and character have a legitimate and vital place in Australian politics and society. On this account, Anglo-Australian culture is duly recognised both inside and beyond the sphere of government, but so is the input of non-Anglo-Australians and the evolving nature of Australian identity and character. Suggested, to some extent, in the *National Agenda* multicultural policy of 1989, something like this multifaceted map of the domains of national identity is also *implicitly* respected by many Australian political leaders, institutions, and practices today. The controversies arise typically when it is not.

Nevertheless, there is no gainsaying that the term 'multiculturalism' lends itself to controversy and misinterpretation. Indeed, the word has always harboured an ambiguity. On the one hand, the 'ism' was simply meant to designate a broad commitment to the idea of cultural recognition, accommodation, and state support. On the other hand, the 'culturalism' in the word often has been read as signifying distinct and homogeneous cultures to which all else should defer. This is why the term 'interculturalism', which is rather more common in continental Europe than in the Anglophone democracies and has long been preferred to 'multiculturalism' in Quebec[66], is not much help. The perceived trouble with multiculturalism is not – or not only – that communities do not adequately interact with each other; it is that they exist and interact as if they were monolithic, self-absorbed, and independent units. Having different cultural fiefdoms interrelate with each other as suggested by 'interculturalism' repeats rather than solves the problem. The term 'multiculturalism' will continue, then, to grate on publics and governments. It may be that we will need to speak of 'multicultural integration' or the like instead.

---

66   For example, Bouchard, Gérard and Taylor, Charles (2008). *Building the Future. A Time for Reconciliation.* Abridged Report. Montréal: Commission de consultation sur les practique l'accommodement reliées aux differences culturelles.

Chapter 5: Attitudes to Multiculturalism and Cultural Diversity

Andrew Markus

It is a complex matter to unravel attitudes to multiculturalism and cultural diversity. Taking specific poll findings at face value can lead to misrepresentation, evidenced in the contending claims made from time to time concerning the level of support for multiculturalism.

Representatives of ethnic communities, not surprisingly, will seek to stress poll findings that indicate high levels of support for cultural diversity. Thus in February 2008, Sam Afra, Chairman of the Ethnic Communities' Council of Victoria, issued a press release to rebut findings of a local study released in February 2008 which indicated little support for government funding for cultural maintenance:

> Recent VicHealth research with a broader representative sample found that 89% of Victorians think cultural diversity is a good thing. In that research only a minority of Victorians oppose cultural diversity ... Victoria has a proud history of settling people from different backgrounds successfully and harmoniously. Our cultural diversity enriches us socially, culturally and economically[1].

The lumping together of separate issues escaped notice.

In a February 2009 statement Hieu Van Le, Chairman of the South Australian Multicultural and Ethnic Affairs Commission, released an almost identical finding of a South Australian survey:

> 87.7% of South Australians believe cultural diversity is a positive influence in our community. Nearly half of those surveyed had more than five friends or colleagues with different cultural backgrounds. More than 40% believe diversity has produced a greater range of skills and knowledge in South Australia. These results demonstrate something that we have known for a long time – South Australia is one of the most harmonious societies on Earth. However, this level of appreciation of

---

1 Afra, Sam (2008). Letter published in *The Herald Sun*, 7 February 2008, Ethnic Communities Council of Victoria, http://eccv.org.au/community/letters/letter-published-in-the-herald-sun-7-february-2008/, accessed 25 January 2010.

the benefits of cultural diversity is not something we can be complacent about. We have worked long and hard to create and maintain our enviable high level of understanding and appreciation of the benefits and richness that cultural diversity brings[2].

As in the press release from Sam Afra, a range of issues are mixed. If it is the case, for example, that 'diversity has produced a greater range of skills and knowledge in South Australia', then why 'more than 40%', not a majority, agree with this proposition? How does this finding relate to the view of 88 per cent of respondents that 'cultural diversity is a positive influence in our community'?

On the other the hand, there has been no shortage of commentators to present the view that only a minority of Australians support multiculturalism. The journalist Alan Wood, writing in the *The Australian* in September 2007, based his analysis on the findings of the 1988 FitzGerald Committee inquiry into immigration which 'found a key problem in maintaining support for immigration was a profound distrust by Australians of the policy of multiculturalism'. Wood referred to the 1994 argument of the historian John Hirst that the problem with multiculturalism was that it reduced mainstream Australians to an 'ethnic group', labeled 'Anglo-Celt', demeaned its heritage and denied its right to primacy[3]. Other political scientists and historians, notably Professor Geoffrey Blainey, commenting on the policies of the Keating and Hawke governments, had developed a critique of multiculturalism in similar terms[4]. Such critique reached its fullest development with the rise of Pauline Hanson's One Nation movement in the years 1996-98.

Of the critics of multiculturalism the most detailed analysis of public opinion surveys is to be found in the work of Katharine Betts, particularly her 1988 study *Ideology and Immigration,* republished in 1999 in an expanded and revised edition as *The Great Divide.* Betts argued that multiculturalism developed in government policy in the 1970s on the promise that cultural diversity would enrich society. Yet 'the majority of old Australians showed little enthusiasm for this development and, as their understanding of it increased, their limited enthusiasm diminished'[5]. There was a clear split in support for cultural diversity between the university educated - labeled

---

2   Hieu Van Le (2009). 'Multicultural South Australia', *Multicultural SA Newsletter*, February 2009, http://www.multicultural.sa.gov.au/documents/MulticulturalSANewsletterFeb2009.pdf, accessed 8 April 2009.

3   Wood, Alan (2007). 'Multiculturalism becomes poison for social capital', *The Australian*, 26 September 2007.

4   Markus, Andrew (2001). *Race: John Howard and the remaking of Australia*, Allen and Unwin, Sydney.

5   Betts, Katharine (1999). *The Great Divide: Immigration politics in Australia*, Duffy and Snellgrove, Sydney: 124-5.

'the new class'- and the rest of the population. In her analysis the lack of support for multiculturalism contributed to the 'growing majority distaste for immigration'.

Following Hirst, Betts distinguished two meanings of multiculturalism, the first of which received widespread support while the latter did not: (a) the idea that we should be tolerant ('soft multiculturalism'); (b) the idea that we should welcome cultural diversity, including support the provision of government funding and other forms of assistance to immigrant groups to facilitate cultural maintenance ('hard multiculturalism')[6].

Betts used findings from a 1994 poll to support her argument concerning the division in Australian society. The poll found that nearly three fifths of university-educated respondents favoured 'hard multiculturalism' compared to a quarter of non-university educated people[7]. Betts concluded that 'Australian surveys and opinion polls on immigration since the 1960s document increasing opposition among the majority of respondents and a growing split between the opinion of university-educated people and that of the majority'[8].

Recent polls provide further support for Betts' argument concerning division of opinion and bring into question the sweeping assertions of the advocates of multiculturalism. They also, however, provide evidence of change, which, contrary to predictions in the 1980s and 1990s, has seen a lessening of division on settlement and immigration issues and can be expected to contribute to further lessening. For the present, 'hard multiculturalism' is an issue that sharply differentiates the attitudes of immigrants of non-English speaking background (NESB) and those of English-speaking background (ESB), notably long-time Australians. The political significance of this division has, however, been neutered by the Howard and Rudd/Gillard governments in their avoidance of policies of 'hard multiculturalism'. The recognition that government provisions of funds to immigrant groups for ethno-specific ends is an issue easily politicised is reflected in the cautious approach of the Rudd/Gillard Labor government (compared to the earlier policies of Hawke and Keating Labor). Caution seems to be based on the recognition that multiculturalism is difficult to sell in the electorate, although strongly favoured within many immigrant communities.

---

6   *Ibid*: 126.
7   *Ibid*: 130.
8   *Ibid*: 97.

Analysis of public opinion

The following discussion isolates for analysis public opinion on four separate issues:

1. Cultural and ethnic diversity.

2. Multiculturalism considered in general or abstract terms.

3. 'Hard' multiculturalism.

4. Assimilation of immigrants.

Before proceeding, however, it is important to establish that in Australia the value of immigration is widely endorsed in times of economic prosperity. Cross-national surveys locate Australia in the category of countries with a positive view of immigration. The 2003 International Social Survey Program (ISSP) provides the basis for cross-national analysis; in the following, comparison is made between attitudes in Australia, Canada, Great Britain and the states of Germany which, prior to reunification, comprised West Germany[9].

In response to the question of whether the number of immigrants should be increased, remain the same or be reduced, a minority of Australians (39 per cent) and of Canadians (34 per cent) favoured reduction, compared with a majority in Great Britain (77 per cent) and Germany (70 per cent).

In response to the proposition that immigrants are good for a country's economy, 71 per cent of Australians and 61 per cent of Canadians were in agreement, compared with 22 per cent of Britons and 29 per cent of Germans.

When presented with the proposition that immigrants improve the country by 'bringing in new ideas and cultures', 75 per cent of Australians and 68 per cent of Canadians were in agreement, compared with 34 per cent of Britons and 57 per cent of Germans.

Cultural and ethnic diversity

Australian surveys indicate wide endorsement of the value of immigration for bringing new ideas and cultural diversity. Five surveys between 1995 and 2003 tested responses to the general proposition that 'immigrants make Australia open to new ideas and cultures' and found consistently strong endorsement.

---

9   International Social Survey Programme (2003). *National Identity II*, SPSS data file, http://www.issp.org/data.shtml, accessed 8 April 2009.

These surveys elicited positive responses in the range 70–80 per cent. In 2007, in response to the proposition that 'accepting immigrants from many different countries makes Australia stronger', 69 per cent were in agreement.

A series of surveys undertaken by Professor Kevin Dunn and Associate Professor Jim Forrest, between 2001 and 2008, found agreement above 84 per cent with the general proposition that 'it is a good thing for society to be made up of different cultures'[10].

A 2008 South Australian government survey found that 88 per cent of respondents believe cultural diversity is a positive influence in the community. The survey with the largest number of respondents, Community Indicators Victoria conducted in 2007 and with over 24,000 respondents, produced an almost identical level of agreement with the proposition that 'it is a good thing for a society to be made up of people from different cultures'[11].

These surveys indicate that when the issue of cultural diversity is raised in the abstract and most general terms, the level of agreement reaches the range 70-90 per cent. But, indicative of the lack of surety and strength of opinion, when the issue was raised in negative terms in 1988, a large majority of respondents (69 per cent) agreed with the proposition that 'having lots of cultural groups in Australia causes lots of problems.'

Multiculturalism considered in general or abstract terms

A second type of question relates to multiculturalism (as distinct from cultural diversity) raised in general terms. This issue elicits similar high levels of endorsement to questions relating to cultural diversity raised in general terms.

When in 1988-89 respondents were presented with the statement that 'multiculturalism is necessary if people from different cultures are to live in harmony', 77 per cent were in agreement. In 1997, asked whether 'multiculturalism has been good or bad for Australia?, 78 per cent agreed that it had been good. In 2005 the same question found 70 per cent in agreement. A second survey in 2005 asked respondents if they supported or opposed 'a policy of multiculturalism in Australia' — 80 per cent were in support[12].

---

10   Dunn, K, Forrest, J, Ip, D, Babacan, H, Paradies, Y and Pedersen, A (2008). 'Challenging Racism: The anti-racism project', conference paper, 4Rs conference, 30 September 2008, http://www.uws.edu.au/__data/ assets/pdf_file/0020/42185/State_level_comparison_for_4Rs_conference.pdf, accessed 8 April 2009.

11   Vic Health (2007). *More Than Tolerance: Embracing diversity for health. A summary report*, Victorian Health Promotion Foundation, Carlton South: 35.

12   For details of specific polls, see Goot, Murray (1999). 'Migrant numbers, Asian immigration and multiculturalism: trends in the polls, 1943-1998', National Multicultural Advisory Council, *Australian*

But when there is suggestion of government action which might encourage separatism, support declines. In 1996, in response to the statement that 'successive Australian governments have adopted a policy of multiculturalism, [a policy that] involves encouraging migrants to become Australians without having to give up their own culture', 61 per cent of respondents were in agreement. In 2002 a poll asked respondents 'how much should migrants be encouraged to keep their cultural identity; 52 per cent were in support of substantial cultural maintenance, 48 per cent were equivocal or against.

'Hard' multiculturalism

A third type of question elicits views concerning government support for cultural maintenance; in response to such a question support shrinks to a small minority. Four polls in 1995, 2003, 2007 and 2009 asked for response to the statement that 'ethnic minorities should be given government assistance to preserve their customs and traditions'; the first two polls found a small minority of 16 per cent in support, the third poll 32 per cent and the fourth 33 per cent in support.

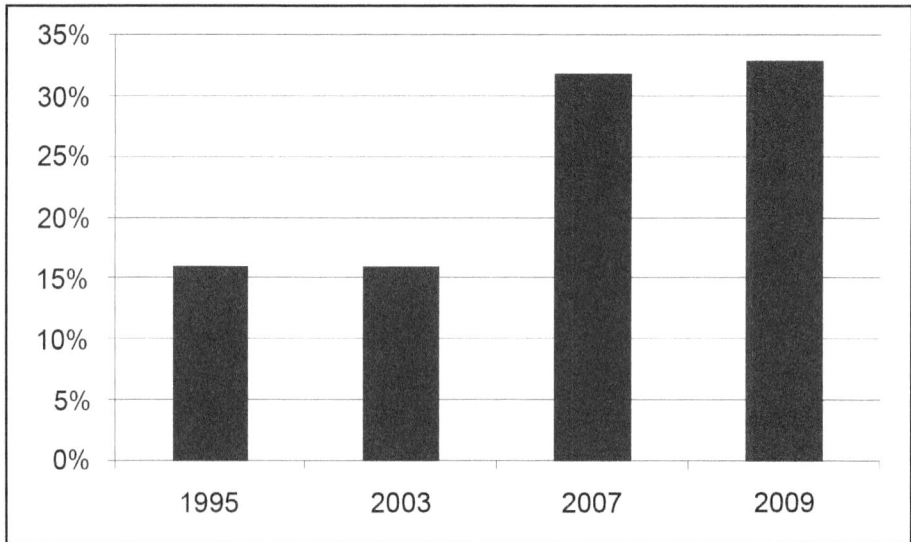

Figure 1 Government assistance to ethnic minorities to preserve their customs and traditions, 1995, 2003, 2007, 2009

Source: *Mapping Social Cohesion* (2009)

Multiculturalism for a New Century, Statistical Appendix part 2, http://www.immi.gov.au/media/publications/multicultural/nmac/statistics.pdf, accessed 8 April 2009; Markus, Andrew, Jupp, James and McDonald, Peter (2009). *Australia's Immigration Revolution*, Allen and Unwin, Sydney: Ch. 7.

The logic of questions which raise the issue of government funding to minorities means that there will necessarily be limited support, and the response to such question needs to be carefully interpreted. The negative finding may relate more to the dynamics of majority opinion, which will not support funding and the conferring of other benefits on 'others'; thus it may be that the negative finding relates less to the specific issues raised and more to the nature of such questions. But additional evidence is provided by a fourth type of question relating to the idea that immigrants should assimilate to the dominant culture.

Assimilation of immigrants

When in 1988 respondents were asked whether 'people who come to Australia should change their behaviour to be more like other Australians', a clear majority, 66 per cent, were in agreement. When two polls conducted in 1992 and 1993 posed the general proposition that 'Immigrants to this country should be prepared to adopt the way of life of this country' there was a very high level of agreement, 87 per cent in the first poll and 86 per cent in the second; 13 per cent and 14 per cent respectively were in disagreement.

A poll in 1994 made possible a clearer testing of opinion, providing respondents not with a statement but with options. Respondents were asked which of two statements came closer to their view: 'Migrants should learn to live and behave like the majority of Australians' or 'We should welcome and respect migrants who have different ways of living and behaving'. Sixty-one per cent of respondents favoured the first proposition, that migrants should live like the majority, 35 per cent were in agreement with the view that there should be a welcome and respect extended to those who have different ways.

The 2003 International Social Science Program survey posed two similarly differentiated options:

> Some people say that it is better for a country if different racial or ethnic groups maintain their distinct customs and traditions. Others say it is better if these groups adapt and blend into the larger society. Which of these views comes closest to your own?[13]

This question, although framed in general terms, yielded an even sharper differentiation of opinion, with 18 per cent in agreement with maintenance of traditions and 82 per cent in support of adaptation. This question was posed most recently in 2009, in a different survey context; 15 per cent of respondents

---

13   ISSP (2003). *Op cit.*

agreed with maintenance of traditions, 59 per cent considered that it was better if there was adaptation, while a further 26 per cent volunteered that they agreed with both propositions[14].

A series of polls conducted in 1993, 1998 and 2006, in a Melbourne suburb adjacent to a region of high immigrant concentration, considered the attitudes of respondents who were born in Australia, with one or both parents born in Australia[15]. The respondents were almost exclusively of Anglo-Celtic background. This group was presented with three options for settlement policy. Immigrants should be 'Encouraged to fit into the community as soon as possible', 'Left to fit in at their own pace', or 'Assisted by government funds to maintain their own culture during their first years in Australia'. A narrow time period, 'their first years in Australia', was thus specified. Across the three polls, the consistent finding was that almost no respondents (2 per cent, 1 per cent, 3 per cent) supported the government funding option. In contrast, 79 per cent, 80 per cent and 83 per cent supported encouragement to fit into the community as soon as possible. The maximum support reached in the three polls for the laissez-faire solution - 'left to fit in as soon as possible'- was 13 per cent.

Three national polls conducted in 1994, 1996 and 1997 elicited a response to the forthright statement that 'Immigrants to Australia should adopt our way of life even if they have to put their own traditions and culture behind them'. The results were consistent across the three polls, with 59-62 per cent in agreement.

There is thus majority support for the view that immigrants should assimilate to Australian norms of behaviour at the cost of their own customs – depending on the wording of the question, around 60-80 per cent are in agreement, with a few poll findings above 85 per cent.

Variables

In considering public opinion, it is important to consider the distribution of attitudes across sub-groups in the population. This close analysis provides indication of possible direction of change and may be of importance for the targeting of information strategies and other government programs. Sub-groups

---

14   Markus, Andrew (2009). *Mapping Social Cohesion 2009*, Institute for the Study of Global Movements, Monash University, http://www.globalmovements.monash.edu.au/news/, accessed 25 January 2010.
15   Markus, Andrew and Dharmalingham, Arunachalam (2007). Attitudinal divergence in a Melbourne region of high immigrant concentration: A case study', *People and Place*, vol. 15, 4: 38-48.

are considered in the context of two recent surveys which provide variables for analysis: the 2007 national social cohesion survey and the 2007 Community Indicators Victoria survey[16].

Divergence in attitude across ethnic groups is first considered. This issue is explored by comparing those whose first language is English with those whose first language is other than English (termed ESB and NSEB in the following discussion), and with regard to two questions.

First, responses are considered to the general proposition that 'immigrants from many countries make Australia stronger' (Table 1). This is the sort of question that yields a high level of agreement: some 66% per cent of ESB and 75 per cent of NESB; difference is more marked when level of 'strong agreement' (20 per cent, 34 per cent) and disagreement (28 per cent, 15 per cent) is considered, with differentiation in the range 10-15 percentage points.

Table 1 Accepting immigrants from many different countries makes Australia stronger. Response cross-tabulated by first language.

	English	Other than English
Strongly agree	19.7%	34.4%
Agree	45.9%	40.5%
(Neither agree or disagree)	3.5%	2.4%
Disagree	19.1%	11.9%
Strongly disagree	8.6%	3.4%
(None of the above/ Don't know)	2.9%	7.5%
(Refused)	0.2%	0.0%
Total	100.0%	100.0%
N	1695	294

Source: Scanlon Foundation social cohesion survey – national (2007)

The issue of government assistance to ethnic minorities for maintenance of customs and traditions (identified in the previous discussion as a question that receives endorsement only from a minority) yields more marked differentiation – at the level of 30-40 percentage points. (Table 2). Thus the relative level of 'strong agreement' for the ESB/ NESB groups is 6 per cent/24 per cent, the level of aggregated agreement is 26 per cent/64 per cent. The level of aggregated disagreement is of similar (but inverse) proportion, 68 per cent/29 per cent. Thus opinion on what has been termed 'hard' multiculturalism sees sharply divided opinion, as Betts argued, between the ESB and NESB groups.

---

16   Markus, Andrew and Dharmalingham, Arunachalam (2008). *Mapping Social Cohesion*, Institute for the Study of Global Movements, Monash University, http://www.globalmovements.monash.edu.au/, accessed 8 April 2009; Community Indicators Victoria (2007). SPSS data file, The McCaughey Centre, VicHealth Centre for the Promotion of Mental Health and Community Wellbeing, University of Melbourne.

Table 2 Ethnic minorities in Australia should be given Australian government assistance to maintain their customs and traditions. Response cross-tabulated by first language.

	English	Other than English
Strongly agree	6.4%	24.1%
Agree	20.0%	40.0%
(Neither agree or disagree)	3.4%	1.7%
Disagree	39.1%	16.6%
Strongly disagree	28.7%	12.2%
(None of the above/ Don't know)	2.2%	5.4%
(Refused)	0.2%	0.0%
Total	100.0%	100.0%
N	1692	295

Source: Scanlon Foundation social cohesion survey – national (2007)

Analysis of the 2007 Community Indicators Victoria, with its large respondent base, enables closer analysis of the majority group, those whose 'main language spoken at home' is English, constituting over 23,000 respondents. Four key variables - gender, age, education and income – are considered in response to the general proposition that 'it is a good thing for a society to be made up of people from different cultures' (Table 3). As noted, this question elicited a very high level of aggregated agreement, at 88 per cent of respondents. In the following analysis attention is directed to those indicating the strongest level of agreement (on a five point scale), as this level provides evidence of substantial variation and thus provides clearer insight into the basis of variation.

This analysis yields the following conclusions: there is minimal variation by gender; analysis by age group yields more variation, at 20 percentage points amongst those in 'strong agreement', with three demarcations, those aged 18-44, 45-64, and 65 and above; consideration of gross household income indicates that level of 'strong agreement' increases with income; and, the sharpest differentiation is yielded by level of education, with strong agreement ranging from 33 per cent amongst those with some high school education to 63 per cent of those with some tertiary education.

Table 3 'Strongly agree' and combined 'Strongly agree and Agree' that 'it is a good thing for a society to be made up of people from different cultures. Cross-tabulations for respondents who indicated English as the main language spoken at home.

Gender	Male	Female					
Strongly agree Total agree	48.5% 86.1%	48.9% 89.7%					
Age	18-24	25-34	35-44	45-54	55-64	65-74	75 plus
Strongly agree Total agree	57.9% 91.7%	59.5% 92.5%	55.8% 91.1%	46.4% 86.9%	42.0% 85.1%	33.9% 81.8%	29.0% 81.9%
Gross household income	$0-$20k	$20-$40k	$40-$60k	$60-$80k	$80k-$100k	$100k-$120k	+$120k
Strongly agree Total agree	37.2% 82.8%	40.8% 85.7%	47.9% 88.1%	52.8% 90.0%	54.4% 89.9%	59.1% 92.2%	62.7% 92.9%
Highest level education	Completed Primary	Some high school	Completed high school	Trade certificate Diploma	Some tertiary		
Strongly agree Total agree	18.3% 81.8%	32.5% 81.5%	50.2% 88.9%	45.6% 87.5%	63.1% 93.0%		

Source: Community Indicators Victoria (2007)

This data also provides indication of direction of change over time. With the increasing levels of university level education across Australian society there is expectation of higher levels of support for the various aspects of multicultural policy. Indicative of the pace of change, over the ten years 1996-2006 Victorian residents with a university degree increased by nearly 75 per cent, or from 392,656 to 678,392. In 2006 19 per cent of the Victorian population aged 15 and above had a university degree[17].

Patterns of response

In addition to the work of Betts already noted, a number of researchers have considered attitudes towards settlement policy. Professor Ien Ang, one of the authors of the 2002 SBS sponsored study *Living Diversity*, concluded that '… there is a high degree of ambivalence about cultural diversity in Australia'[18]. A leading Melbourne pollster, Irving Saulwick, has commented on the strong

---

17 Australian Bureau of Statistics (2007). *2006 Census Community Profile Series. Victoria. Time series profile*, cat: 2003.0, Commonwealth of Australia.

18 Ang, Ien, Brand, Jeffrey E, Noble, Greg and Wilding, Derek (2002). *Living Diversity. Australia's multicultural future*, Special Broadcasting Service Artarmon, http://www20.sbs.com.au/sbscorporate/index.php?id=547, accessed 8 April 2009: 22.

desire for unity in Australia. His findings indicated that 'the concept of multiculturalism raised in many minds an emphasis on separateness rather than togetherness'[19].

In 1999 Professor Murray Goot drew attention to the contradictory character of public opinion:

> On the question of assimilation versus multiculturalism, the surveys suggest that the public subscribes to both. It appears to recognise the inevitability, even the advantages, of a society which in many respects is culturally diverse while at the same time wanting migrants in other respects to be 'one of us'[20].

More recently, in a 2005 article, Goot and Ian Watson concluded that 'Depending on how it is presented to survey respondents, statements about multiculturalism can be widely accepted, widely opposed, or can divide opinion down the middle'[21].

This judgement, with its depiction of variation to all points of the compass, is open to the criticism that it is too sweeping. Rather, there is a largely consistent pattern of response – types of question yield predictable types of response. This is further illustrated by the findings of the 2002 *Living Diversity* study: broad questions, for example the question of general benefit to Australia of immigration, yield positive responses at the level of 80 per cent; statements about the enjoyment of eating food from other cultures are endorsed by 72 per cent; more specific statements, for example, concerning the benefit of cultural diversity, finds majority support, but at 59 per cent; a general statement concerning the encouragement to migrants to retain cultural identity splits opinion, with 52 per cent in favour and 48 per cent undecided or against. And as has been shown, when the prospect of government funding is introduced, there is majority opposition. The underlying reality, as noted by Irving Saulwick, is the strong desire for unity. Survey findings indicate that unity is understood in terms of a common culture.

In addition to these generalisations concerning the nature of response to a range of general and specific propositions, variance within the population needs to be recognised. The marked division between those of English-speaking and non-English speaking background, highlighted by Betts and others, is a key social variable. Within specific ethnic groups, level of education provides a key indicator of openness to other cultures and support for cultural maintenance.

---

19   Saulwick in National Multicultural Advisory Council (1999), *Australian Multiculturalism for a New Century*, http://www.immi.gov.au/media/publications/multicultural/nmac/report.pdf, accessed 25 January 2010: 91, 96.
20   Goot, Murray (1999). *Op cit:* 31.
21   Goot, Murray, and Watson, Ian (2005). 'Immigration, multiculturalism and national identity', in S Wilson, G Meagher, R Gibson, D Denemark and M Western (eds), *Australian Social Attitudes. The first report*, UNSW Press, Sydney: 185.

Chapter 6: Intermarriage, Integration and Multiculturalism: A Demographic Perspective[1]

Siew-Ean Khoo

Introduction

The demography discipline provides one of the most powerful indicators of integration of immigrants or ethnic groups in multicultural societies: intermarriage between people of different national origins or ethnic background. Marriage is an important demographic and life course event, usually signalling the start of family formation and childbearing. As with births and deaths, two other important demographic events, marriages are recorded with the registrar of births, deaths and marriages in countries that keep records of these vital events. These records are usually referred to as vital registration statistics and are one of the most important collections of demographic data for any country.

Intermarriage is considered as one of the most definitive measures of the dissolution of social and cultural barriers – and therefore of social and cultural integration – because it is the result of close social interaction between people of two different ethnicities[2]. Early studies of inter-ethnic marriage in the United States of America considered it an important element in the 'melting pot' theory of assimilation[3] and, in 1982, Australian demographer Charles Price wrote that 'intermarriage is still the best measure of ethnic intermixture because it breaks down ethnic exclusiveness and mixes the various ethnic populations more effectively than any other social process'[4]. Intermarried partners, although coming from different ethnic, social or cultural backgrounds, are likely to share some common values and aspirations, important elements in building

---

1   I would like to dedicate this chapter to the memory of Dr Charles Price, FASSA (1920-2009), who pioneered the study of the demography of intermarriage in Australia.

2   Bean, F and Stevens, G (2003). *America's Newcomers and the Dynamics of Diversity*. New York: Russell Sage Foundation; Kalmijn, M and Flap, H (2001). 'Assortative Meeting and Mating: Unintended Consequences of Organized Settings for Partner Choices.' *Social Forces*, 79: 1289-1312.

3   Drachsler, J quoted in Jones, F L (1994). 'Multiculturalism and ethnic intermarriage: Melting pot or nation of tribes?', paper presented at the Seventh National Conference of the Australian Population Association, Canberra, 22 September.

4   Price, C A (1982). The *Fertility and Marriage Patterns of Australia's Ethnic Groups*. Canberra: Department of Demography, ANU: 100.

social cohesion and contributing to social integration in multicultural societies. Inter-ethnic marriage also affects the social and cultural identities of the next generation who will be of mixed or multiethnic origins.

As an indicator of integration, intermarriage is also an indicator of the progress of multiculturalism in ethnically diverse societies. Intermarriage is more likely to occur in multicultural societies where there are opportunities for social interaction between people of different ethnicities. This interaction is facilitated by various factors including access to education, training and employment opportunities for young people of all ethnic backgrounds, and opportunities for people to participate in social and community activities regardless of ethnic background. Thus, social, cultural and religious factors and institutions, and government policies and programs that facilitate access to these opportunities are likely to increase the intermarriage rate. Conversely, cultural or religious institutions that focus on intra-group activities and maintaining intra-group cohesion – sometimes preferred by the elders in some ethnic communities in order to preserve the group's language and culture – can lead to reduced opportunities for their youth to interact socially with other young people in the local community who are of different ethnic or religious background, and to lower intermarriage rates.

Factors such as the size of, and gender imbalance in, the ethnic community and its residential concentration can also affect the availability and choice of marriage partners within the community, thereby affecting the group's intermarriage rate[5]. The larger the ethnic community and the more concentrated it is in terms of residential location, the more opportunity there is of finding a marriage partner within the community. An imbalance in the sex ratio of single people in the ethnic community, on the other hand, will affect the supply of potential spouses and can lead to greater intermarriage with members of the local community. For example, where single men outnumber single women in the ethnic community, some of the men will have to find marriage partners from outside the ethnic community or otherwise remain unmarried. This will result in a higher intermarriage rate for men than women.

While these demographic or geographic factors may have affected the intermarriage rate in the past, today's marriage market is no longer local but global. People now look abroad for marriage partners if the local marriage market is limited from their perspective. Former migrants now maintain transnational contacts with friends and relatives in the country of origin through the use of email, internet, mobile phones and cheap airfares and can easily return to their homeland to find a marriage partner if there is no suitable partner locally. Some immigrant parents who are concerned with maintaining cultural traditions

---

5   Penny, J and Khoo, S E (1996). *Intermarriage: A Study of Migration and Integration*, AGPS, Canberra.

within the family have also looked to their country of origin for marriage partners for their children when they reach marriage age. These practices are associated with lesser integration and contribute to a lower intermarriage rate.

Intermarriage is therefore regarded as an important index or indicator of integration particularly in a country of immigration such as Australia, where 40 per cent of the population is either first (born overseas) or second generation (born in Australia with one or both parents born overseas) Australians. Because of Australia's long history with immigration, country of birth is an important demographic identifier of people's origin. Data on country of birth are collected in the Australian census. The country of birth of the bride and groom is also specified in marriage registration records (and previously also the country of birth of the parents of the bride and groom, although this is no longer the case). The availability of these data ignited the interest of demographers in Australia some forty years ago in the study of intermarriage between immigrants and native-born Australians as an indicator of immigrant integration[6]. Information on each person's ancestry is also now available from the Australian census (since 2001), providing the opportunity for demographers to examine intermarriage by ethnic origin as well as birthplace. Because it is also possible to identify the second and third or more generations from census data, it is now also possible to examine intergenerational trends in intermarriage, allowing us to observe the extent that successive generations of each ethnic group are integrating into the country of settlement through intermarriage.

The next section of this paper introduces and discusses the two methodological approaches used by demographers to measure intermarriage rates, and their strengths and limitations. This is followed by a review of previous demographic studies of intermarriage in Australia. I then present and discuss current rates of intermarriage by birthplace and ethnicity based on the two methodological approaches and the latest available demographic data. This is followed by an examination of outcomes and implications for the next generation – the children of intermarriages – in terms of their ethnic identification and language spoken at home. The paper concludes with a discussion of the implications of current patterns of intermarriage for immigrant integration and the progress of multiculturalism in Australia.

---

6   Price, C A and Zubrzycki, J (1962a). 'The use of intermarriage statistics as an index of assimilation', *Population Studies* 16 (1): 58-69; Price, C A and Zubrzycki, J (1962b). 'Intermarriage patterns in Australia', *Population Studies* 16 (2): 123-133.

The demography of intermarriage

In 1962, Price and Zubrzycki published a paper, 'The use of inter-marriage statistics as an index of assimilation', which marked the beginning of the study of intermarriage in Australia[7]. The paper discusses the two different demographic approaches to measuring intermarriage.

The two approaches are based on different sources of demographic data. The first uses marriage registration statistics to measure the *incidence* of intermarriage during a specific period, for example, a particular year. It provides a measure of intermarriage that is based on marriages that take place in the country of settlement only. For example, the rate for Australia is calculated as the percentage of brides or grooms marrying in Australia each year (or over a two- or five-year period) who is marrying a person born in a different country. Since it is based on the bride's and groom's country of birth, it is a measure of intermarriage by birthplace. The intermarriage rate that is calculated as the percentage of overseas-born brides or grooms who marry a person who is born in Australia is usually considered as an index of immigrant integration because it measures the extent of intermarriage between immigrants and native-born Australians, with the marriages taking place in Australia after the migration of the overseas-born spouse.

The second approach uses census or survey data to measure the *prevalence* of intermarriage at the time of the census or survey. The intermarriage rate is obtained as the percentage of married men or women born in country x (or of ancestry/ethnic origin a) whose spouse is not born in country x (or of ancestry/ ethnic origin a). The intermarriage rate obtained in this way includes marriages that have occurred in the country of settlement as well as marriages that have taken place overseas before the migration of the overseas-born spouse or couple. Price and Zubrzycki[8] suggested that the intermarriage rate obtained in this way is a better measure of immigrant integration because the people who are already married in the country of origin before migrating are just as important in maintaining ethnic values as are those who choose to marry within their own ethnic background in the place of settlement. Price and Zubrzycki[9] considered this approach 'the most appropriate for measuring the extent of intermarriage amongst an ethnic group at any given moment of time' and referred to the intermarriage rate obtained in this way as the true rate. Being based on the entire population of married men or women of a given birthplace or ethnicity, this rate is also more stable, particularly for small birthplace or ethnic groups, and is not affected by year to year fluctuations in the number of men and women of any

---

7   Price, C A and Zubrzycki, J (1962a). *Op cit.*
8   *Ibid.*
9   *Ibid:* 67.

given birthplace or ethnicity who marry each year as in the first approach. When using data from recent Australian censuses to obtain intermarriage rates in this way, the rate includes couples in de facto relationships, while the intermarriage rate based on marriage registration statistics is based on registered marriages only and excludes couples in de facto relationships.

Intermarriage rates are usually calculated separately for men and women so gender differences can be observed. These differences usually reflect the different roles and status of men and women in the family in different cultures. The rates can also be obtained for men and women of each generation so that intergenerational trends in intermarriage can be observed. The immigrant generation – the overseas-born – is referred to as the first generation. The second generation refers to people born in the country of settlement to one or both immigrant parents. The third generation refers to the native-born whose parents are also native-born but whose grandparents are the immigrant generation. Studies of intermarriage by generation have shown that intermarriage rates usually increase with each successive generation but there is also variation by ethnic origin[10]. Intermarriage rates can also be examined by educational attainment, or other descriptors of the socio-economic status of the couple, to observe the nature of the relation between intermarriage, socio-economic status and ethnicity.

Previous studies of intermarriage in Australia

The first study of intermarriage in Australia by Price and Zubrzycki[11] examined the intermarriage rates based on data on the country of birth of brides and grooms whose marriages occurred in Australia during the period 1947-60. At that time, just after the Second World War, the overseas-born population in Australia was mainly from European countries so the focus of the study was on intermarriages between the European migrants and native-born Australians. The paper showed that, among the European migrants, those born in Italy and Greece had lower rates of intermarriage than migrants from Western or Eastern European countries such as the Netherlands or Poland.

Subsequent studies by Price[12], based on marriage registration statistics, show the same pattern of lower intermarriage rates among Southern European migrants than Western European migrants, indicating that Southern European

---

10   Bean, F and Stevens, G (2003). *Op cit*; Khoo, S E (2004). 'Intermarriage in Australia: Patterns by ancestry, gender and generation', *People and Place* 12 (2): 35-44; Khoo, S E, Birrell, B and Heard, G (2009). 'Intermarriage by birthplace and ancestry in Australia', *People and Place* 17 (1): 15-27.

11   Price, C A and Zubrzycki, J (1962b). *Op cit.*

12   Price, C A (1981). *Australian Immigration: A Digest,* ANU, Canberra; Price, C A (1982). *Op cit*; Price, C A (1989). *Ethnic Groups in Australia,* Office of Multicultural Affairs, Canberra.

migrants were integrating more slowly than other European migrants through marriage with native-born Australians. The studies by Price[13] on intermarriage among the second generation during the 1980s and early 1990s also show that the second generation of Southern European and Middle Eastern background had lower intermarriage rates than those of Western European background, although there was an increase in the intermarriage rate from the first to the second generation. His analysis also showed a small increase in in-marriage among the Greek, Lebanese and Yugoslav second generation between the 1980s and early 1990s and he attributed it partly to the increase in second-generation numbers and the geographic concentration of these groups. He also suggested that 'cultural and religious factors have a very strong influence on in-marriage, and that the larger a culturally strong ethnic group becomes, the more it can open clubs, churches and schools and the more it can keep its young people together and discourage mixed marriages'[14].

A question on ancestry was asked for the first time in the Australian census in 1986, providing the first opportunity to examine inter-ethnic marriage based on people's ethnic origin. These data were used in a number of studies to examine the effects of generation, group size, residential concentration, education and social distance on inter-ethnic marriage[15]. The rate of intermarriage between a particular ethnic group and the dominant ethnic group was found to be related to the social distance between the two groups: the greater the social distance the less likely intermarriage will occur[16]. In the studies, social distance between groups was indicated by ethnic group characteristics such as the percentage speaking only English at home, the percentage Catholic and the percentage living in metropolitan areas. Pre-1986, group size was found to have an impact on the intermarriage rate, with larger groups having lower rates of intermarriage[17]. The study also showed that groups which had a more dispersed pattern of residential settlement, such as the Dutch and Germans, had higher rates of intermarriage, but gender imbalance had no impact. Education had a strong effect only in those groups that had relatively low educational attainment.

The ancestry question was asked again in the 2001 census. Analysis of the data shows that intermarriage rates increase from the first to the second to

---

13   Price, C A (1993). 'Ethnic intermixture in Australia', *People and Place* 1 (1): 6-8; Price, C A, (1994). 'Ethnic intermixture in Australia', *People and Place* 2 (4): 8-11.

14   Price, C A (1994). *Op cit: 10.*

15   Jones, F L (1994). 'Multiculturalism and ethnic intermarriage: Melting pot or nation of tribes?' Paper presented at the Seventh National Conference of the Australian Population Association, Canberra, 22 September; Jones, F L and Luijkx, R (1996). 'Postwar patterns of intermarriage in Australia: The Mediterranean experience'. *European Sociological Review* 12 (1): 67-86; Giorgas, D and Jones, F L (2002). 'Intermarriage patterns and social cohesion among first, second and later generation Australians', *Journal of Population Research* 19 (1): 47-64.

16   Jones, F L and Luijkx, R (1996). *Op cit;* Giorgas, D and Jones, F L (2002). *Op cit.*

17   Jones, F L (1994). *Op cit.*

the third generation for all ancestry groups examined[18]. Although differences in the intermarriage rate persist from the first to the second generation, there is convergence in the rates by the third generation, with 70 per cent or more of the third generation of ethnic groups that migrated to Australia before 1970 married to spouses of a different ancestry. Of particular interest is that the majority of third generation men and women who reported Southern or Eastern European, Middle Eastern or Asian (Chinese or Indian) ancestry, and who had intermarried, had spouses who were of Australian or English-speaking ancestries. This indicates a high degree of social integration of these groups with Australian society by the third generation.

Current patterns of intermarriage in Australia

Current patterns of intermarriage can be examined using the two demographic approaches described earlier and the 2006 census data and 2006-07 marriage registration statistics. Table 1 shows the extent of intermarriage between immigrants and native-born Australians based on a comparison of the country of birth of spouses in all married and de facto couples enumerated in the 2006 population census. As noted earlier, according to Price and Zubrzycki[19], this measure indicates the extent that migrant communities are becoming integrated through intermarriage with the native-born population.

The table ranks the birthplace groups from the highest percentage to the lowest for overseas-born women with a spouse born in Australia. Men and women from North America have the highest rate of intermarriage with the Australian-born, followed by men and women born in the United Kingdom and other Western European countries such as the Netherlands, France and Germany. This pattern is consistent with those observed in previous studies and indicates close social interaction between Australians and people from Western European and North American countries.

In contrast to migrants from the UK and other Western European countries, migrants from Southern and Eastern European countries are less likely to have Australian-born spouses. This is partly a reflection of the migration of families from these countries in the 1950s and 1960s.

A relatively low percentage of immigrants from Lebanon and Turkey, and more recent source countries of migration such as China, India and Sri Lanka, are married to Australian-born men and women. Many have spouses born in the same country and are married before their migration to Australia. There is also

---

18   Khoo, S E (2004). *Op cit.*
19   Price, C A and Zubrzycki, J (1962a). *Op cit.*

some evidence that immigrants from these countries are more likely to look to their country of origin for marriage partners. Statistics on spouse and fiancé(e) visa grants since the 1990s show that China has been the second largest country of origin (after the UK), and Viet Nam, India and Lebanon are among the top ten source countries, of recipients of the spouse and fiancé(e) visas[20]. A study of spouse migration also shows that more than 85 per cent of migrants arriving on partner visas in 1993-95 from Turkey, China, Viet Nam, Lebanon, India, Sri Lanka and Cambodia were sponsored by previous migrants from the same country[21].

Women from three Asian countries - Thailand, Japan and the Philippines - have high intermarriage rates with the Australian-born, but this is not the case for the men from these countries. The high female intermarriage rate is related to marriage migration of women from these countries to marry Australian men and this pattern has been observed since the 1970s for women from the Philippines and since 1990 for the other two countries[22]. In recent years, there has also been a similar pattern of marriage migration of women from Russia and this is indicated in a similar gender differential in the intermarriage rate as shown in Table 1.

Table 1 Percent of overseas-born men and women in couple families with an Australian-born partner, by country of birth, 2006

Country of birth of overseas-born men/women	Male	Female
	% intermarried with Australian-born	
Canada	60.6	60.1
United States of America	57.3	56.6
Thailand	15.6	47.4
Netherlands	50.3	42.3
United Kingdom	43.4	40.8
Japan	14.9	40.6
France	43.8	39.5
Germany	45.2	38.6
New Zealand	42.9	38.3
Philippines	8.1	35.6
Ireland	42.3	34.8
Singapore	23.5	28.2
Spain	30.6	26.0

20 Department of Immigration and Citizenship (2008). *Community Projects* 2007-2008, http://www.immi. gov.au/media/publications/multicultural/pdf_doc/Community; Department of Immigration and Multicultural Affairs, various years.
21 Khoo, S E (2001). 'The context of spouse migration to Australia', *International Migration* 39 (1): 111-132.
22 Penny, J and Khoo, S E (1996). *Op cit.*

Indonesia	17.4	24.0
Malaysia	17.0	23.7
Malta	32.7	23.4
Hungary	28.5	22.4
Russian Federation	8.9	21.4
South Africa	22.5	20.7
Chile	19.7	18.3
Poland	18.7	18.0
Fiji	14.2	16.8
Egypt	23.3	14.4
Italy	29.6	13.5
Lebanon	24.3	12.2
Hong Kong	8.5	12.0
Croatia	18.3	10.9
Korea, Republic of	1.6	9.9
Turkey	16.8	9.9
Greece	19.4	9.1
Serbia	13.8	9.0
Sri Lanka	10.4	8.9
India	10.7	8.8
Fmr Yugo Rep of Macedonia	15.0	8.4
China	2.4	7.3
Pakistan	10.8	7.0
Iran	9.3	6.8
Viet Nam	2.0	5.2
Cambodia	2.2	5.2
Bosnia and Herzegovina	6.4	4.6
Iraq	4.7	2.1
Sudan	3.7	1.9
Afghanistan	2.7	0.9

Source: Khoo *et al*, (2009)[23]

23   Khoo, S E, Birrell, B and Heard, G (2009). 'Intermarriage by birthplace and ancestry in Australia', *People and Place*, vol. 17, 1: 15-27.

Higher female than male rates are also observed for migrants from other Southeast and East Asian countries, although the female rate is not as high as that for migrants from Thailand, Japan and Philippines. This gender differential reflects cultural norms in East Asian societies in relation to women's and men's roles and status, namely that women leave the family when they marry whereas men are expected to remain in the family to carry on the lineage so it is more important that they marry women of the same ethnic background[24]. The reverse gender pattern is observed for migrants from South Asia and the Middle Eastern countries. In these societies, daughters are considered a kind of family asset and are more protected to safeguard the family's reputation while sons are given more freedom to mix outside the ethnic community[25]. Therefore, the men are more likely to intermarry than the women.

Birthplace groups with the lowest rates of intermarriage with the Australian-born population are mostly from countries that have been the sources of recent refugee and other humanitarian migration, such as Afghanistan, Sudan, Iraq and Bosnia. Their low intermarriage rate reflects the migration of families from these countries, most of whom arrived during the past ten years for resettlement under Australia's humanitarian migration program. Older refugee groups, such as those from Cambodia and Viet Nam, also have low intermarriage rates with the Australian-born which may partly reflect the slower social and economic integration of these migrant communities.

Patterns of inter-ethnic marriage are shown in Table 2 by ancestry and generation for groups that have at least a second generation of marriage age. In the first generation, intermarriage is more common among men and women of Western European ancestries than among men and women of Southern or Eastern ancestries. Among the European migrants, the first generation Greek and Macedonian ancestries are the least likely to marry outside the ethnic community. The proportion intermarried is also low among the first generation of Middle Eastern and Asian ancestries such as the Lebanese, Turks, Vietnamese, Chinese and Indians. This is partly a reflection of the recent migration of families and partly of the propensity of these groups for intra-ethnic marriage, sometimes achieved through sponsorship of spouses from the country of origin, as referred to earlier.

---

24   *Ibid.*
25   *Ibid.*

Table 2 Percentage of partnered men and women with spouse of a different ancestry, by ancestry and generation, 2006

Ancestry	1st generation		2nd generation		3rd + generation	
	Male	Female	Male	Female	Male	Female
English	41	36	49	48	20	21
Irish	62	59	86	83	71	67
Scottish	65	60	90	88	80	75
Welsh	71	66	96	96	96	94
Dutch	62	55	89	88	95	95
French	61	60	91	93	98	98
German	59	56	91	90	72	69
Greek	12	9	37	31	67	61
Italian	22	12	51	42	77	74
Maltese	33	28	67	64	79	77
Spanish	36	37	87	85	96	98
Bosnian	15	14	44	42	*	*
Croatian	26	21	60	59	88	88
Macedonian	10	8	39	35	*	*
Serbian	26	17	67	62	96	91
Czech	52	47	96	96	*	*
Hungarian	47	36	89	88	*	*
Polish	34	34	84	80	95	94
Russian	28	43	74	76	97	94
Armenian	21	15	48	47	*	*
Egyptian	24	14	66	58	*	*
Lebanese	11	8	31	21	68	58
Turkish	11	7	25	16	*	*
Filipino	8	52	47	76	*	*
Indonesian	24	53	58	64	*	*
Vietnamese	7	13	48	48	*	*
Chinese	6	13	35	48	69	73
Indian	11	11	56	58	*	*
Sinhalese	14	13	95	86	*	*
South African	30	34	92	97	*	*
Maori	53	50	89	88	*	*
New Zealander	70	69	97	96	*	*

a. Based on sole ancestry response

* Less than 100 persons

Source: Khoo *et al*, (2009)

The most significant pattern shown in Table 2 is the increase in intermarriage with each successive generation. This indicates increased social interaction among people of different ethnicities with each successive generation. The increase in intermarriage is seen in all ancestry groups and it is quite large for some groups such as those of Greek, Lebanese or Chinese ancestry, where the proportion intermarried increases from about 10 per cent in the first generation to 30 per cent or more in the second generation to 60 per cent or more by the third generation. These patterns are similar to those indicated in the analysis of the 2001 census ancestry data discussed earlier[26]. Significant increases in the proportion intermarried are also seen from the first to the second generation of the other Asian, Middle Eastern and Southern and Eastern European groups that do not yet have a sizeable third generation of marriage age, indicating that social interaction is occurring between members of the second generation of these ethnic groups and other Australians.

Over 90 per cent of the third or more generation of most Western and Eastern European ancestries have spouses of a different ancestry. The exception is the third or more generation of English ancestry; the relatively low proportion intermarried is likely a reflection of the large number of third or more generation Australians who are of English ancestry.

Current patterns of intermarriage as indicated by marriage registration statistics for 2006 and 2007 are shown in Table 3. The first two columns show the percentages of overseas-born brides and grooms marrying persons born in Australia. Persons born in the United States were the most likely to marry persons born in Australia, followed by persons born in the United Kingdom and other European countries, New Zealand and South Africa. Very few men born in China or Viet Nam were marrying Australian-born women. Women from these two countries were more likely than the men to marry native-born Australians. This gender differential is also observed for the other East and Southeast Asian birthplace groups and is consistent with the pattern shown in the intermarriage rates based on census data (Table 1). However, the figures based on marriages registered in 2006-07 are higher than those based on all couples in the census because the latter include marriages that occurred overseas before the couples' migration and that are more likely to involve spouses from the same country of birth.

---

26   Khoo, S E (2004). *Op cit.*

Table 3 Per cent of brides and grooms marrying persons born in Australia or different country: Marriages registered in Australia, 2006-07

Country or region of birth of bride or groom	% marrying person born in Australia		% marrying person from another overseas country		% marrying person from a different country*		Number of:	
	Brides	Grooms	Brides	Grooms	Brides	Grooms	brides	grooms
New Zealand	57.9	62.6	18.1	18.7	76.0	81.3	5354	6860
Other Oceania	40.3	45.7	27.5	15.1	67.8	60.8	1679	1751
Germany	52.1	46.4	24.5	32.2	76.6	78.6	1198	1309
Ireland	56.6	61.4	23.7	25.6	80.3	87.0	599	909
United Kingdom	58.4	60.8	16.8	21.1	75.2	81.9	10744	14725
Other NW Europe	58.6	55.6	24.5	30.9	83.1	86.5	1697	2121
Greece	56.8	61.4	21.8	27.5	78.6	88.9	220	425
Italy	56.8	55.1	22.3	35.0	79.1	90.1	387	818
Other S&E Europe	45.2	37.9	28.7	32.2	73.9	70.1	4096	3581
Lebanon	45.0	63.7	14.1	12.3	59.1	76.0	773	1315
Other Middle East	26.1	33.8	24.9	27.0	51.0	60.8	2106	2633
Malaysia	37.2	23.0	38.6	46.2	75.8	69.2	1791	1410
Philippines	51.2	20.8	23.7	11.9	74.9	32.7	3494	1305
Viet Nam	17.8	7.3	16.8	16.1	34.6	23.4	3405	2906
Other SE Asia	43.0	17.7	31.5	32.7	74.5	50.4	5214	2680
China	17.0	1.9	23.1	10.5	40.1	12.4	6084	4162
Hong Kong	26.2	12.3	34.1	47.4	60.3	59.7	1184	1167
Other NE Asia	36.6	8.3	29.4	24.7	66.0	33.0	3557	1808
India	15.9	22.0	15.8	23.3	31.7	45.3	1664	2079
Other S. Asia	21.3	22.7	23.3	29.9	44.6	52.6	1308	1531
USA	69.1	66.4	19.6	23.9	88.7	90.3	1433	1666
Other Americas	48.3	47.0	25.6	25.2	73.9	72.2	2947	2774
South Africa	57.7	59.6	24.3	23.1	82.0	82.7	1441	1500
Other Africa	37.4	39.7	29.1	30.2	66.5	69.9	1386	1543

* Includes marrying persons born in Australia

Sources: Calculated from marriage registration statistics published by ABS (2007; 2008)

The intermarriage figures according to marriages in 2006-07 are also relatively low for migrants from India and other South Asian countries and also for the Other Middle East group, although they are relatively high for brides and grooms born in Lebanon. It is likely that the brides and grooms born in Lebanon may be marrying men and women who are second generation of Lebanese background. Analysis of the 2001 census data shows that 42 per cent of married women of Lebanese ancestry who are of the second generation are married to first generation (overseas-born) Lebanese men, while 22 per cent of married men of Lebanese ancestry who are of the second generation are married to first generation (overseas-born) Lebanese women[27]. It is likely that some of these second generation Lebanese men and women have looked to their parents' homeland to find marriage partners[28].

Table 3 also shows the percentage of brides and grooms in 2006-07 marrying a person born in a different overseas country, a possible indicator of the extent of social interaction between members of different migrant communities. About 20-30 per cent of overseas-born brides and grooms marrying in 2006-07 were marrying migrants from another overseas country. The exceptions were brides and grooms born in Lebanon, and grooms born in China or the Philippines, of whom less than 15 per cent were marrying migrants from a different overseas country. However, a marriage between persons born in different countries does not necessarily indicate an inter-ethnic marriage. It is possible that the relatively high percentage of brides and grooms from Malaysia or Hong Kong marrying migrants from another overseas country may be marrying co-ethnic Chinese. Many migrants from Malaysia or Hong Kong are ethnic Chinese[29] and their marriage to migrants from Singapore or China, for example, may be to co-ethnics from these countries. The marriage registration statistics do not have information on the ethnicity of the brides and grooms to enable examination of this issue.

Both demographic approaches to measuring intermarriage between migrants and native-born Australians show similar patterns of differences by migrants' birthplace. It is apparent that some migrant groups have integrated socially to a greater degree with Australian society than others who have tended to marry within their community or look for marriage partners from their country of origin. Migrant communities of more recent origin, and particularly those formed through mainly family reunion or refugee/humanitarian migration, are less likely to mix socially with local Australians, as indicated by their

---

27   *Ibid.*

28   Khoo, S E (2001). *Op cit.*

29   See Department of Immigration and Citizenship (2009a). 'Community Information Summary: Hong Kong-born Community'. At http://www.immi.gov.au/media/publications/statistics/comm-summ/summary. htm; Department of Immigration and Citizenship (2009b). 'Community Information Summary: Malaysia-born Community'. At http://www.immi.gov.au/media/publications/statistics/comm-summ/summary.htm.

intermarriage rates. Language may be a barrier to such social interaction as members of these migrant groups are generally less proficient in English. A recent study has shown that migrants who are less proficient in English are less likely to participate in social and community groups and activities; they are more likely to participate in religious groups and ethnic/multicultural clubs and organisations, which involves interaction mainly with people of similar religious beliefs or co-ethnics and other migrants since less than three per cent of native-born Australians participate in ethnic/multicultural clubs[30].

Outcomes and implications for the next generation

Intermarriage has important implications for the next generation who will have mixed or multiple ethnicities. With marriage registration statistics in the early 1990s showing that at least two-thirds of the second generation are marrying outside their ethnic group, this will result in an increase in the number of Australians of mixed ethnic origins[31]. Price estimated that 37 per cent of Australia's population in 1988 were of mixed ethnic origins and that this proportion would exceed 40 per cent by the year 2000. He also suggested that 'not only will this element soon become the largest ethnic element in the population but it will have more and more influence in determining Australia's identity and values'[32].

Just 28 per cent of the Australian population reported mixed or multiple ancestries in the 2006 census. This is likely to be a considerable underestimate of Australians who are of mixed or multiple ancestries. Studies comparing the ancestries of parents and children in the 1986 and 2001 censuses have shown that when parents are of different ancestries, they do not always report their children as having both their ancestries; instead there is a tendency to simplify their children's ancestry by reporting just one ancestry[33]. Of particular interest in relation to the issue of integration, these parents are also likely to report their children's ancestry as 'Australian', particularly when one parent is identified as Australian[34]. A study in the United States has also shown that second generation children of intermarriages between immigrants and native-born Americans are

---

30 Khoo, S E and Temple, J (2008). '"Immigrants" social and community participation in Australia', Paper presented at the Australian Population Association Biennial National Conference, Alice Springs.

31 Price, C A (1994). *Op cit.*

32 *Ibid*: 11.

33 Khoo, S E (1991). 'Consistency of ancestry reporting between parents and children in the 1986 census', *Journal of the Australian Population Association* 8 (2): 129-139; Khoo, S E and Lucas, D (2004). *Australians' Ancestries, 2001.* Australian Census Analytic Program. Canberra: Australian Bureau of Statistics.

34 Khoo, S E and Lucas, D (2004). *Op cit.*

more likely to identify as American than children with two immigrant parents[35]. Table 4 shows this comparison for the second generation in Australia in 2006. More than 50 per cent of the second generation who have one Australian-born parent identified their ancestry (or were identified by their parents) as Australian compared with less than 10 per cent of the second generation with both parents born overseas. More than 60 per cent of the second generation who have one Australian-born parent and one overseas-born parent reported multiple ancestries compared with just over 20 per cent of the second generation who have two overseas-born parents.

Table 4 Second generation Australians: Per cent with multiple ancestries or Australian ancestry, by age and parents' birthplace, 2006 census

Age of person (years)	Father born overseas, mother born in Aust.	Mother born overseas, father born in Aust.	Both parents born overseas
% with multiple ancestries			
0-14	62.6	63.3	22.6
15-29	64.1	66.0	26.1
30-44	66.1	67.0	20.5
45 +	59.8	59.0	20.3
Total	63.0	63.8	22.4
% with Aust. ancestry			
0-14	59.6	61.8	8.6
15-29	54.9	57.7	6.1
30-44	52.1	53.6	4.1
45 +	51.2	52.7	4.7
Total	54.6	57.2	5.9

Source: 2006 census, customised table

In case studies of the family context in intermarriages between immigrants and native-born Australians, Penny and Khoo[36] observed that the cultural identity of the children of mixed marriages depends on their upbringing as well as on their physical appearance. Those of mixed race face different concerns and issues from those who are not because of how others see and respond to them. The majority of the couples in the study have raised their children to be 'Australians, because they live here' rather than according to the customs of the immigrant parent. Others have tried to combine 'the best of both cultures' taking what they value from the culture of the immigrant parent and 'the openness, freedom,

---

35   Portes, A and Rumbaut, R (2001). *Legacies: The Story of the Immigrant Second Generation*. Berkeley: University of California Press.
36   Penny, J and Khoo, S E (1996).

self-confidence and practical approach to life of the Australian culture'[37]. Some families have also given their children a combination of 'ethnic' and Australian names to reflect their mixed ethnic-Australian parentage.

Other studies have shown that intermarriage also has important implications for the maintenance of the ethnic language. In studies of the second generation in Australia, Clyne and Kipp[38] and Khoo[39] compared children whose parents were born in the same overseas country with children with one parent born in that country and the other parent born in another overseas country or Australia on whether they spoke the ethnic language or English at home. They found that the shift to speaking English only at home was greater among the children of parents born in different countries or those with one parent born in Australia than those with two parents born in the same overseas country. However, the shift to speaking English among the children also varies by the overseas-born parent's birthplace. The pattern of these variations was similar to the pattern of intermarriage by birthplace discussed earlier. Children whose fathers or mothers were born in Viet Nam, Lebanon, Greece or Turkey – groups that have a low rate of intermarriage with the Australian-born – were more likely to retain the language of the overseas-born parent than children whose overseas-born parent was from migrant communities that have a higher rate of intermarriage with the Australian-born. Still, more than 40 per cent of Australian-born children with one Australian-born parent and one parent born in Viet Nam, Lebanon or Greece, spoke English only at home, compared with less than 10 per cent of Australian-born children with both parents born in these countries[40], indicating the importance of intermarriage in terms of the next generation's shift to speaking English at home.

Penny and Khoo's[41] study of intermarriage between immigrants and Australians also found that 'reverse assimilation' can occur, where the Australian-born partner has adopted the language, religion and culture of the migrant partner. Hence they warn that it may be an oversimplification to assume that intermarriage between immigrants and Australians always leads to immigrant integration. However, the strong statistical evidence in terms of the tendency to identify as Australians amongst the second generation who are children of marriages between immigrants and Australians, and their greater shift to speaking English at home, indicates the important role of intermarriage in the integration of the second generation.

---

37   *Ibid*: 206.
38   Clyne, M and Kipp, S (1995). 'The extent of community language maintenance in Australia', *People and Place*, 3 (4): 4-8.
39   Khoo, S E (1995). 'Language maintenance amongst the second generation', *People and Place*, 3 (4): 9-12.
40   Penny, J and Khoo, S E (1996). *Op cit*: 52.
41   *Ibid*.

Conclusion

Australian demographers have had a long-standing interest in research on intermarriage and its potential as a measure of immigrant integration, an important issue for a country of immigration. The result has been a rich body of knowledge of the intermarriage behaviour of immigrants, based on data on the country of birth of brides and grooms marrying in Australia since the 1920s. More recently, the availability of census data on ancestry has made it possible to examine intermarriage rates by ethnic origin of the Australian-born second and third generations, providing information on the integration of successive generations through inter-ethnic marriage.

In a country of immigration and increasing ethnic diversity such as Australia, intermarriage is not an uncommon occurrence. The spouses were of different ancestries in 30 per cent of all couples enumerated in the 2006 census, and 30 per cent of all marriages that took place in Australia in 2007 were between people who were born in different countries: 23 per cent were between a person born overseas and a person born in Australia and 7 per cent were between people born in two different overseas countries who had migrated to Australia. This level of prevalence and incidence of intermarriage is an indication of the progress of integration and multiculturalism in Australia up to the present time and the continuing role that intermarriage will have in the social and cultural integration of immigrants and ethnic communities in the country's future.

Intermarried couples have overcome social and cultural barriers in their partnering decisions. This process, building on shared aspirations and values, respect and tolerance, surely also contributes to the progress of multiculturalism, which advocates respect and tolerance of all cultures. Intermarriage is of course also more likely in multicultural societies where different ethnic groups are more likely to come into daily contact with one another in schools, workplaces and social and community activities than in societies where ethnic minorities are residentially and/or socially more segregated. Thus, multiculturalism both promotes and is advanced by intermarriage.

Intermarriage also contributes to the development of an Australian identity in that many children of intermarriages, with their bi- or multi-cultural identities, become Australians by their parents' or their own definition, as indicated when they are asked to identify their ancestry in the population census. This is particularly the case when one parent identifies as Australian or when one parent is overseas-born and the other is Australian-born. These outcomes also demonstrate the important role of intermarriage in the integration of immigrants and ethnic groups in multicultural societies.

Recent census data show increasing intermarriage with each successive generation in Australia regardless of ethnic background. Whether this trend will continue in the future in relation to ethnic communities of more recent migrant origin, that do not as yet have a second or third generation of marriage age, is unknown at this time. It will be a few more decades before the intermarriage patterns of the second and third generations of recent immigrant groups can be observed. Much depends on the extent of social interaction between young people from these communities and young Australians of different ethnic backgrounds in schools, tertiary training institutions, workplaces and the community. Policies, institutions, attitudes and cultural-religious norms that encourage equal access to education, training and employment opportunities and participation in social and community groups and activities for young men and women of all ethnic backgrounds will increase their social interaction and encourage intermarriage while those that lead to ethnic or gender segregation and social exclusion are unlikely to contribute to an increase in the intermarriage rate.

Chapter 7: The Cost of Fluency

Kim Kirsner

Granted that fluency in the dominant language of a country is a *necessary* if not *sufficient* condition for integration, questions about the cost of fluency are pertinent. The aim of this chapter is to determine the amount of engagement required to achieve fluency in a second language.

Measurement of second language skills depends critically on the test procedure, and the target problem. Many procedures involve de-contextualised tasks, and they therefore fail to capture the speaker's fluency under natural language conditions. Other procedures rely on subjective judgement, and they are correspondingly unreliable. The procedure outlined here involves measurement of fluency for short natural language samples, and provides a range of estimates of the cost in time of first language fluency in a second language.Engagement was assessed via a structured and in-depth interview designed to provide an estimate in hours of each participant's exposure to his or her second language. The fluency procedure was designed to provide objective and semi-automatic measurement of pause duration, and effective information transmission was also calculated. We have recently implemented and tested a fully automatic procedure.

We describe a pilot study involving 24 English-Italian or Italian-English bilinguals in Australia. The final study will involve 400 people including one EFL and eight ESL groups. The interview yielded second language practice estimates from 250 to 100,000 hours for all forms of engagement in second language activities. We obtained five-minute speech samples from each participant in English and Italian. Our results indicated between 8,000 and 80,000 hours of engagement are required before second language skills meet first language levels.

The discussion focused on questions about technical developments required to transform the language learning equation.

Fluency and integration are complex concepts. Fluency in the language of the host country is certainly critical to effective integration, however other factors including family upbringing, access to local customs and traditions, emotional attachments, values and religion will also enter the equation. Fluency is also complex, particularly where spontaneous speaking is concerned. It reflects motor, cognitive and vocabulary capabilities where these variables will in turn reflect the amount of engagement the individual has had with the host culture. The core concepts of integration and fluency are, we assume, associated to some extent, however the extent of that association and the causal links between the concepts are likely to be variable and unpredictable. The landscape of the relationship between integration and fluency is further compromised by the role of identity.

The aim of this project is to take a first and tentative step down the road to empirical measurement of a sample of these variables. In the pilot study described below we have concentrated on the relationship between Engagement and Fluency. Using a new and objective approach to the measurement of fluency – to what extent is fluency moderated by engagement in the host language?

The extent to which immigrants adapt to and integrate in their host society depends on a variety of individual, social, educational, emotional and cultural variables. One of the most potent of these variables involves the extent to which an individual has mastered the language of his or her host community. Mastery is a complex issue however, and involves many dimensions of communication. Here we focus on what is arguably the most demanding task in second language learning, language production.

Language production reflects both *competence*, an individual's knowledge of his or her own language, and *performance*, the transformation of competence into everyday speech[1]. In our approach we have focused on performance, and, even more narrowly, fluency. In this study consideration is restricted to just two dimensions of fluency, the amount of time required to deliver one *Correct Information Unit*, a measure that excludes material that is unintelligible, ungrammatical or not appropriate to the communication task, and *pause duration*, periods of silence during continuous speech.

Design

The results described here involve speech samples from eighteen English-Italian and six Italian-English speakers[2]. The speakers ranged in age from 17 to 56.

The participants were selected in order to provide a wide cross-section based on the extent of the participant's engagement in English. In practice, the range for the participants described in this chapter is from 250 hours for a recent arrival in Australia to 100,000 hours for one participant who left Italy 40 years ago.

---

1   Chomsky, N (1965). *Aspects of the Theory of Syntax*, MIT Press, Cambridge (Mass.).

2   Bujalka, H (2006). A Quantitative Assessment of the Development of Fluency in English/Italian and Italian/English. Unpublished Thesis, University of Western Australia, School of Psychology.

Each participant completed a questionnaire in collaboration with an interviewer in order to determine; first, the extent of his or her engagement in language activities involving all of her languages, and, second, his experience of, attitudes to, and integration with the Australian community.

Each participant subsequently provided five speech samples, one in his or her first language, and the balance in English. The samples were provided in response to questions about everyday topics. The following is a summary:

Question 1: First Language Response: Imagine your ideal holiday in the country of your first language (eg, Arabic, Italian, Greek, etc). Imagine a place you have never actually visited. Where would you go, what would you do there; and what would you expect to see?

Question 2: English Second Language Response: Imagine your ideal holiday in Australia. Imagine a place you have never actually visited. Where would you go, what would you do there; and what would you expect to see?

Question 3: English Second Language Response: Think about what you have done over the last two or three weeks. Where have you been? What did you see or hear that was new? What was difficult and what was easy? What did you enjoy and what did you find boring?

Question 4: English Second Language Response: Think about a typical day in your life. Think about a typical social event, a picnic, an outing, a visit to the beach, a party, or a meal for example, a visit to your favourite club or pub.

Question 5: English Second Language Response: I would be most grateful if you could tell me about your experience of Australia? How do you feel about Australia? Have you been accepted? Have you experienced difficulties in regard to education or work that appear to stem from the fact that English is not your first language? Just give me a general impression of your experience please.

Results

Estimation of second language engagement

A structured interview was designed and implemented to estimate the amount of practice each participant had had in English or Italian. The interviewer followed a chronological structure, and included questions about language use during each phase of the interviewee's life. The interviewees were specifically asked to estimate the amount of time associated with each language for each phase. The structure of the interview included provision for questions about the interviewee's home, school, family, social, working and holiday roles as well as language instruction. The interview data was used to estimate engagement (in hours) for each participant.

Transmission of information

The amount of information conveyed in a message is not tied directly to the temporal dynamics of language production[3]. In Broca's aphasia for example, speech is often slow and difficult to follow but analysis can nevertheless reveal that a considerable amount of information has been transmitted. In Wernicke's aphasia on the other hand, fluency including the number of words spoken per minute may be very high, but the amount of information conveyed very low, as the actual words sound like 'gibberish'.

We therefore adopted an independent measure of communicative efficiency. The measure, based on work by Nicholas and Brookshire[4], involves the concept of a Correct Information Unit. The Correct Information Unit count for a speech sample is restricted to *words* that are intelligible, and accurate, relevant and informative relative to the eliciting stimulus. For comparative purposes we divided speaking time by Correct Information Units to give *seconds per Correct Information Unit*.

Figure 1 shows the impact of practice on Communicative Efficiency. The dashed function is a measure of Communicative Efficiency for the speaker's first language. On average, each unit requires about 0.4 seconds, and first language performance is more or less indifferent to practice in the speaker's second language. However, while speakers produce about 2.5 units per second in their first language, second language performance commences at about one unit every two seconds following a few hundred hours of second language practice and it does not intersect with first language performance until somewhere between 10,000 and 100,000 hours of practice. Communicative Efficiency in second language production evidently involves a significant outlay of time even for cognate languages such as English and Italian.

---

3   For example, Ano, K (2002). Relationship between fluency and accuracy in spoken English of High School Learners, Step Bulletin 14: 39-49.

4   Nicholas, L E and Brookshire, R H (1993). A system for quantifying the informativeness and efficiency of the connected speech of adults with aphasia. *Journal of Speech and Hearing Research*, 36: 338-350.

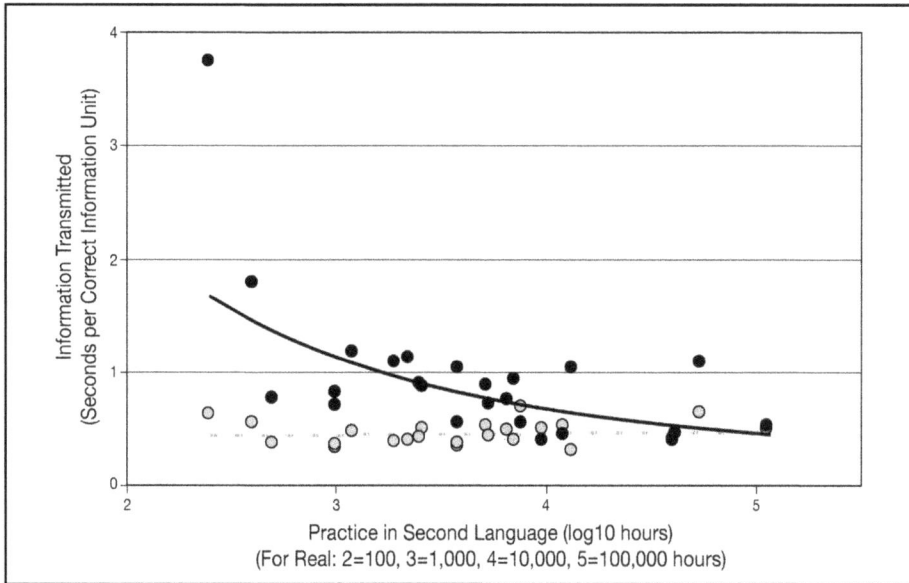

Figure 1 Relationship between practice and information transmitted

Role of fluency in second language learning

Measurement of the temporal dynamics is more challenging. Consideration of work by Lennon and Clark and Clifford[5] indicated that fluency can be used to refer to frequency of pauses, the duration of pauses, utterance length, semantic density, situational appropriateness and several other variables. There is some consensus however, that it refers to *performance* rather than *competence*[6]; that it is a measure of language as it is processed in real time[7]; and that it reflects interactions among a number of processes[8]. Uncertainty about the measurement of fluency extends to the measurement of second language skills. The assessment procedure for immigrants to Australia assigns individuals to bands. To achieve a particular band an individual must demonstrate mastery of specific features associated with a particular band. Is it possible to develop an objective procedure for measuring fluency?

One of our objectives is to develop a measurement system that is not only objective but automatic as well. We have developed acoustic and mathematical procedures[9], and we are currently refining an automatic implementation. We have

---

5   Lennon, P (1990). Investigating Fluency in EFL: A quantitative approach, *Language Learning*, 40: 387-417; Clark, JLD and Clifford, R (1988). 'The PSI/ILR/ACTFL proficiency scales and testing techniques: development, current status and needed research'. *Studies in Second Language Acquisition*, 10: 129-147.

6   Chomsky, N (1965). *Op cit*.

7   Schmidt, R (1992). Psychological mechanisms underlying second language fluency. *Studies inSecond LanguageAcquisition*, 14: 357-385.

8   Lennon, P (1990). *Op cit*.

9   For example, Kirsner, K, Dunn, J, Hird, K, Parkin, T and Clark, C (2002). 'Time for a Pause...', 9th International Conference on Speech Science, Melbourne; Kirsner, K, Dunn, J and Hird, K (2005). Language Production: a complex dynamic system with a chronometric footprint. *Proceedings of the 7th International*

however applied an interim stage of the procedure to a variety of communication problems including simultaneous interpretation and the acquisition of second language fluency

The temporal dynamics of language production are very complex, similar in some respects to output from an Electrocardiogram (EKG). Spontaneous speaking is composed of alternating periods of silence and speech. But there are several vexing measurement problems. The first of these has been recognised since the pioneering work of Lounsbury, and Goldman-Eisler[10]. The problem is that silence emanates from three or possibly more qualitatively different sources, including 'breathing', 'articulation' and 'cognition'.

The second problem is that pause duration distributions are massively skewed, precluding the use of arithmetic means to assess pause duration in natural language. This problem was first recognised by Quinting[11] but it has rarely been recognised in subsequent research.

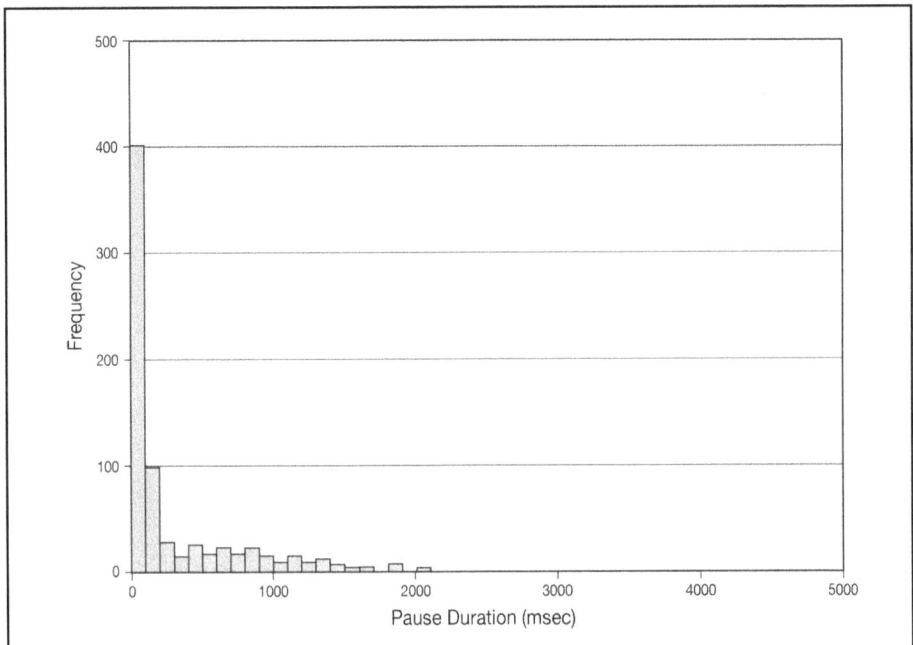

Figure 2 Typical pause duration distribution in real time

Conference on Cognitive Systems, New Delhi (India); Kirsner, K, Dunn, J J, Hird, K and Hennesy, N (2003). Temporal co-ordination; the lynch-pin of language production. In Palethorpe, S and Tabian, M (eds.), *Proceedings of the 6th International Seminar on SpeechProduction*, Macquarie University, CD-ROM: 19-24.

10   Lounsbury, FG (1954). Transitional probability, linguistic structures. In C Osgood and T A Sebeock (eds.), *Psycholinguistics: a survey of theory and research problems*: 93-101, Waverley Press, Baltimore (MD); Goldman-Eisler, F (1968). *Psycholinguistics: Experiments in spontaneous speech*, Academic Press, New York. Goldman-Eisler, F (1968). *Psycholinguistics*, Academic Press, London/New York.

11   Quinting, G (1971). *Hesitation phenomena in adult aphasic and normal speech*, Mouton, The Hague.

Figure 2 shows the pause duration distribution for one three-minute speech sample. The figure indicates frequency of occurrence for each bin. Hand analysis of pause duration is a challenging task of course, hence our motivation to produce an automatic system. Preparation of the figure involved reference to two hundred and thirty-nine 25 msec 'bins' between 25 msec and 6,000 msec or six seconds. As depicted in Figure 2, the vast majority of the hand-measured pauses fall into the first (26-50 msec), second (51-75 msec) or third bin (76-100 msec).

The assumption that two distributions are involved is not obvious in Figure 2. In Figure 3 however, following natural log transformation, the presence of two distributions is apparent[12].

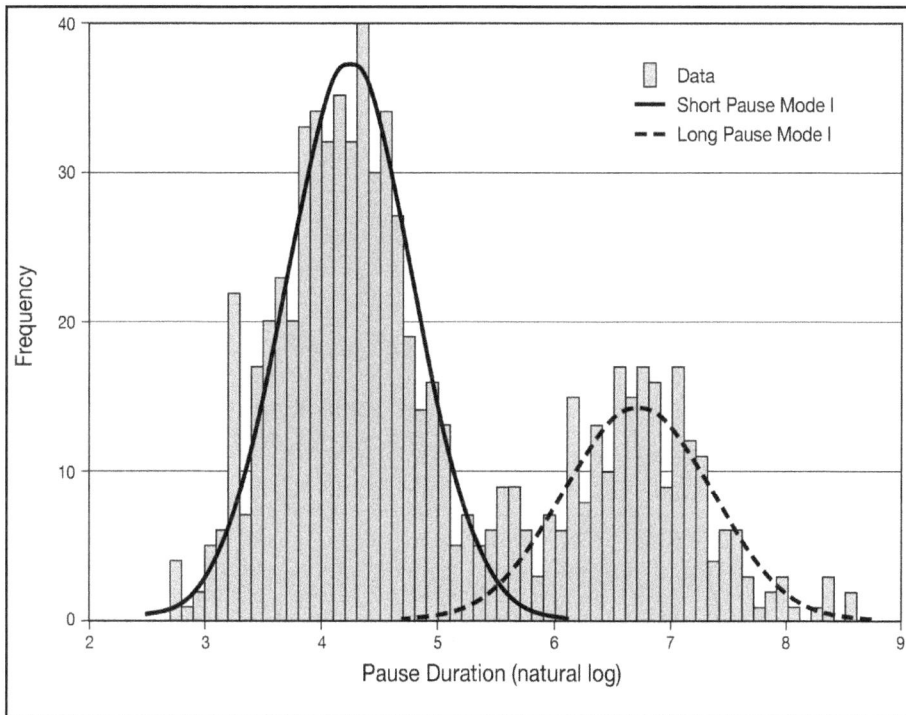

Figure 3 Typical pause duration distribution in natural log

The modes of the two-pause duration distributions fall at about log 4.1 (60 msec) and log 6.2 (600 msec) respectively. Recent work by our group indicates that most, although perhaps not all, the pauses in the short pause distribution constitute what Goldman-Eisler[13] would have called 'articulation' pauses, and that very few of the pauses in the long pause distribution fit the notion of

---

12   Kirsner, K et al (2002). Op cit.
13   Goldman-Eisler, F (1968). Op cit.

an 'articulation' pause. As a working hypothesis, it is our assumption that the short and long pause distributions reflect articulation and extra-articulation sources of variance respectively.

The solution to the measurement problem is apparent in Figure 3. The two distributions are approximately lognormal, and it is clear that they intersect at about log 5.5 or 250 msec, the value adopted by Goldman-Eisler to exclude articulation pauses from her analyses.

One more problem merits consideration. Complex biological systems are variable and unstable. Everything from nerve transmission time to conceptual planning varies from person to person, and occasion to occasion, and the actual point of intersection between the two distributions can fall anywhere between 100 and 400 msec for different individuals. Thus, although Goldman-Eisler[14] chose an appropriate mean value for the threshold – to exclude articulation pauses – adoption of the same value for each and every speech sample or participant inevitably leads to misclassification, of short pauses as long pauses, and vice versa.

We have used the Maximum-Equalisation algorithm[15] to optimise separation of the pause duration distributions. Given an estimate of the threshold that best defines the boundary between the two distributions, we define the means and standard deviations for the pause duration distributions (in natural log), the mean and standard for the speech segment duration distribution defined by the long pause duration distribution (in natural log), and a number of other statistics.

Long pause duration

The fact that the long pause duration distribution is lognormal complicates interpretation. Because the distribution is lognormal, it follows that the underlying process reflects interactions involving a number of variables. A provisional list of candidates would include conceptualisation, planning, intention, attention, lexical search and syntactic formulation, although breathing too is likely to be a factor. Unlike modular models that rely on fractionation or decomposition, therefore, it is not appropriate to identify a single hypothetical process with the result. Thus, unlike modular approaches to language production, it is not our assumption that the procedure measures a single process. Rather, our approach assumes that the distribution statistics reflect interactions involving many or even all of the processes listed above.

---

14   *Ibid.*
15   McLachlan, G and Peel, D (2000). *Finite Mixture Models*, Wiley, New York.

Figure 4 depicts the impact of practice on mean Long Pause duration for each individual's first and second language. Each participant has contributed two points to the figure, one for her or his first language, English or Italian, and a second one for her or his second language, Italian or English. The figure shows that trend lines fitted to the two sets of data intersect at approximately log 3.9 (base 10) or 7,000 hours of practice.

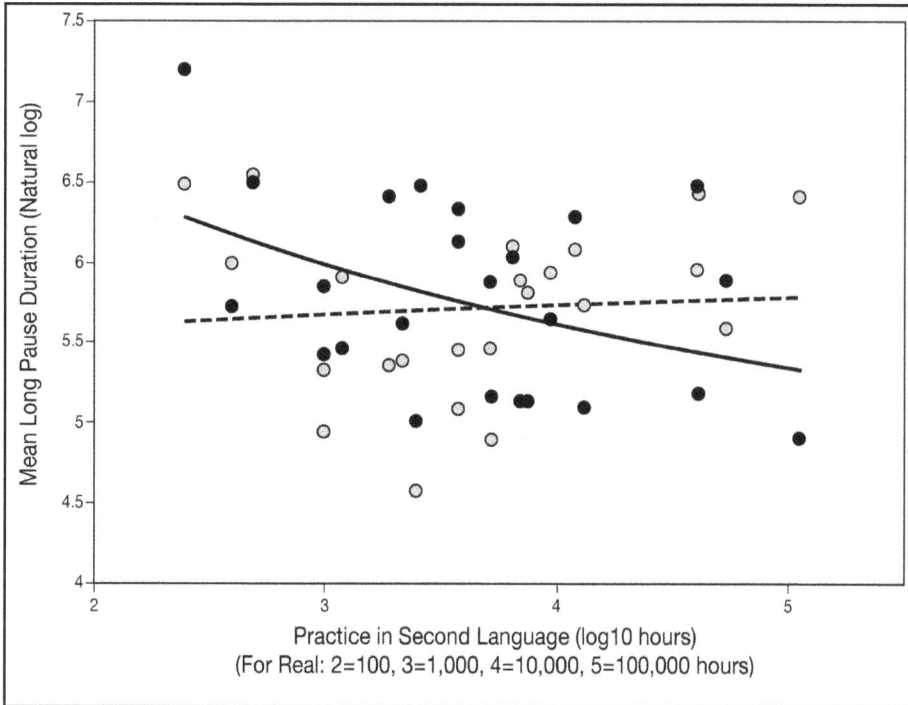

Figure 4 Relationship between practice and pause duration for L1 (open circles) and L2 (filled circles)

Discussion

Acquisition of second language skills

Our project is based on the premise that second language learning can be treated as a skill, and that measurement of practice is therefore critical[16].

Our first objective concerned the time required to attain fluency in English. Two parameters from a large potential suite suggest that people with Italian

---

16 Speelman, C and Kirsner, K (2005). *Beyond the learning curve: the construction of mind*, Oxford University Press.

First Language skills require at least 7000 hours to attain fluency in English. Assuming 50 hours of engagement in English per week (for an immigrant, not a second language student), this estimate rounds out to a minimum of three years.

Other studies provide even more depressing answers. Magiste[17], for example, used de-contextualised, as distinct from natural, language tasks and found that people who migrated from Germany to Sweden early in life did not reach the performance levels of native Swedes even after 20 years. But engagement is unspecified for Magiste's samples; some or all of them could have remained in German speaking communities.

Magiste's experiment included two groups of people, Swedish First Language Speakers (SFL, who had lived in Sweden from birth), and German First Language–Swedish Second Language Speakers (GFL-SSL, who had been born in Germany). She did not estimate number of hours of engagement in Swedish, and, as acknowledged by her, individual variation in this variable would have been considerable. Instead, she assigned each GFL-SSL participant to a group based on 'number of years in Sweden', and measured their performance on a series of de-contextualised tasks including Picture Naming Latency. The results were striking. Picture Naming Latency for the GFL-SSL group declined steadily as a function of practice, across the seven sub-groups that had been in Sweden for one to 20 years. The most significant result for our argument is that the performance levels for the GFL-SSL group never approached the values achieved by the Swedish First Language group, even after 20 years.

An even more depressing note was sounded by Thomas and Collier[18]. Children who entered the USA at age 12 showed steady gains in English throughout their secondary school years, however they actually fell further and further behind their English First Language peers throughout the same period. 'These findings show that there is no shortcut to the development of cognitive academic second language proficiency and to academic achievement in the second language. It is a process that takes a long, long time'[19].

Language differences and transfer between languages

Several authors have highlighted the role of similarity between a student's first and target languages. A significant part of the argument against the study of Mandarin, Cantonese and Japanese depends on the assumption that English First Language speakers find these languages significantly harder than languages that

17   Magiste, E (1979). The competing language systems of the multilingual: a developmental study of decoding and encoding processes. *Journal of Verbal Learning and Verbal Behaviour*, 18(1): 78-89.
18   Thomas, W and Collier, V (1997). *School effectiveness for language minority students*. NCBE Resource Collection Series Number 9, Washington DC.
19   Thomas, W and Collier, V (1997). *Ibid*: 638.

belong to one or other of the Indo-European family of languages. The extent to which this analysis depends on the need to master reading and writing as well as speech is unclear. The value of transfer between languages depends on numerous factors including vocabulary, syntax, prosody and pronunciation. The assumption that languages such as Mandarin, Cantonese and Japanese are an order of magnitude harder to learn is insecure, and may depend on the detailed transfer patterns between the languages involved, and the level of mastery required.

Consider the following result from an unpublished study by a Japanese student visiting our laboratory. Australian students of Japanese were asked to read words from Hiragana (Japanese words) and Katakana (loan words). The results showed that Australian students experienced reading problems with Katakana, the script used to depict Japanese loan words. Ice cream or *aisukuri-mu* is an obvious example. The word is borrowed from English but, while it is easy to learn, it is actually difficult for English speakers to pronounce. Transfer patterns between English and other languages are not in all cases obvious. Our overall study will provide evidence on the comparative difficulty of reaching first language proficiency in a variety of languages.

It is important to note however that the US-based Defense Language Institute provides tuition for six to sixteen months, depending on language, and that the longer period includes languages such as Japanese, Chinese and Korean.

The relationship between fluency and integration

The questions designed to elicit information about integration were not included in the pilot study reported here. But the question goes to the heart of the objectives of the overall project; what is the role of language in integration and multiculturalism? Does integration simply follow the language function, for example as if the two processes are coupled? Perhaps language leads to integration so that integration is only possible after a certain level of English proficiency is acquired. When we have collected integration measures as well as fluency measures for people from numerous language and cultural groups, we will be in a position to address the broader issue.

Will new technologies or combinations of technologies transform the time taken to master second languages?

The most important issue raised by our study involves the sheer amount of time it takes to master a second language. Whether the precise figure is 7000 hours or 70000 hours or it involves different amounts of time for different language skills is not the issue; it invariably involves a significant cost to the student. Yet the case for second language learning, and for a broad distribution of second language skills in the Australian community is overwhelming for educational, social, cultural and security reasons.

Perhaps surprisingly the security case does not involve terrorism, for recent events indicate that proficiency in a language provides no protection against extreme acts of hostility toward host communities. But these acts involve less than 1/10th of one per cent of the immigrant community, and cannot be used to shape *integration* policies.

A more appropriate challenge involves the facilitation of proficiency in English among the immigrant community generally, in a climate of limited resources, in regard to both teachers and funds. Four factors merit consideration, and, like most technical challenges, significant change is likely to involve interaction among several factors.

Virtual worlds

A recent article by Easteal[20] provides part of the answer. Technology has reached the point where it is possible to establish virtual environments between individuals and groups more or less anywhere in the world. Easteal, a legal expert from the University of Canberra undertook a 'virtual sabbatical' at Durham University in the UK, and participated in a wide range of social and academic events. I inhabit the same world when my London-based son calls me from his CISCO office. Virtual environments have barely been sampled for learning purposes. Given a camera on my head, a microphone on my lapel, and a transmitter on my back, I can include anybody anywhere in my everyday life.

Situational and contextualised learning

The second factor involves situated or contextualised learning. The trade world has honoured the apprenticeship model for centuries, with on-the-job training for electricians, mechanics and a host of other 'trades'. But over recent decades the medical profession has gradually embraced a variant of this model as well.

The Clinical Training and Evaluation Centre at UWA (ie, CTEC) provides an interesting example of the concept. Traditionally the medical model followed the trade model with supervised practice in an apprenticeship system. However, owing to decreasing patient availability, increasing demand for complex and hazardous procedures, and the rising number of trainees, the opportunity to become competent in a medical skill using traditional training methods

---

20   Easteal, P (2009). *Voices of the Survivors*, Spinifex Press, Melbourne.

has diminished. The solution for medicine involved the development of simulated environments including, for example, operating theatres. Simulated environments are designed to mimic the real thing while enabling minimal patient involvement during the early stages of skill acquisition, providing numerous opportunities for unlimited practice without risks to patients, and providing expert feedback to improve accuracy and reduce errors.

The language learning equivalent could place engineering students in China at the 'coalface' in Rio Tinto, Chinese Second Language students in Australian restaurants in Guangdong, and it could tailor the environment available to each student according to his or her preferences and needs, for cooking or system management in an iron ore mine for example. Importantly too, because such a system provides a form of social system, it has the potential drawing power associated with pen pals and even the Web dating world. While these opportunities involve risks, they also offer the type of motivation that fuels learning in all forms in the teenage community.

Collaborative learning

A third factor involves Collaborative Learning. The potential to create tailored groups is considerable. Groups would generally need a language expert to be 'on call' for planned support but many of the support skills could be met by individuals at more advanced levels of proficiency. Collaborative Learning, though, is not without its problems[21].

Conclusion

In conclusion, it is our contention that the critical issue involves transformation of the concept of a community. When I can share part of my daily life with a remote 'cousin' in Quangdong, and work and play in a remote community, I will in be in a position to master the language skills required to live and work in that environment. This is, of course, equivalent to living in a foreign country, but without the cost and time limits usually associated with international travel.

---

21   Roberts, T S and McInnerney, J M (2007). Seven problems of online group learning (and their solutions). *Educational Technology and Society*, 10 (4): 257-268.

Chapter 8: Religion and Integration in a Multifaith Society

James Jupp

Australia has been defined in many different ways over the past two centuries. From 1788 to the separation of Queensland in 1859 it developed as a series of British colonies, each one answerable to London rather than to anywhere else. Being British was its defining ethnic feature and anyone who was not British, and preferably of Anglo-Celtic origin, was not always welcome, though not excluded. Preference was given to the Protestant Germans and Scandinavians, but Catholic Italians and Croatians were less welcome and there was considerable criticism of the Irish despite them being British subjects. Within a generation Australia was further refined as a 'white' British society with many local common links additional to those with the United Kingdom. This was consolidated by Federation in 1901 and continued to be essentially maintained until the Second World War. Non-Europeans were rigidly excluded, while white British immigrants were generously subsidised to settle[1].

The Aboriginal population declined rapidly and was expected to die out. The great majority of Australians subscribed to one or other religious denomination imported from the British Isles, of which the largest at Federation were Anglicans, Catholics, Methodists, Presbyterians and Baptists. Australia was a very homogeneous society in terms of origins, languages and religions and certainly much more so than the two major immigrant societies of the time in the United States and Canada[2].

Social cohesion

Only one 'cultural' factor threatened the social cohesion of this British outpost – hostility between Protestants and Catholics[3]. Underlying this was hostility between British and Irish and the conflicting interests of labour and capital. But ethnic and religious conflict was muted by the exclusion of all elements believed to threaten peace and harmony, namely non-Europeans and, *de facto*, non-Christians. This did not mean that Australia was a deeply religious society. On the contrary, secularism was strongly entrenched in the political élite and

---

1   Jupp, J (1998). *Immigration*, Oxford University Press, Sydney.
2   Jupp, J (ed) (2009a). *The Encyclopedia of Religion in Australia*, Cambridge University Press, Melbourne.
3   Hogan, M (1987). *The Sectarian Strand*, Penguin, Ringwood, Victoria.

led to the withdrawal of public funding from religious schools throughout the second half of the nineteenth century. This particularly alienated the already distinctive Catholic quarter of the population, whose politics were thereafter determined by what they regarded as an injustice[4]. This resentment lasted into the 1960s, making religion a simmering political issue but one which was largely submerged by the tensions between labour and capital.

One intellectual consequence of this history is that academic historians have dealt with religious issues to only a limited extent, while other social scientists have concentrated on secular, and especially economic, questions or attempts to define Australia in uniform terms which ignored the religious divide. One major exception to this blinkered view was the historian Manning Clark, but he was more concerned with spiritual and moral dimensions than with denominational struggles. Despite a growing group of religious historians, other historians tended to marginalise religious issues, with few exceptions like Douglas Pike's history of the South Australian 'paradise of dissent'[5]. With the growth of the political science profession in the 1960s, attention was largely focused on the political role of Catholics, especially in Victoria[6]. Opinion polling, which had once shown Catholics to be predominantly Labor voters, increasingly excluded a religious question. The sociology of religion was also neglected[7].

Managing diversity

Despite the apparent uniformity of Australia into the 1950s, there was always a concern with external threats and with internal stability and cohesion[8]. Since 1901 immigration has been 'micromanaged' in the sense that there has never been an 'open door' for everyone who has wished to settle, despite the recognition that Australia had a very small population relative to its size and proximity to heavily populated Asian societies. This has meant that at every stage some types of people are welcome while others are not or are excluded altogether. The criteria have always been the utility of immigrants for Australia. This was generously defined for the British at least until the 1970s. Their utility was that they came from the founding stock and required no special services. They spoke English (unlike many Irish, Highland Scots and Welsh in the nineteenth century), were nominally Christian and could, therefore, be absorbed into existing institutions, jobs and neighbourhoods with little expense

4   O'Farrell, P (1992). *The Catholic Church and the Community*, University of New South Wales Press, Sydney.
5   Pike, D (1957). *Paradise of Dissent*, Melbourne University Press, Melbourne.
6   Truman, T (1959). *Catholic Action and Politics*, Georgian House, Melbourne.
7   Mol, H (1985). *The Faith of Australians*, George Allen and Unwin, Sydney.
8   Jupp, J, Nieuwenhuysen, J and Dawson, E (eds) (2007). *Social Cohesion in Australia*, Cambridge University Press, Melbourne.

or trouble. The extent to which others met these criteria was usually important for being selected or rejected. Everyone arriving lawfully since 1901 has had to be inspected at the entry point, except for a handful of seamen jumping ship – which was illegal under British maritime law. Others, arriving 'unlawfully' (without a visa) have recently been subjected to increasingly draconian controls beyond the normal procedures of deportation.

Religion was not one of the measures used to determine the status of immigrants. Religious discrimination by the Commonwealth was unconstitutional under the 1901 constitution s.116, but this was of only marginal importance, especially as Irish migration had dropped off in the 1890s never to recover. A minor exception to 'whiteness' was made for Lebanese Christians (Maronite and Melkite Catholics) who formed a small but distinct community in Sydney from the 1890s[9]. Some Muslims were accepted as 'white', including several Albanian families in the 1920s and others from the Balkans. A small number of Muslims, who had established residence before 1901, were allowed (like resident Chinese) to enter and leave under a permit system[10]. Sikhs who had served in the British Indian army were given some concessions in the 1920s for their service to the empire. But the entire non-Christian population did not exceed one per cent until the admission of Turks (who were defined as 'white') in the late 1960s. Of the non-Christians at least half were Jewish[11].

Religious variety only became significant with the ending of the White Australia policy between 1966 and 1972. Physical appearance and descent had been central, but many Asians of 'mixed race' and Christian religion were admitted in the 1960s. These, like the British migrants they resembled in most respects except birthplace, did not need 'managing' nor were they seen as presenting a problem. Many became active in the already established Christian churches. Chinese and other Asian students were required to return home once their studies were completed. Australian Jewish Welfare was active in bringing in refugees from Nazism in 1938 and Holocaust survivors after 1945[12]. The Jewish community was expected to service the welfare needs of their own people and there was marked opposition to their arrival from conservative politicians and media. The Australian Council of Churches also sponsored Orthodox Russian Christians from China after the Communist victory of 1949, continuing a long tradition of Protestant support for the Orthodox.

Essentially the management of diversity did not become an issue until the 1950s (except in Aboriginal affairs). Religious organisations took an important role in welcoming immigrants and assisted in the creation of churches and congregations,

9   Batrouney, A and Batrouney, T (1985). *The Lebanese in Australia,* AE Press, Melbourne.
10 Raikovski, P (1987). *In the Tracks of the Camel Men,* Angus and Robertson, Sydney.
11 Tavan, G (2005). *The Long, Slow Death of White Australia,* Scribe, Melbourne.
12 Benjamin, R (1998). *'A Serious Influx of Jews',* Allen and Unwin, Sydney.

including those of different denominations, as with the Anglican support for some of the smaller Orthodox groups from Eastern Europe. In that sense, the first wave of post-war entrants integrated through already existing networks. A substantial majority of the refugee Displaced Persons were Catholics[13]. The existing churches also took a role in the Good Neighbour Councils set up with Commonwealth funding from 1950. These embraced existing religious and charitable institutions, strongly favoured assimilation and declined to accept affiliation from ethnic organisations. Their major beneficiaries were British, Dutch and German immigrants and Displaced Persons, who were favoured in public opinion but started to decline in numbers by the 1970s. This exercise in integration depended on bringing individuals into already established religious networks with strong charitable traditions.

The central problems perceived by governments in those early days were communication and acceptance. Communication was tackled by the Adult Migrant English Programme, which became the largest item in the budget of the Immigration Department. This taught 'survival English' and still does, although it now offers a wider range of courses. Acceptance was tackled via a propaganda campaign showing that all new migrants loved Australia and were 'just like us' (including 'spot the Aussie' picture displays at Good Neighbour meetings). As many of the anti-Communist refugees were blonde and blue-eyed this was not too difficult. There was some hostility, especially to the use of other languages in public. Religion was not an issue, as all were presumed to be Christians and most were Catholics. However, behind the assimilationist façade, there was the steady creation of ethnic and religious organisations and networks, most of which still exist. There was, then, integration but not full assimilation.

This system of encouraged assimilation steadily eroded as immigration shifted towards southern Europe and the arrival of hundreds of thousands of Italians, Greeks, Maltese and Yugoslavs. All were deemed to be 'white', even the Turks who were assisted in substantial numbers from 1968. Turks were the first (and only) Muslim group to be assisted with publicly funded fares. But there was very little opposition. They were supported by the Returned Services League (for their bravery at Gallipoli) and by the motor industry (for their role in German car factories) and have remained a rather unproblematic community in concentrated working class districts of Melbourne and Sydney. What their 'values' are is scarcely understood and they are essentially a classic industrial proletariat with limited English. The Greeks and Italians and large contingents of Lebanese and Vietnamese refugees, admitted under relaxed conditions in the mid-1970s, were important in dismantling the Good Neighbour assimilationist movement. They were the backbone of the multicultural movement which had

---

13   Kunz, E F (1988). *Displaced Persons: Calwell's New Australians*, Australian National University Press, Sydney.

been launched in Melbourne in the early 1970s and was enthusiastically encouraged by Malcolm Fraser later in the decade[14]. The major policy document of this period was the Galbally report of 1978, which has shaped policy ever since[15].

Here again, religion was not emphasised. Solutions were secular, including welfare, the creation of local migrant service points, the subsidy of Ethnic Communities Councils and their national body, extended translation and interpreting services, the multilingual Special Broadcasting Service, funding assistance to ethnic welfare bodies on the same basis as others and, eventually, funding of religious schools (Christian and otherwise) on an equal basis. This latter was in financial terms and its long-term implications much more important than many of the Galbally proposals, but it escaped critical comment and was not mentioned by Galbally. Most of the conservative opponents of multiculturalism were strong proponents of religious schools.

Many supporters of multiculturalism deplored public subsidies to religious institutions, although the main benefits came from tax concessions rather than direct grants. Distinct education, social and welfare provision grew rapidly, but multiculturalism was seen by most Australians as involving dances, festivals and food. The protection of s.116 ensured that non-Christian schools were generously supported, which had not been the case in Britain or other European states. This did not arise in the United States where there was no public provision for religious institutions other than very generous tax breaks, some of which were comparable to those in Australia.

The new global conflict

The official definition of 'culture' as somehow excluding religion naturally influenced public policy towards 'ethnic groups'. These were defined in terms of national origins, language and citizenship, replacing the racial basis officially used for most of the century before the 1970s. Yet this definition was increasingly irrelevant to classifying many immigrants from outside Europe, who began to dominate the intake. The old argument as to whether Jews were a race, a religion or an ethnic group had been glossed over for many years and probably worried Jews more than anyone else. However, in 1996 Samuel Huntington launched a new approach to cultures which became increasingly important in Australia as in other immigrant receiving societies[16]. In his view the lines of future conflict would correspond to those between 'religious/cultural' traditions rather than nation states. Such states were often 'cleft' or 'torn' between alternative cultures,

---

14   Lopez, M (2000). *The Origins of Multiculturalism in Australian Politics 1945–75*, Melbourne University Press, Melbourne.

15   Galbally, F (chair) (1978). *Migrant Services and Programs*, AGPS, Canberra.

16   Huntington, S P (1996). *The Clash of Civilizations and the Remaking of World Order*, Simon and Schuster, New York.

most relevantly in the case of Yugoslavia. In a rather fanciful passage he even extended this analysis to Australia, which was 'torn' between its European origins and its Asian location.

Huntington's approach was influential on policy makers in the United States and seemed increasingly relevant as Islamic militancy influenced the Islamic revival which had been spreading since the 1920s from the Middle East and South Asia and was now reaching developed Christian societies through globalised migration. Huntington's general propositions gained enormous influence through the destruction of the World Trade Centre in New York in 2001 and the resulting 'war on terrorism'. This 'war' had been going on for many years in the Middle East but had been largely ignored by the major powers, which were preoccupied with the Cold War between liberal democracy and communism. However it became threatening just as that 'war' came to an end and it rationalised a continuing militant stance by the United States in world affairs. The new 'war' began to impinge on domestic politics of Europe and North America, with terrorist acts in the US, Britain, Spain, the Netherlands, Germany, France and Russia. Religious hostilities were also central to the violent collapse of the state of Yugoslavia, which Huntington had correctly defined as a meeting place for the three 'cultures' of Catholicism, Orthodoxy and Islam.

The impact of all of this on public policy was detrimental to the development of multiculturalism, which had been proceeding slowly but surely in Europe, North America and Australasia. The first reaction was to define the crisis as requiring more vigorous immigration controls, as the 9/11 bombers were Arabic immigrants to the USA. However, the European incidents shifted the emphasis to locally born Muslims, opening up the fear that there were large and growing elements who had not only not been assimilated or integrated but might be hostile to the dominant society and all its values. This view was strongly endorsed by John Howard for Australia, as it was by a range of Western politicians. Howard had been publicly hostile to multiculturalism ever since the Bicentennial debates of 1988 and now saw the political opportunity to reverse public policy without unduly alienating 'ethnic' voters.

At a political level, then, it does not need a very sharp analytical mind to understand why states like the Netherlands totally reversed their previous welcome to non-European immigrants and to religious diversity. When prominent individuals were being murdered in the streets or threatened with death for criticising Islam, such a dedicated plural democracy rapidly reassessed its previous tolerance. A major factor in shifting attitudes was the rapid increase in the votes of racist parties in states such as Austria, Switzerland and Denmark. However this did not apply to Britain, Canada or Australia. The rise and fall of One Nation in Australia was over before 9/11[17].

---

17   Leach, M, Stokes, G, and Ward, I (2000). *The Rise and Fall of One Nation*, University of Queensland Press, St Lucia (Qld).

No similar movement affected Canada. But what did affect all these liberal democracies, which had adopted multicultural approaches, was a shifting of the political debate in favour of the new concept of 'integration' and the centrality of 'values'. These developments gave an incentive to social scientists to take a new interest in religion, but few did so in Australia[18]. Politicians and public servants continued to generalise rather than to specifically attack Islam. Efforts were made to encourage and consult 'moderate' Muslims. Muslims were appointed to advisory positions, but none succeeded in entering the national parliament, until 2010.

Integrating religion and the religious

From 9/11 onwards, the management of diversity shifted ground in most democracies from concern with language and welfare services to anxiety about religion, values and loyalty. In the early suspicious days of non-British immigration there had been concern about Communist sympathies among Greeks and Italians, some of whom were excluded via security clearance. Many got in nevertheless, making the Greeks a bastion of the ALP Left in Victoria and South Australia. There was much less concern officially about fascist and Nazi sympathies, except in the Jewish community. Later concerns were expressed about possible war criminals coming in from Viet Nam, Lebanon and Yugoslavia. But all of these undemocratic entrants remained law abiding, confining their views within their own communities and in their own languages. Communism, fascism and nationalism are all secular creeds, held by minorities. However the Middle Eastern and Asian immigrants who became so prominent from the 1970s, were frequently defined by their religion rather than by their nationality or secular ideologies. The Lebanese had been disrupted by a series of civil wars based entirely on religious adherence, which they brought with them to Australia. Indians, Sri Lankans, Egyptians, Malaysians, Iranians, Ethiopians, Yugoslavs and Sudanese all came from societies in which self definition by religion was often more important than formal nationality. In many cases they also came from civil war situations in which human values had become seriously distorted.

Ethnic minority threats to Australian social stability and an ordered society were quite limited and found mainly among criminals in the drug trade. The gang wars, which killed thirty people in Melbourne within a few years, had a significant Lebanese and southern European element, although at least one criminal family was of Irish descent. The rather less vicious marijuana industry had a strong Calabrian influence, which extended to some city markets and rural areas. Vietnamese criminals were significant in some suburbs of Sydney and

---

18   Hassan, R (2008). *Inside Muslim Minds,* Melbourne University Press, Melbourne.

Melbourne. Few were notably religious, although several had Catholic funerals. In the most violent confrontation between Anglo-Australians and Lebanese – the Cronulla riot of 2005 – the aggressors were locally born Anglo-Australians. Compared with such problems in Europe or North America, Australia was quiet and cohesive. Religion had nothing much to do with any of these crises, although anti-Muslim slogans were used at Cronulla.

The 'war on terror' had to have a target, like all wars. Australian authorities (as elsewhere) were careful not to identify the 'enemy' in religious terms. The Tamil Tigers of Sri Lanka (who were not Muslims) were charged with supporting a terrorist organisation, albeit one which was not proscribed in Australia. But all organisations proscribed by Australia were Muslim, which was not the case for the much larger American list. No terrorist act was recorded on Australian soil. But the rapid expansion of anti-terrorist laws made advocacy and financial support for 'terrorist' organisations very serious and heavily punishable offences. It was under this legislation that a Muslim imam, Benbrika, and his disciples were prosecuted and sentenced to long prison terms in 2008.

Despite past suspicions about the Irish, the Italians, the Vietnamese and the Lebanese, no ethnic group had in the past been officially nominated a threat to Australian social cohesion, and certainly no religious group since at least the 1890s. Whatever unpublished instructions may have been sent to overseas posts, no public condemnation of entire ethnic or religious communities was made at the official level. However the long-term consequence of the 'war on terror'(as elsewhere), was to strengthen the requirements for entry and naturalisation, to institute a test of knowledge and values for intending citizens, and to seek 'moderate' Islamic leaders who might act as influences against the terrorist minority (whoever they might be). Public formulation shifted from multiculturalism to integration, accomplishing in a short period what the Howard government's slow death approach had not yet achieved. Positively, academic centres of Islamic studies shot up everywhere and experts on terrorism appeared from nowhere. With some rare and unfortunate exceptions, the major Christian denominations remained aloof from attacks on the Muslim religion. The growing ecumenical movements began to expand outwards from their Christian bases[19]. But there was no agreed Islamic leadership and government attempts to create one were unproductive.

---

19   Cahill, D, Bouma, G, Dellal, H and Leahy, M (2004). *Religion, Cultural Diversity and Safeguarding Australia*, Australian Multicultural Foundation, Melbourne.

Religious integration

Apart from the draconian new laws and a rapid expansion of security agencies, the main objective of government was to manage religious diversity by encouraging 'integration'. This magic word had been used officially in Australia in the interim between assimilation (to 1966) and multiculturalism (from 1973). It was never clearly defined, nor has it been yet, at least in Australia. However its popularity at the annual Metropolis conference in Bonn (Germany) in October 2008 suggests that it has secured considerable support. Metropolis is an agency of the Canadian government, where multiculturalism was invented in 1968. It brings together a wide range of academics and officials to debate ethnic affairs and immigration. It has, regrettably, had little support from Australia except when it met in Melbourne, but its deliberations are certainly reported to the Immigration Department.

Obviously integration is a more appropriate term than assimilation when dealing with religious communities. Jews have maintained their distinctive life in Australia for two centuries. Assimilation sounds the death knell to their religion in the opinion of most Jews. Muslims are not going to become Christians and neither are Hindus or Buddhists. Within Christianity there are more ecumenical relationships than ever before. But the Orthodox and Catholics have been negotiating reunion since the 15th century and nothing much will happen in a hurry. Nor are the Sydney Anglicans likely to unite with the Catholics, despite agreement on several issues such as sexual morality and the ordination of women. So the old question 'assimilate to what?' will not produce an answer in religious affairs.

Integration holds out the prospect of close co-operation with agreement to differ, which is already advancing among the major denominations and distinct religions. This means, however, that there will still be substantial religious variety, with allegiances to various centres outside Australia and the use of languages other than English. It may also mean that some practices, inconsistent with liberal democracy and social equity, will go on being condoned by the more conservative clergy or their overseas superiors. One hope expressed by government is that native-born clergy will be trained in Australia, thus emulating the policy of the New South Wales Catholic Church nearly a century ago. As in the United States, churches which previously conducted their affairs in another language will move over to English to retain the support of the young. To some extent this has already happened. However some of the most dangerous militants have been locally born and perfectly fluent in English. The incorporation of non-Christian religious leaders into positions of authority, including as elected politicians, is a long way off. There is only one Muslim in the Commonwealth parliament and the first such member of the New South Wales upper house was only elected in 2009. This is a worse record than in Britain, Canada or New Zealand.

An ambiguity in the concept of integration is whether this refers primarily to individuals or to social groups. The assimilationist expectations of the 1950s were that within a few years 'New Australians' would be indistinguishable from their local fellows. This did not (and could not) happen for many of them. It is even less likely now that immigrants are drawn from a much wider range. Accepting the values of democracy in an affluent and secure society is more probable. This is problematic when Muslims see the Australian government, in alliance with others, bombing Muslim villages and occupying Muslim countries. Muslims can hardly fail to have noticed that most of the asylum seekers interned under the Howard government were Muslims, although the Immigration Department never publishes official figures based on religion. The unjustified treatment of Dr Haneef in 2007-2008 was also specifically directed against a Muslim[20]. The 'war against terrorism' recruits its own terrorists. Presumably one expectation of integration is that a sense of unity with co-religionists somewhere else should wither and die. This has not yet happened for Irish Catholics, Muslims, Jews, Armenians or most of the Orthodox Christians.

The tables following this chapter suggest that a high degree of collective integration is already taking place. But this is not the same as saying that individual members of religious communities will integrate at the same rate or with the same enthusiasm. The level of Australian citizenship is exceptionally high for some of the European religions (such as the Greek, Macedonian and Serbian Orthodox), which grew in size in Australia mainly in the 1960s (see Table 1). The level is lower for more recent arrivals such as Buddhists and Hindus, mainly from China, India, Malaysia and Fiji, but this is a consequence of recent arrival rather than reluctance to naturalise. Australian citizenship had become easy to achieve, at least until the waiting period was doubled by the Howard government. No matter how 'exotic' a religion may be by previous Australian standards, its adherents were anxious to become citizens, often seen as a measure of integration. The low levels of citizenship for Hindus reflect the recent arrival of Indians in general and of temporary students in particular. But Melkite Catholics (95.3 per cent), Ukrainian Orthodox (93.1 per cent). Druse (90.5 per cent) and Armenians (94.6 per cent) all have very high levels of citizenship, despite being unmistakably 'ethnic' churches. One important factor in the future, created by public policy, will be the very large numbers admitted under temporary visas who may not be eligible for citizenship.

---

20   Ewart, J (2009). *Haneef: A Question of Character*, Halstead Press, Canberra.

The Tables in general show that 'traditional' religions from the British Isles still retain the overall loyalty of the majority of Australians. Non-Christian religions rose from 1.4 per cent of the total in 1901 to 5.6 per cent in 2006, more than one million and the highest level in Australian modern history. But this covers a wide variety of belief systems, often very decentralised. Christian denominations were more likely to feel pressure from the well-funded and efficient 'American' religions and especially Pentecostalism, than from Buddhism, Hinduism or Islam. Apart from acquiring citizenship, another measure of integration is educational and occupational success. By this standard, Jews (with 33 per cent graduates) and Hindus (41 per cent) are exceptionally well integrated, while Pentecostalists, Buddhists and Muslims are at the national level (Table 3). The Hindu figures represent the very large numbers of students now coming from India, many of whom will be eligible for permanent residence once they graduate, but who are less likely to have dependent children counted for their religion. Briefly, non-British and non-Christian religions seem well integrated into Australian society, while often retaining many quite distinctive traditions and cultures of their own. There is little reason to suppose that religious denominations as a whole may reject democratic values, but no guarantee that some individuals may not be attracted to violence and terror.

Conclusions

As public policy discourses move from 'multiculturalism' to 'integration', nationally and internationally, the religious factor in cultural diversity still remains at the margin of Australian public debate. Yet the very change in approved terminology would not have happened had it not been for the rise of Islamist militancy and the violent attacks on institutions and individuals in the past decade. The proverbial 'elephant in the room' grows larger by the hour. Its presence is the major factor in the tightening of citizenship requirements in previously liberal societies like Australia, Canada and the Netherlands. Australia has so far escaped the reactions of European societies like Switzerland, France and Denmark, which aim to erase visual evidence of the Muslim presence. But 'values' are tested as a requirement for final integration into majority society as a legal citizen. These values are all conceived of as secular, liberal and democratic and are reinforced by general knowledge requirements, which skirt around religion altogether by emphasising history, politics and even sport.

The basic dilemma is that all Western democracies conceive of themselves officially as secular, with a clearly defined division between 'church and state'[21]. This applies especially strongly to states such as the United States, the United

---

21   Fergusson, D (2004). *Church, State and Civil Society,* Cambridge University Press, Melbourne.

Kingdom and its former colonies, Germany and the Scandinavian democracies. Yet many of these still retain established churches, while the United States is usually presented as the most deeply religious of all democratic societies, with the obligatory exhortation 'God Bless America' at all political gatherings. This contradictory tradition means, among other things, that religions are free of requirements to sustain equality between men and women or even to pay many taxes, while being eligible for a wide range of subsidies[22]. Religions are truly privileged and this is rarely challenged, except in the typically rigorous French Republic.

These contradictory approaches to one of the major cultural divisions in society – organised religion – makes the public discussion of issues surrounding social cohesion increasingly bizarre. The argument is really about whether Islam and Muslims can be 'integrated' into Christian and Enlightenment inheritances. Yet official multiculturalism in all its variants has skirted around the 'elephant', concentrating on languages, values, customs and 'culture' and social justice issues such as racism, refugees and equality of access to social and economic goods. The basic assumption of policy makers has been that religious issues should be left alone and 'mainstream' religious organisations should be privileged and secure from political interference while, at the same time, being allowed to exert legitimate pressures upon the political process[23].

The social science disciplines have been just as cautious in approaching these dilemmas as politicians and public servants. In the Enlightenment tradition many academics in Western democracies are secular rationalists, with only the Catholic Church presenting a carefully crafted alternative set of views. Thus economists see integration as equal access to the labour market for the equally qualified, and immigration policy as contributing to improving the quality of the labour force and expanding demand and productivity. Demographers see immigration as essential to limit the effects of falling birth rates. Political scientists see religions as influences on public opinion – and hence on voting – or as elements in pluralist bargaining for measurable advantages. Sociologists and psychologists explain religious loyalties, without fully coming to grips with the question why such loyalties may persist over centuries when secular beliefs change quite rapidly. Many social scientists are uncomfortable with the concept of values, as well they might be.

Thus when governments develop 'evidence based' integration policies they normally do so in a rather confused state where the object is to make minorities become 'just like us' – namely, rational human beings driven primarily by

---

22   Industry Commission (1995). *Charitable Organisations in Australia Report No.45*, Industry Commission, Canberra.

23   Maddox, M (2005). *God Under Howard; the Rise of the Religious Right in Australian Politics*, Allen and Unwin, Sydney.

economic factors, subscribing to values developed within a predominantly Christian tradition, a dominant language and a common loyalty to a defined 'nation', which over-rides other loyalties and former homelands. The clearest enunciation of such expectations can be gained from the speeches on Australian values delivered by John Howard from his Esperance address of 1988 to his election campaigning of 2007[24]. Essentially these are demands for cultural minorities to change their ways and for the majority to accept them graciously when they do. Politically this works well where the majority is either irreligious or subscribes to broadly defined versions of the dominant (usually Christian) creed. It ceased to work for Howard and his mentor George Bush when their official versions of national values became too narrow to cater for increasingly diverse electorates[25].

If integration is to have any agreed meaning it must distinguish between assimilation – where individuals become indistinguishable from a national norm – and multiculturalism – where different cultures (including languages and religions) persist and are encouraged by authority to do so 'within strictly defined limits' as the Galbally definition of 1978 puts it. Obviously these two extremes are ideal types rather than legislated policies. Canada recognises that 'visible minorities' will not be fully assimilated because they look different from the majority, who consequently may treat them differently. No other society has adopted this common sensical but controversial approach, nor is it likely that Australia will. It lumps together Somali refugees, Indian academics and Aborigines, with very little in common except for potential vulnerability to prejudice. Today it would need to include Muslims and others wearing religiously distinctive clothing. Being 'visual' is defined by the perceptions of the majority population. In Australia the defining common denominator was language, through the category Non-English Speaking Background (NESB), now replaced by Culturally and Linguistically Diverse (CALD). These also lump together a wide variety of 'different' people.

Multiculturalism has had to be defended against claims that it is divisive, encourages loyalties to societies other than Australia, preserves conservative and reactionary values and practices and, of course, delays assimilation[26]. The 'strictly defined limits' have never been defined in practice and many involve religious beliefs and practices. The expectation that immigrants will accept equality of the sexes as a basic value began to appear in the late 1980s as Muslim immigration increased following the wars in Lebanon, Somalia and Afghanistan. Yet the two largest religious denominations – the Catholic Church and the Sydney Anglican diocese – do not accept gender equality within

---

24   Markus, A (2001). Race: John Howard and the Remaking of Australia, Allen and Unwin, Sydney.

25   Lohrey, A (2006). *Voting for Jesus*, Quarterly Essay, Melbourne.

26   Parekh, Lord B (2006). *Rethinking Multiculturalism*, Palgrave Macmillan, Basingstoke (UK).

their organisations, as they have no women clergy. Neither do the Orthodox Churches. Some prestigious gentlemen's clubs in the major cities still do not accept women members. Religious and social organisations are, consequently, exempted from the prohibition on gender discrimination. Whether religious spokespersons can lawfully abuse other religions (as they have been doing for centuries) became controversial with the case of the Islamic Council of Victoria's legal action against two Pentecostalist ministers in Melbourne[27].

Apart from the important religious dimension, there is an uncertain emphasis on individual or collective responsibility in recent formulations. Assimilation in its classic Australian form, between 1947 and the 1960s, assumed a common physical appearance within the terms of the White Australia policy; this is now redundant. It assumed the adoption of English to the exclusion of other languages; this has finally sunk in that many people can converse adequately in more than one language. It assumed that immigrants who arrived after 20-30 years of socialisation elsewhere would drop everything they knew and adopt a uniquely Australian culture; the popularity of ethnic festivals and food has laid that to rest. This extreme assimilationism had become dysfunctional by the 1960s. There is no likelihood of any government urging its return, though there were echoes of it in the tests introduced for intending citizens by the Howard government and subsequently revised by Labor. The assumption that all concessions would be made by minority groups and individuals was talked out in a series of official enquiries in the 1970s and 1980s.

At this stage of policy discourse it is hard to see what distinguishes the newly fashionable approach of integration from its predecessor multiculturalism. Clearly it is directed at changing the attitudes of many Muslims and thus gaining their acceptance by the majority population. The Commonwealth-State *National Action Plan to Build on Social Cohesion, Harmony and Security,* developed in 2005-2006, 'seeks to foster connections and understanding between Muslim and non-Muslim Australians and reinforce major contributions that all Australian can make to our country's future'. This joint effort by the Commonwealth and State governments focuses on 'education, employment, integration and security' through a modest programme of projects[28].

While cultural diversity is mentioned in the DIAC introductory kit, multiculturalism is not. But nothing in official policy envisages the disappearance of Islam as a significant Australian religion. Nor does it require Christians to change their ancient attitudes towards Islam, provided they do not express these in unacceptably harsh terms. If religious activities are to continue unaffected, religious schools to be subsidised, religions to be tax exempt, free to advocate

---

27   Deen, H (2008). *The Jihad Seminar,* University of Western Australia Press, Perth.

28   Department of Immigration and Citizenship (2008). *Community Projects* 2007-2008, http://www.immi. gov.au/media/publications/multicultural/pdf_doc/Community.

a range of highly controversial views, conduct their affairs in languages other than English and answer to leaders outside Australia, then integration will look rather like multiculturalism. No government is likely to change this situation even if the descriptive words are changed. As Shakespeare so wisely put it 'what's in a name? That which we call a rose by any other name would smell as sweet'. Religious variety will have saved secular multiculturalism. It has already posed a challenge to assimilation.

Table 1 Twenty largest religions in Australia by declared adherents and by the percentage of Australian citizenship for the total

Religion	Declared adherents	Percentage of Australian citizenship for the total
(Western) Catholics	5 087 114	92.3%
Anglican	3 716 379	92.2%
Uniting Church	1 135 426	94.8%
Presbyterian	583 397	87.7%
Buddhist	418 757	76.3%
Greek Orthodox	374 576	96.1%
Islam	340 392	77.2%
Baptist	316 741	89.9%
Lutheran	251 105	90.4%
Hinduism	148 125	57.9%
Assemblies of God	94 893	87.5%
Judaism	88 829	90.7%
Undefined Pentecostal	88 534	86.5%
Jehovah's Witnesses	80 916	88.4%
Salvation Army	64 200	94.4%
Seventh Day Adventists	55 254	86.7%
Latter Day Saints (Mormons)	52 147	76.4%
Macedonian Orthodox	48 082	96.1%
Churches of Christ	47 772	94.6%
Serbian Orthodox	39 967	93.6%
(No Religion - as stated)	3 706 554	89.6%

Source: 2006 Commonwealth Census of Population and Housing

Table 2 Religions grouped by 'regions of origin' and largest groups from that region

Region of origin	Largest groups from that region	Declared adherents
Great Britain	Anglican, Uniting	5 886 833
Ireland and Europe	Catholic, Orthodox	6 002 244
North America	Pentecostal, Adventist	451 912
Middle East	Islam, Orthodox	438 639
Asian	Buddhist, Hinduism	602 593
Indigenous and Pacific	Traditional, Aboriginal	12 498
Non-Specific/Australian	Undefined Christians	450 392

The 'region of origin' indicates the region from which most adherents arrived or in which the denomination has its greatest strength (hence the separation of Ireland from Great Britain). Choices are generalised and may be arbitrary.

Source: adapted from the 2006 Commonwealth Census.

Table 3 Numbers with graduate or postgraduate qualifications for major religions and percentage for total figures for adults in that religion

Religion	Graduates	Percentage of adult number
(No Religion)	601 745	16.2%
(Western) Catholic	422 170	8.3%
Anglican	390 563	10.5%
Uniting Church	141 747	12.5%
Buddhist	80 241	19.2%
Presbyterian	67 345	11.5%
Hindu	60 731	41.0%
Baptist	50 101	15.8%
Islam	44 158	13.0%
Greek Orthodox	41 024	10.9%
Lutheran	33 571	13.4%
Judaism	28 243	32.9%
Assemblies of God	13 096	13.8%
Pentecostals*	12 526	14.2%

*not further defined

Source: 2006 Commonwealth Census of Population and Housing

Chapter 9: The Incorporation of Australian Youth in a Multicultural and Transnational World

Christine Inglis

This chapter explores how integration and multiculturalism intersect with, affect and, in turn, are influenced by their encounter with Australian youth. This focus on a social category, rather than being restricted to a particular dimension of incorporation, reflects a realisation that in the modern world youth has emerged as a distinctive social grouping in transition between childhood and adult life with its own cultural features, interests and challenges. Key social changes contributing to the construction of this distinct social group include the extension of universal education, increasing longevity, changes in family formation and the world of work as well as expanding prosperity and consumerism. The age-based definition of 'youth' can extend from 12-35[1]. In this paper the focus is on those aged from 18-35 who, as legal adults with their schooling behind them, still face the challenge of entering the world of work, and establishing a separate household and family.

As this chapter will argue, the way youth do this in contemporary Australia does not necessarily fit with many of the older assumptions about how those from migrant backgrounds are incorporated into Australian society. While apparently straightforward, the title of this project, *Integration and Multiculturalism: A harmonious combination?,* allows for diverse interpretations. Both 'integration' and 'multiculturalism' refer to Australian policy responses to diversity. But they also have descriptive and normative or ideological referents which affect the precise conceptual and policy issues to examine in relation to the experiences of youth from diverse ethnic backgrounds. Following a consideration of these and their implications for evaluating the incorporation of ethnic minority youth in Australia, the remainder of the chapter focuses on the young people, their experiences and the dynamics underlying their incorporation in Australian society.

---

1   Nilan, P and Feixa, C (eds) (2006). *Global Youth? Hybrid identities, plural worlds*, Routledge, London: 1.

Sociological perspectives on integration and multiculturalism

One of the challenges posed by this project is to locate it within the context of social science disciplinary debates. From a sociological perspective these involve theoretical debates surrounding the efforts of theorists to capture the essence of the massive social changes occurring in the 19th century. Their interest focused on the transformation of 'traditional' societies into a modern world in which individual merit and free association replaced a reliance on ascribed status and homogeneity as a basis for stability and social continuity. These changes have prompted a continuing theoretical and empirical interest in how the pre-conditions for ensuring social harmony, if not social survival, can exist within a democratic framework. But, if sociologists within Western industrial societies often ignored the potential significance of ethnically based diversity, the continuing social and political significance of ethnic diversity continued to be evident in other societies[2]. And by the end of the 20th century, as the exponential expansion of migration generated new inter-ethnic encounters and social conflicts, there was a renewed theoretical interest in the social and political significance of ethnic diversity. Underlying this interest were debates concerning the root causes of ethnic conflict. Does it result from the absence of shared culture and values as suggested by theorists such as Durkheim and Parsons? Or is it because of socio-economic inequality and conflicting material interests as those influenced by Marx argue?

By the late 20th century the theoretical debates were broadened to take account of two phenomena whose existence could no longer be ignored. These were globalisation and transnationalism. These processes called into question the previous theoretical focus on 'intact' societies and their states as they highlighted the movements of people, information, ideas, cultural forms and, potentially, conflicts across state and societal borders. A key question associated with globalisation is how these factors transform ethnic groups and their position within society. The transnational paradigm directs attention to the existence of ethnic ties stretching beyond the boundaries of the local/national society and state thus raising questions about their impact on the society of residence and, also, on the 'homeland' and third countries[3].

---

2   Inglis, C (2000). 'The "rediscovery" of ethnicity: Theorising and analysis at the end of the twentieth century', in S Quah and A Sales (eds), *The International Handbook of Sociology*, Sage, London: 151-170.
3   Dunn, K (2005). A Paradigm of Transnationalism for Migration Studies. *New Zealand Population Review, 31*(2): 15-31; Inglis, C (2007). Transnationalism in an Uncertain Environment: Relationship between Migration, Policy and Theory. *IJMS: International Journal on Multicultural Societies 9*, 2: 185-204.

Despite their generality these theoretical debates provide a framework for mid-level theorisation and empirical inquiry into such issues of inter-ethnic relations as:

- Does the continuing existence of ethnic diversity necessarily contribute to internal/domestic social conflict?

- Are ethnic processes and phenomena susceptible to 'management', particularly through government policies?

- If they are susceptible to such management, what type of policies limit or moderate the appearance of social conflict?

In doing so they provide a link between the theoretical and policy levels of debate and analysis, since, once inter-ethnic relations are identified as a social 'problem', the way is open for policy makers to seek appropriate policy responses to overcome social conflict, especially in a manner commensurate with democratic principles. In Australia, as in many other Western industrial societies, *assimilation* was the dominant policy response until the late 1960s. Like other policy models it includes a descriptive dimension as well as an ideological or normative statement concerning the appropriate outcome to ensure stability and social harmony. Based on research by the Chicago school of sociology in the early 20th century, assimilation theory argued that ethnic minorities would become 'invisible' as they took on the values and behaviours of the larger society. Given that assimilation was viewed as inevitable there was a denial of the need for any active policy interventions by the majority society since the responsibility for change lay with the minority group[4]. Cultural change was at the heart of assimilation theory and highlights its links to theorists such as Durkheim. A similar link to Durkheim's work has been noted in an Australian study addressing the recent interest in *social cohesion*, if not as a policy model, then certainly as a policy objective and normative outcome[5]. Nevertheless, there remains considerable disagreement about the term and its actual policy focus, although in addition to focusing on the existence of shared values there is also an emphasis on 'commitment' and 'belonging'[6] which typically carries the connotation that this is the responsibility of the minority group member.

In Australia, following the criticisms of assimilation policy based on the disjuncture between its theorising and the social reality of immigrant settlement experiences, *integration* was briefly adopted in the late 1960s as its replacement. Although integration policy was never fully articulated and was soon replaced in the 1970s by multicultural policy, its underlying premises appeared to be

---

4   Martin, J (1978). *The Migrant Presence*. Allen and Unwin, Sydney.

5   Jupp, J, Nieuwenhuysen, J and Dawson, E (eds). (2007). *Social Cohesion in Australia*, Cambridge University Press, Melbourne.

6   Markus, A and Kirpitchenko, L (2007). Conceptualising Social Cohesion. In J Jupp, J Nieuwenhuysen and E Dawson (eds), *Social Cohesion in Australia*, Cambridge University Press, Melbourne: 21-32.

that minority members might retain their cultural practices in the privacy of the home even if, in public, they were still expected to conform to Australian society and institutions. More recently, following its appearance in European migration debates, integration has once again entered Australian policy discussions. The European Union now describes integration as a 'two way' process involving change by both the minority and majority groups in society[7]. However, there remains in Europe a tendency for supporters of 'integration' to assign to it assimilationist expectations and objectives in which the one-way process is the responsibility of the minority individual[8]. This is not surprising since 'integration' played a prominent role in the structural-functional theory of Talcott Parsons which emphasised the importance of social consensus and underplayed the role of power in social relations.

Contrasting with the emphasis on shared culture and values evident in assimilation theories and policies and the associated social cohesion and integration approaches are policies addressing *social exclusion* and its obverse *social inclusion*. The theoretical underpinnings of these approaches derive from neo-Marxian class theories of society which identify power relations and material inequalities as key factors influencing inter-ethnic relations. The policy priorities to achieve stability and harmony thus focus on overcoming material differences and inequalities and removing the barriers to the participation of minority group members in key social institutions and structures. Since its election in 2007 the Labor government has announced an Australian Social Inclusion Agenda intended to reduce disadvantage, increase social, civil and economic participation and to give people a greater say in identifying their needs and participating in policy making while also having the responsibility to take advantage of available opportunities[9]. While the Agenda targets a broad range of social groups and is not limited to ethnic minorities it obviously has relevance to policies relating to inter-ethnic relations.

The importance of overcoming ethnic disadvantage was one of the key factors leading to Australia's shifting in the 1970s from integration to multicultural policy. As multicultural policy has evolved over four decades, there have been changes in the emphases placed on overcoming disadvantage and the support and maintenance of cultural diversity. This policy focus on both disadvantage and cultural diversity is a distinctive feature of Australian and Canadian

---

7   European Commission (2005). Communication from the Commission to the Council, the European Parliament, the European Economic and Social Committee and the Committee of the Regions: A common agenda for integration-framework for the integration of third-country nationals in the European Union.

8   Brubaker, R (2001). The Return of Assimilation? Changing Perspectives on Immigration and Its Sequels in France, Germany, and the United States. *Ethnic and Racial Studies, 24* (4): 531-548; Wright, S (2008). Citizenship Tests in Europe – Editorial Introduction. *IJMS: International Journal on Multicultural Societies,* vol 10, 1: 109.

9   Australian Government (2009). *Social Inclusion Principles for Australia.* Retrieved 21 August 2009.

multicultural policies[10]. In both countries multicultural policies were developed in response to political considerations which, in a marked departure from the descriptive dimensions of the assimilation model, recognised the ongoing social and political significance of diverse ethnic groups. This descriptive difference highlighted the need for policies which provided ethnic minorities with opportunities for incorporation while at the same time avoiding conflict and ensuring social stability. An important dimension of these policies was that the responsibility for change shifted from the minority to the majority and, in particular, involved institutional reform to reflect the diversity in the society. Initially conceived as a policy for migrants, by 1989 the *National Agenda for a Multicultural Australia*[11] marked a major normative and ideological shift as it proclaimed that multiculturalism was a policy for *all* Australians. The distinctive ideological feature of the policy was describing cultural diversity as a benefit to the society as a whole. In itself, this was a major change from commonly held views that such diversity is a potential threat to social stability and survival.

Dimensions of incorporation

The present examination of the experiences of Australia's ethnically diverse youth takes place after nearly four decades, or two generations, of multicultural policies. Because of the ambiguities surrounding 'integration' and its key dimensions and to avoid confounding it with assimilation, this chapter uses the term 'incorporation' rather than 'integration' when exploring how young Australians (both overseas and locally born) from diverse ethnic backgrounds are incorporated into Australian society. The experiences of the locally born second generation in Australia and elsewhere attract considerable theoretical interest as they provide a litmus test to evaluate the impact of official policies for managing diversity. This is because as they have grown up and been locally educated it is assumed they have overcome barriers to incorporation such as poor English and overseas qualifications which may penalise their overseas-born peers. They also largely avoid the material and social disruptions experienced by the overseas born other than those referred to as the '1b' or '1.5' generation who arrived in Australia when very young and were also educated in Australia.

Despite the lack of consensus as to the conceptual framework to privilege in evaluating the process of incorporation, there is nevertheless considerable agreement concerning the types of phenomena which are important dimensions in the settlement process. This is exemplified in the way the actual dimensions identified in the detailed seven stage assimilation model developed by Milton

---

10   Wieviorka, M (1998). Is multiculturalism the solution? *Ethnic and Racial Studies*, 21, 5: 880-910.
11   Office of Multicultural Affairs (1989). *National Agenda for a Multicultural Australia*. Canberra: Australian Government Publishing Service.

Gordon[12] are still widely used as indicators even if set within a different theoretical framework[13]. Three main dimensions of incorporation are examined here. The first concerns the extent of socio-economic disadvantage experienced by ethnic minority groups. This involves exploring education and labour market involvement, since economic and educational capital directly affect the material circumstances of individuals and their ability to participate in society. The second dimension involves individuals' social networks, cultural practices and values. It addresses the extent to which individuals' social relations are constrained within their own ethnic group or extend across other minority and majority groups. These relations and cultural attributes also have the potential to provide social and cultural capital which complement individuals' material resources and economic capital. However, whether such capital exists depends on the institutional structures of the wider society which construct the capital 'markets'. Here prejudice and discrimination targeting the minority groups are also relevant. The third dimension of incorporation examined here involves citizenship, identification and other subjective aspects of belonging which are affected by prejudice and discrimination in the wider society. The impacts of globalisation and transnationalism are also potentially important for the ways in which they foster and sustain linkages and attachments outside Australia. They do this through the new technologies which have greatly enhanced opportunities for immediate and cheap international contacts involving the internet and international travel.

Ethnic youth research

Before examining each of these dimensions it is important to note that one of the major features of research involving Australian youth, and especially those of immigrant background, has been its *problem* orientation and, in particular, a focus on how young people are *'at risk*[14]. Initially, the area of greatest concern involved the first dimension of incorporation, the educational participation and attainment of those from non-English speaking migrant backgrounds. Because of their linguistic differences, and how these were taken as indicators of other cultural differences, these young people were often depicted as being torn between the two worlds variously described as 'home' and 'school'; the

---

12 Gordon, M (1964). *Assimilation in American Life*. Oxford University Press, NY.

13 Kaya, A (2009). *Islam, Migration and Integration: The Age of Securitization*. Palgrave Macmillan, Basingstoke: 35.

14 Butcher, M and Thomas, M (eds) (2003). *Ingenious: Emerging youth cultures in urban Australia*. Melbourne: Pluto Press; Sherington, G (1995). *Youth Policy and Ethnic Youth: A history*, in C Guerra and R White (eds), *Ethnic Minority Youth in Australia: Challenges and myths*, National Clearinghouse for Youth Studies, Hobart: 25-34; White, R (ed) (1999b). *Australian Youth Subcultures: On the margins and in the mainstream*. Australian Clearinghouse for Youth Studies, Hobart.

culture of the 'homeland' and Australia; or traditional and modern values[15]. These cultural differences were seen as creating problems for them in adjusting to school and succeeding educationally. These included the view that they were more prone to become school dropouts as problems at school were exacerbated by conflict with their own, often poorly educated, parents who brought different norms and expectations to Australia. From this starting point youth research separated in two directions. One focused on the extent of educational inequality amongst ethnic minorities while the second was concerned with their identity formation and how this was linked to their involvement in the home and wider Australian society.

By the 1970s educational inequality was seen as a major policy issue which affected girls, working class and rural students as well as those from ethnic minority backgrounds[16]. The particular problems facing students from Non English Speaking Backgrounds (NESB) provided a major impetus for the development of a range of migrant and multicultural education policy innovations[17]. The extent to which social class rather than ethnic background was the major factor in the patterns of educational disadvantage involving particular immigrant background children was never really resolved[18]. By the 1990s, the concerns about educational disadvantage for those of ethnic minority backgrounds were less commonly heard, reflecting evidence that, perhaps as a result of the various multicultural educational innovations as well as the increasing arrival of skilled professional migrants with high levels of educational resources and educational capital, there was decreasing evidence of clear patterns of ethnic inequality involving the non-Indigenous population.

The first major collection of papers on ethnic minority youth which addressed the second research focus covered a range of youth experiences with the majority of papers exploring in detail the diverse experiences of young people[19]. It also highlighted the limitations of the overly simplistic conflict view of relations between ethnic minority youth and their parents. This was based on an essentialist and static model of socialisation and cultural diversity implicit in the 'Between Two Worlds' approach which ignored the role of individual agency involved in identity construction. Also focusing on the agency involved

---

15   Brotherhood of St Laurence (1971). *Two Worlds: School and the Migrant Family*. Stockland Holdings, Melbourne.

16   Interim Committee for the Australian Schools Commission (1973). *Schools in Australia: Report of the Interim Committee for the Australian Schools Commission, May 1973, [the Karmel Report]*. AGPS, Canberra.

17   Martin, J (1978). *Op cit*.

18   Jakubowicz, A (1985). *Education and Ethnic Minorities- Issues of Participation and Equity*. Canberra: National Advisory and Coordinating Committee on Multicultural Education; Poole, M E (1981). Educational Opportunities for Minority Groups: Australian Research Reviewed. In J Megarry (ed), *Education of Minorities: World Yearbook of Education*. Kogan Page, London.

19   Guerra, C and White, R (eds) (1995). *Ethnic Minority Youth in Australia: Challenges and Myths*. National Clearing House for Youth Studies, Hobart.

in ethnic minority youth's daily lives, cultural practices and identities was another collection of papers which addressed the way in which the digital revolution, linked to globalisation and transnationalism, played a major role in the life of young men and women from immigrant backgrounds[20].

However, much of the recent research has focused on the problems of transition into the adult world within the older model of conflict between two worlds. In the case of young women, especially those perceived to be from certain 'traditional' cultures, the focus has been on conflicts between them and their families with regard to their future gendered roles as wives and mothers as well as their inability to participate in social activities outside the family and home with the same freedom as their brothers or friends from other backgrounds. This has been described as the 'being allowed to go out issue'[21]. In the case of young men, much of the focus has been on youth 'gangs'. This research has its origins in public concerns about the potential of young men from ethnic minority backgrounds to form gangs which constitute potential threats to social harmony (if not violence and criminal activity) and, more recently, even to national security. Encounters with police have been seen as a particular source of tension and the media has also been implicated in promoting the dangers associated with these gangs whose values are portrayed as opposed to those of the wider society. In Australia, research on ethnic youth gangs began in the 1990s[22]. In fact, one of the main conclusions from the studies undertaken involving a number of different ethnic groups in Melbourne was that 'most often the 'gang' is simply a group of like-minded young people who enjoy each other's company, and who share support and life experiences in common'[23]. Research in Sydney has been concentrated in the outer western suburbs and in particular on young Lebanese. It coincides with extensive media reporting of a series of particularly violent gang rapes linked to Lebanese youth in the late 1990s[24]. Subsequently, the events of 9/11, the commencement of the War on Terror and the Cronulla Riots of 2005 have led to a targeting of Muslims by the

---

20   Butcher, M and Thomas, M (2003). *Op cit.*

21   Tsolidis, G (1986). *Educating Voula: A report on non-English-speaking background girls and education.* Melbourne: Ministerial Advisory Committee on Multicultural and Migrant Education: 59.

22   Pe-Pua, R (1999). Youth and Ethnicity: Images and constructions, in R White (ed) (2000), *Op cit*: 130-137; White, R, Perrone, S, Guerra, C and Lampugnani, R (1999). *Ethnic Youth Gangs in Australia: Do they exist? Overview Report.* Australian Multicultural Foundation, Melbourne.

23   White, R (1999a). Youth Gangs, in R White (ed) (2000), *Op cit*: 44.

24   Collins, J, Noble, G, Poynting, S and Tabar, P (2000). *Kebabs, Kids, Cops and Crime: Youth, Ethnicity and Crime.* Pluto Press, Annandale; Noble, G, Poynting, S and Tabar, P (1999a). Lebanese Youth and Social Identity, in R White (ed) (2000), *Op cit:* 130-137; Noble, G, Poynting, S and Tabar, P (1999b). Youth, Ethnicity and the Mapping of Identities: Strategic essentialism and strategic hybridity among male Arabic-speaking youth in South-western Sydney. *Communal/Plural,* 7(1): 29-44; Poynting, S (2000). Ethnicising Criminality and Criminalising Ethnicity, in J Collins and S Poynting (eds), *The Other Sydney: Communities, Identities and Inequalities in Western Sydney,* Common Ground Publishing, Altona: 63-78.

media, public and government which has led to a continuing research focus on Muslim and, in particular, Lebanese youth and the way they have been depicted in the media and by police[25].

Australia's multicultural youth

Before examining the contemporary patterns of incorporation among Australia's multicultural youth it is useful to know who they are and where they come from. In 2006 the census showed that those aged between 18-35 were a quarter (24.8 per cent) of Australia's population. Within this age group it is useful to distinguish two sub-groups. The first are those aged 18-24 who have normally completed their schooling and are in the process of moving into adult life while frequently continuing their education and commencing work. The second group, those aged between 25 and 35, are included given the new trends to extend education and to delay the start of careers and family life.

These Australian young people reflect the ethnic diversity in the wider population with 27 separate ancestries having at least 10,000 young Australians identifying with them in the 2006 Census (Figure 1). Among the overseas born first generation these represent 80 per cent of the total population. However, among the Australian born, second or higher generation, this figure increases to over 97 per cent, reflecting the more recent diversification of immigration source countries which has resulted in many more small ancestry groups in the first generation. Also very important is the way large numbers of the Australian born chose to identify their primary ancestry as 'Australian' rather than identifying with that of their overseas-born parents. The size of the major ancestry groups differs considerably. The largest group is the English closely followed by Australians then Irish, Italians and Chinese. The greater prominence of both Australians and Australian Aboriginals in the locally born population highlights how important Australian birth is to both identities. In other ancestry groups the greater or lesser prominence of the overseas or locally born reflects changes in the major source countries of Australia's immigrant population. Thus, whereas among Asian groups the first generation outnumbers the Australian born, the reverse is the case in European groups who commenced migration to Australia earlier.

---

25 Poynting, S and Morgan, G (eds) (2007). *Outrageous! Moral panics in Australia*. Hobart: Australian Clearing House for Youth Studies Publishing; Poynting, S, Noble, G, Taylor, C and Collins, J (2004). *Bin Laden in the suburbs: Criminalising the Arab other*. Institute of Criminology, Sydney.

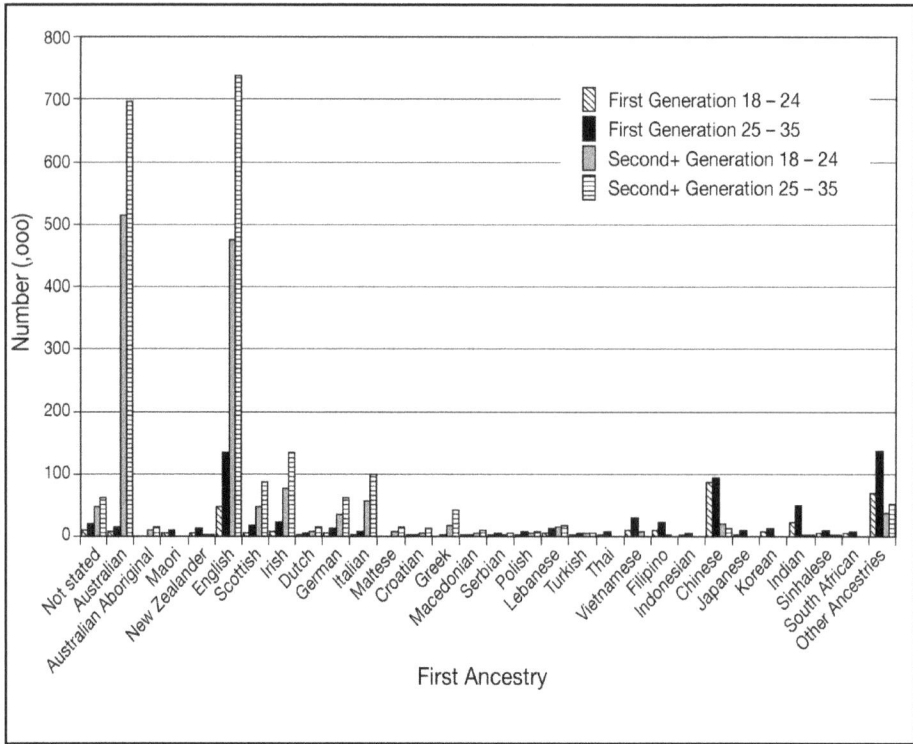

Figure 1 Selected ancestry by generation and age, 2006

Figure 2 shows the percentage of the 18-35 year olds from selected ancestries who reported having only a single ancestry. Among the overseas-born first generation there was considerable diversity in the extent to which they reported having more than one ancestry. Among the Australian born[26] with the exception of Australian, Aboriginal and Greek ancestry groups, there was an increased likelihood that the young people acknowledged more than one ancestry, which points to an increasing incidence of inter-ethnic marriage, itself an indicator of incorporation[27]. By the second generation there was a decline in the number of ancestry groups where more than 90 per cent of young people reported only having a single ancestry. Apart from Australian Aboriginals and Greeks the other ancestry groups where more than 90 per cent of young people reported having only a single ancestry were the Macedonians, Lebanese, Turkish, Vietnamese and Koreans.

---

26   The Census CData2006 used in this analysis did not allow a distinction between the second-generation and third-generation groups where the individual and both their parents were born in Australia. Hence the term 2+ generation is used to refer to those born in Australia when discussing the census data.

27   See chapter 6 in this volume by Siew-Ean Khoo.

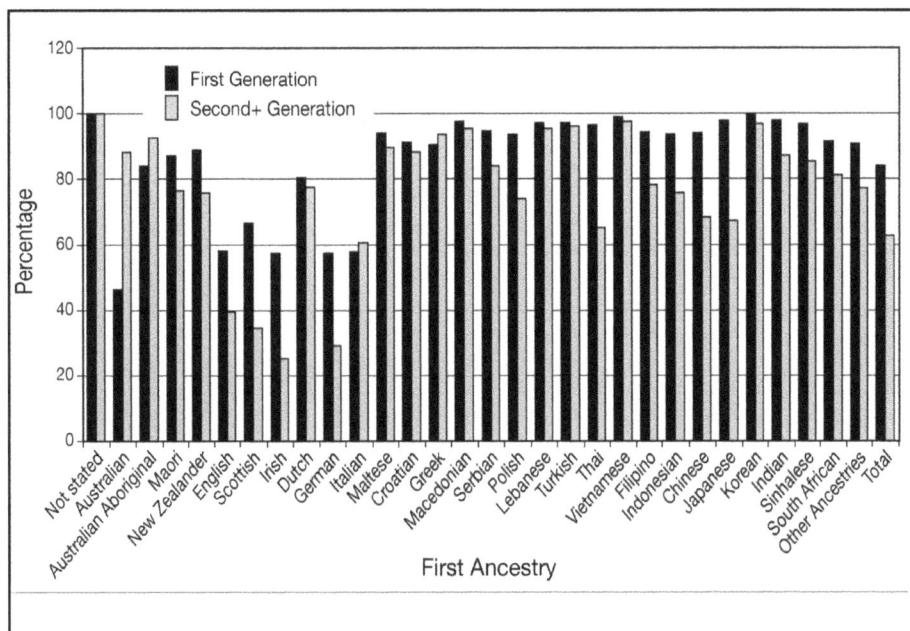

Figure 2 Single ancestry by generation (18-35), 2006

All the Australian born under 35 have grown up during a period when Australia was in the process of developing and implementing its multicultural policies. However, this is not the case for many of the overseas born who have arrived in Australia more recently. Since the end of the 20th century, there have been major changes in Australian immigration policies to provide increased opportunities for skilled settler migration as well as temporary migration for periods in excess of a year for international students and temporary workers[28]. One outcome has been a significant increase in the numbers of young people in many ancestry groups. By 2006, 39.7 per cent of all the overseas born aged 18-35 had arrived since 2000. Among all those aged between 18-24, 60 per cent arrived after 2000, with the figure being even higher for the Thai, Indonesian, Chinese, Japanese and Indian. The percentages were slightly lower among those in the older 25-35 year age group who are less likely to have come to study since 2000. Nevertheless, more than 60 per cent of the Thai, Japanese and Indian had arrived in this time period followed by 50 per cent of the Indonesian and 40 per cent of the Germans, Sinhalese and South Africans (Figure 3). The effect of these changes in patterns of migration means that it can no longer be assumed that all these young people now living in Australia intend to 'settle' or be 'incorporated' in the same way as earlier cohorts. For some of them, the Australian education for which they have paid substantial sums of money may be viewed as a means of obtaining an education which will allow them to secure work in other countries. For

---

28 The census data used in this paper includes those on temporary visas who have lived in Australia for at least one year.

many others, Australian qualifications now make it easier to obtain permanent residence, although, in common with their Australian born peers, they too may have ambitions to travel, if not settle, overseas[29].

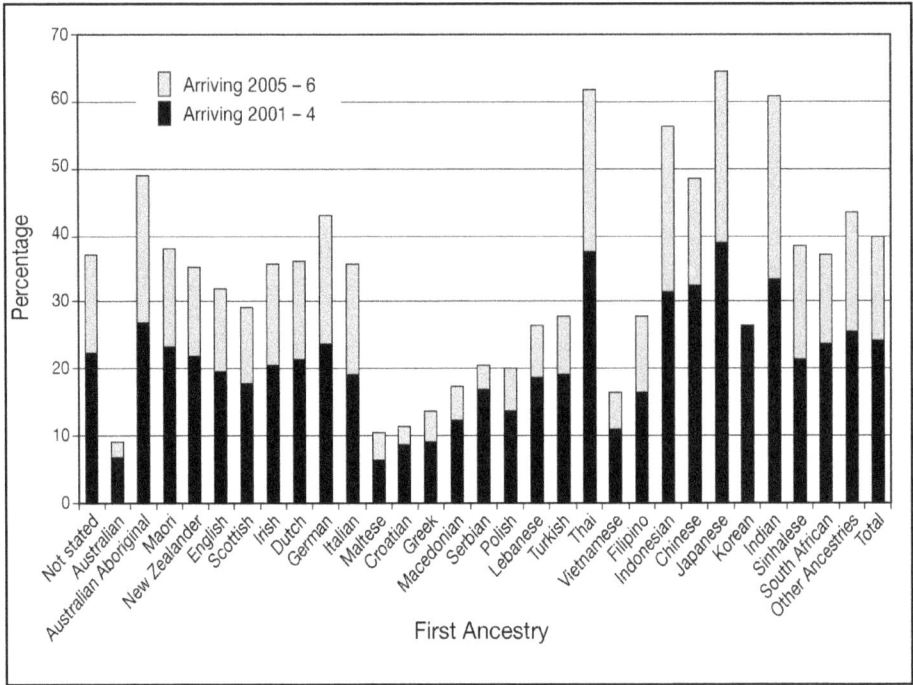

Figure 3 Ancestry and year of arrival (2001-6), 2006

Proficiency in English, the uncontested national language, is an imperative if incorporation is to involve extensive participation in the wider society. As might be anticipated, the Australian born (2+ generation) who speak a language other than English at home typically report high levels of English proficiency (Figure 4). The major exception are those of Australian Aboriginal ancestry. Among the first generation overseas born, the older, 25-35, age group (except in the case of the Italians and Japanese) are more likely than the younger overseas born to report either not speaking English at all or not speaking it well. The first generation groups most likely to report lack of proficiency in English are those of Korean, Vietnamese and Turkish ancestry.

---

29   In 2007-8, 27.5 per cent of all those granted permanent residency were already living in Australia on temporary visas and the percentage was even higher (28.9 per cent) in the following six months. Department of Immigration and Citizenship (2009). *Immigration Update: July to December 2008*. Belconnen, Department of Immigration and Citizenship, ACT: 8.

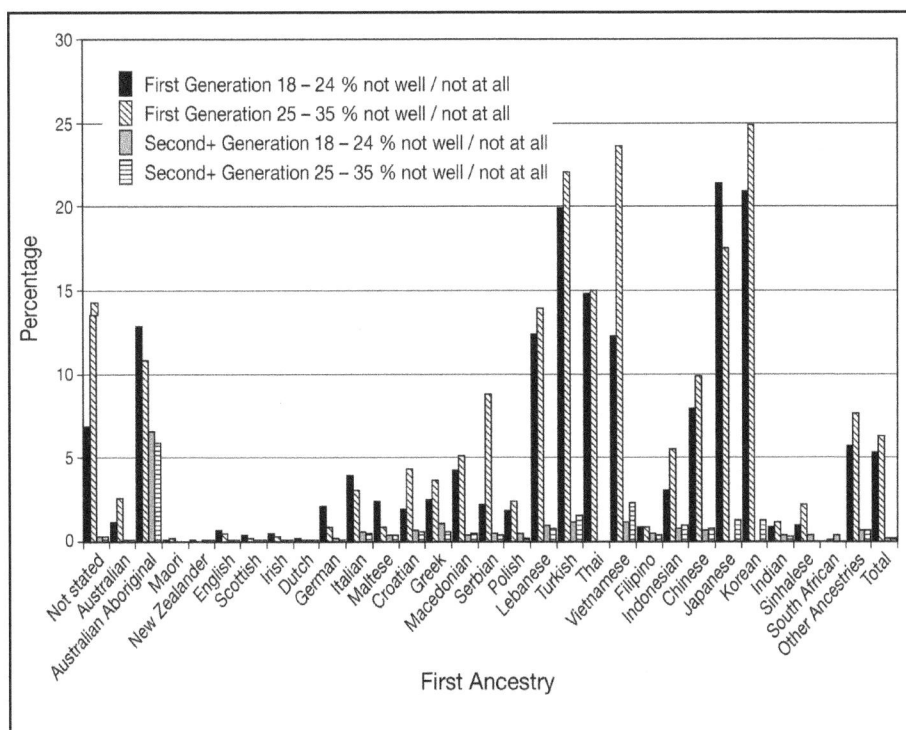

Figure 4 Lack of English proficiency by ancestry and generation, 2006

Socio-economic incorporation

One of the difficulties with many discussions of patterns of socio-economic incorporation is that they focus on the experiences of highly aggregated groups such as those from English speaking and non-English speaking backgrounds (NESB). In doing so, they gloss over the diversity which, as seen above, characterises Australia's multicultural youth. The population data from the 2006 census provides information about three dimensions of socio-economic incorporation: educational participation, lack of educational qualifications and unemployment.

Particularly among the 18-24 age group there is considerable diversity between ancestry groups in the extent of educational participation. The percentage of those who are not studying is particularly low among the first generation in those Asian ancestry groups (other than Vietnamese and Filipinos), which include substantial numbers of international students (Figure 5). Even among the Vietnamese and Filipinos the participation rate among the 2+ generation Australian born is still higher than for most of the other ancestry groups, where usually more than 50 per cent are not continuing with their education. Among those aged between 25-35 the differences in educational participation have largely declined, although the tendency for lower participation among the 2+ generation remains.

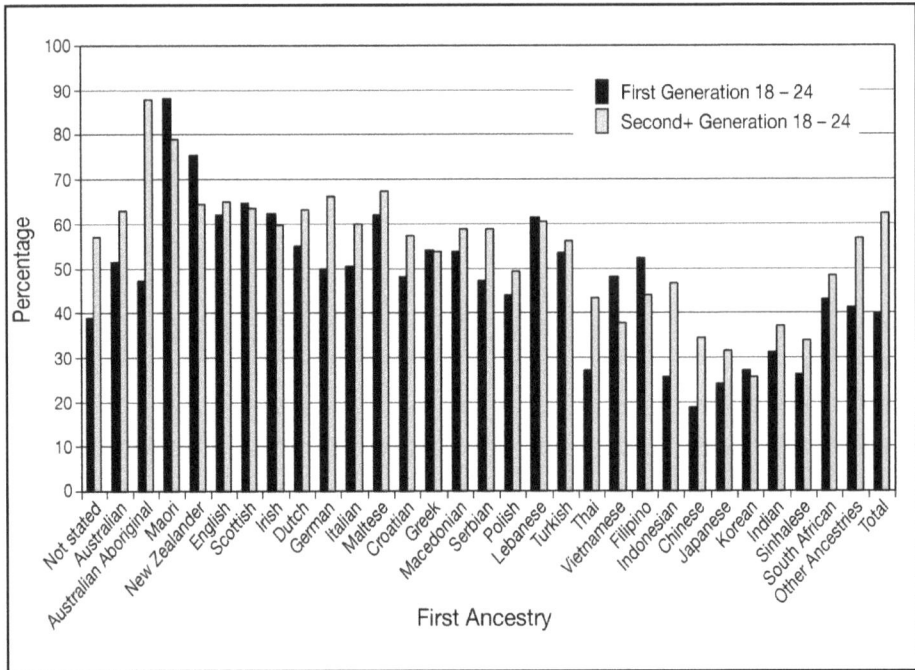

Figure 5 Not studying by generation and age (18-24), 2006

When the focus turns to those who have post-school qualifications the older, 25-35 age group, is less likely to be lacking such qualifications. However, there are generational differences between the ancestry groups (Figure 6). In some of the groups such as the Maori, Lebanese and Turkish, the overseas born first generation is more likely to be unqualified in both age groups - a pattern which suggests that growing up in Australia has contributed positively to gaining educational qualifications and 'capital'. In others, the advantage of the 2+ generation in having qualifications is most evident among the older, 25-35 age group of Vietnamese and Filipinos.

Access to employment is one of the most critical indicators of socio-economic status. In 2006 there was substantial variation in the unemployment rate which ranged from 3 per cent for the Maltese up to almost 9 per cent for those of Turkish ancestry. Groups with above average rates of unemployment included Aborigines, Maoris, Serbians, Lebanese, Turkish and Asian ancestry groups (apart from the Filipinos and Japanese). Being Australian born does not necessarily protect against unemployment as the 2+ generation of Turkish, Vietnamese, New Zealand, Scottish, Irish and Japanese ancestry groups all reported clearly higher percentage levels of unemployment than the first generation (Figure 7). One of the most noteworthy features of these patterns is that high levels of unemployment still characterise those immigrant groups (the Lebanese, Turkish and Vietnamese) and their descendents who were widely seen in their early years of settlement after their arrival in 1970s as experiencing substantial socio-economic disadvantage

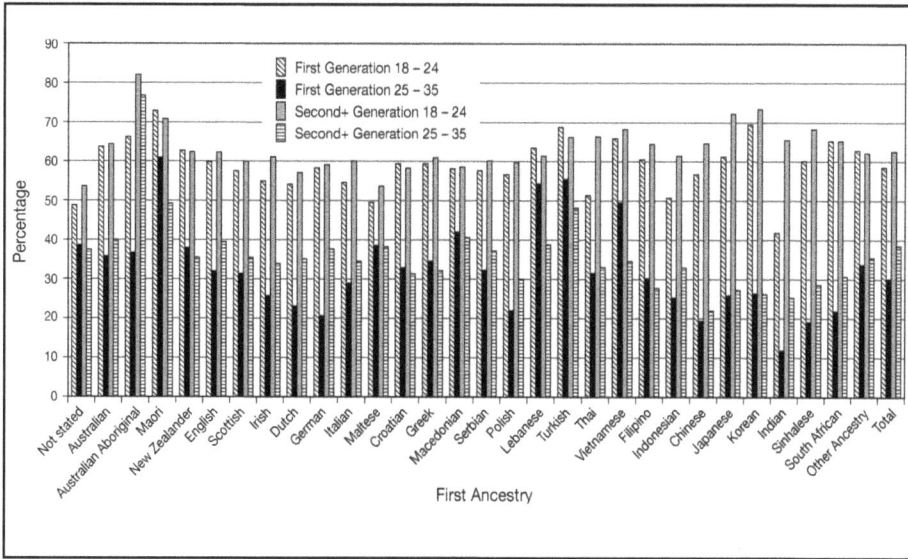

Figure 6 Lack of post-school qualifications by age and generation

Three factors are often suggested to influence access to employment: level of qualifications, fluency in English and year of arrival. Of the three the census data indicates that possessing a post-school educational qualification is the most important factor in avoiding unemployment (Figure 8). Given that substantial numbers of young people have been born and raised in Australia and/or come from predominantly English speaking countries, it is not altogether surprising that in only a few ancestry groups, such as the Serbian, Lebanese, Turkish and the various non-Filipino Asian ancestry groups, is there evidence that lacking English proficiency is a major factor associated with unemployment. It is often thought that length of residence in Australia is associated with declining levels of unemployment since over time individuals improve their English and acquire the social and cultural capital necessary to access the labour market. Length of residence does appear important in reducing unemployment among more recently arrived Asian ancestry groups. However, this is not so evident in the longer established ancestry groups where the Australian born are a significant component of the total numbers unemployed.

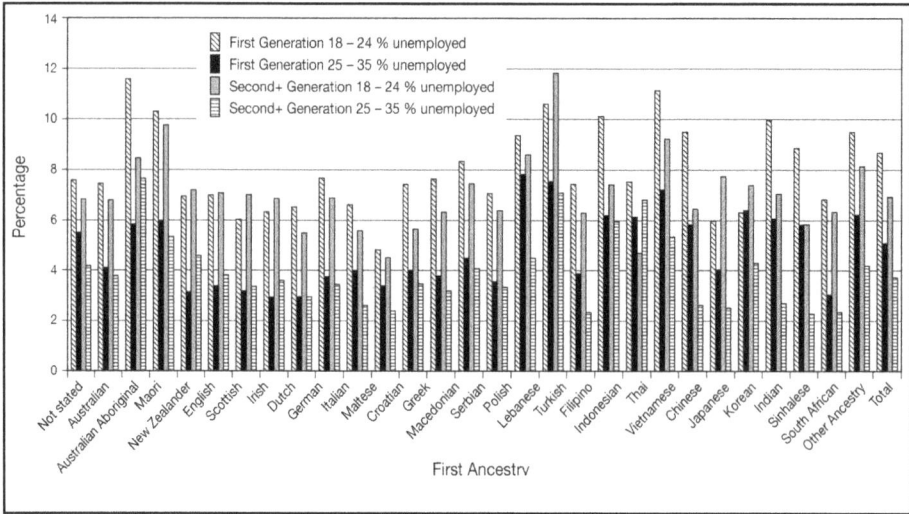

Figure 7 Unemployment by generation (18-35), 2006

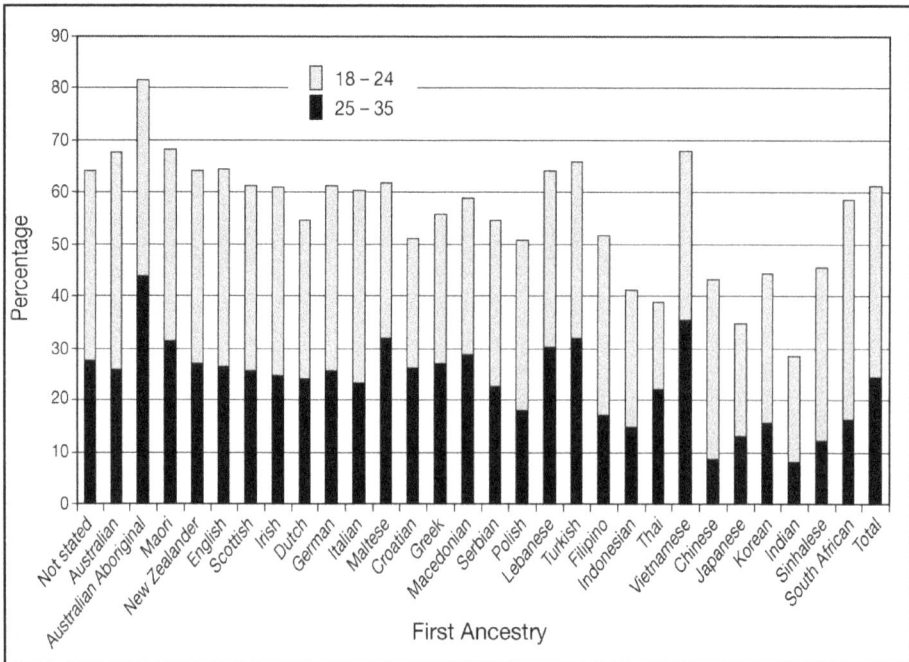

Figure 8 Unemployment by lack of qualifications by age, 2006

Although there is considerable variation in the economic and educational outcomes just described for young people from different ancestries in Australia in 2006, analyses using 1 per cent census sample data from the 2001 census indicated that by the second and third generations there was considerable convergence across the majority of ancestry groups which were examined[30]. This convergence suggests that being born and raised in Australia does contribute to a decline in the 'ethnic penalties' experienced by the first generation. The main exception, apart from Aboriginal Australians, after taking account of age, educational level and marital status was among second-generation Lebanese men and women who were more likely to experience unemployment. However, among this group in 2001 there was evidence of a bipolar pattern since there was little evidence that those who were employed experienced disadvantage relative to other ancestry groups in their occupations and incomes

Given that a major impetus for the adoption of multicultural policies in Australia was a concern to overcome socio-economic disadvantage, the evidence relating to the socio-economic dimension of contemporary incorporation is generally positive in international as well as national comparisons. This was illustrated in the 2007 Inglis and Model study which was part of a thirteen nation study of ethnic minorities in Western labour markets. The editors of that study concluded that Canada and Australia, both of which have a long standing commitment to multicultural policies, emerge as the two countries where the ethnic penalties for immigrant minorities are least evident[31]. However, the experiences of their Indigenous minorities, among whom multicultural policies have not been pursued, are far less favourable and closer to those of guest worker groups in various European countries.

The sustainability of these patterns of incorporation in the face of changes in the economic and social environment needs to be continually monitored. By 2006 the Australian levels of unemployment had improved and preliminary analysis of the comparable 2006 census data suggests that these findings from 2001 will be largely confirmed. Since then, the global financial crisis beginning in 2008 has led to some increase in Australia's levels of unemployment although it is yet too early to see whether this is affecting some ethnic groups more than others.

The social dimension of incorporation

One of the difficulties of assessing the social incorporation of multicultural youth in Australia is the absence of national data covering such diverse aspects of their social experiences as their friendship groups, leisure activities and participation in community organisations and associations. An exception is a recent paper

---

30   Inglis, C and Model, S (2007). Diversity and Mobility in Australia, in A Heath and S Y Cheung (eds), *Unequal Chances: Ethnic minorities in Western labour markets*. Oxford University Press, Oxford for the British Academy. Because of small sample sizes the socio-economic outcomes could only be examined for the larger of the ancestry groups described in more detail in the text.

31   Heath, A and Cheung, S Y (eds) (2007), *Ibid.*

which analyses the 2006 General Social Survey in relation to the social resources of young people[32]. The paper is based on 2175 individuals aged between 18-29 from three groups: the Australian-born (84 per cent of the sample) and permanent Australian residents born either in mainly English speaking (MES) countries (5 per cent) or in other countries (11 per cent). Although the sample size only allows a comparison between these two groups of the overseas-born and does not provide information about the second generation from different ethnic backgrounds, it nevertheless provides an important base-line set of data giving insights into selected aspects of the social lives of young people.

One of the study's key findings is that youth from mainly English speaking countries have similar forms of social connectedness to their Australian-born peers. This includes visits with friends over the last three months, frequency of contacts with family and friends, social activity on the internet, remaining close to former family household members, having close family and friends in whom to confide, an ability to ask for small favours and get support in times of crises. Unemployment appears associated with more restricted, and perhaps less well-resourced, social networks. This finding is an important reminder that both education and work have important contributions to make which extend beyond their instrumental contribution to gaining skills, knowledge and material resources. All young people surveyed felt equally likely to approach government agencies and non-government organisations for assistance, although few had actually done so. Instead, family members and friends are more important sources of support than impersonal groups or institutions.

One surprising finding of this study is that young people from non-English speaking backgrounds apparently feel less able to call on family members for support in times of crisis. This finding conflicts with common assumptions (and indeed some of the data reviewed below) about the existence of tight-knit family bonds in many immigrant communities. One possible explanation is the existence of intergenerational conflict within NESB families[33].Others may be the families' lack of material resources or more generally attenuated social links with immediate family members in Australia or overseas.

As already noted, much of the research on ethnic minority youth has focused on the problematic nature of their experiences in Australia through research on youth 'gangs', particularly among those from Lebanese, Arabic or Muslim backgrounds in disadvantaged areas in western Sydney. This research highlights the social and material disadvantage experienced by the young people and problematises the extent to which they are actually involved in criminal gangs.

---

32   Khoo, S E (2009). Migrant Youth and Social Connectedness, in F Mansouri (ed), *Youth identity and migration: Culture, values and social connectedness*, Common Ground Publishing, Melbourne: 165-177.
33   *Ibid*: 171.

However, it also depicts them as resisting mainstream society as they search for a secure identity, respect and material resources. How they do this is shown to be potentially counter-productive as they risk being marginalised from that society as well as from their own families and communities. More recent research, which revisits one of these small groups of young men after nearly a decade, shows that the dangers of marginalisation and non-incorporation evident in their earlier lives has not, however, eventuated as they are now 'respectable' educated and employed adults[34]. Other research, also drawing on the experiences of young people from diverse ethnic backgrounds in western Sydney, provides a more varied picture of the ways in which they participate in society and their daily activities[35]. Together with other studies[36] there is now emerging a more nuanced understanding of the varied forms of social incorporation characterising Australia's multicultural youth and how ethnicity, gender, class and locality all play a part in contributing to the complexity in their patterns of incorporation.

In the case of Middle Eastern groups such as Lebanese and Turks, which have a long history of being viewed as 'outsiders' even predating events such as the War on Terror and the Cronulla riots[37], it is important to avoid assuming that their patterns of social incorporation necessarily involve either withdrawal and looking inward for protection or actively resisting the wider society. As recent research into the experiences of second generation Lebanese and Turkish youth is showing, the nature of their social incorporation is more complex[38]. The 306 hour-long interviews were undertaken in 2008 in Sydney and Melbourne among young (18-35 year old) Australians from second generation Lebanese (Christian and Muslim) and Turkish backgrounds as well as a third generation group both of whose parents were born in Australia.

When the young people reported on their current group of friends, the majority of the third-generation group (80 per cent) said that many or most of their friends were of Anglo-Celtic background. Among the second-generation groups, one-third of the Turkish and Christian Lebanese group and a quarter of the Muslim Lebanese also reported that most or many of their friends were Anglo-Celtic.

---

34   Noble, G (2007). Respect and Respectability amongst Second-Generation Arab and Muslim Australian Men, *Journal of Intercultural Studies*, 28 (3 August): 331-344.

35   Butcher, M and Thomas, M (2003). *Op cit*.

36   Gilbert, H, Khoo, T and Lo, J (eds) (2000). *Diaspora: Negotiating Asian-Australia*, St Lucia: University of Queensland Press; Guerra, C and White, R (1995). *Op cit*.

37   McAllister, I and Moore, R (1989). *Ethnic Prejudice in Australian Society: Patterns, intensity and explanations*. Office of Multicultural Affairs, Canberra.

38   The study was funded by the Department of Immigration and Citizenship and the preliminary findings referred to here were presented at a conference in Amsterdam in December 2008. Inglis, C (2008). *The Integration of the Australian Second Generation*. Paper presented at the TIES Academic Conference from http://www.tiesproject.eu/component/option,com_docman/task,cat_view/gid,131/Itemid,142/.

The extent of mixing across ethnic groups had increased when compared to their friendship groups in secondary school and suggests that after school there are more opportunities to meet and develop more ethnically diverse friendships.

While it may see somewhat paradoxical in the light of recent events, two thirds of the second-generation Turks, half of the Christian Lebanese and almost half of the Muslim Lebanese described relations between Anglo-Celts and their own groups as 'friendly' or 'very friendly'. However, this positive assessment was stronger in Melbourne than in Sydney where the events linked to the Cronulla riots in 2005 remain in people's memories as indicated by the way a higher percentage of Sydney than Melbourne respondents from all groups also felt that these friendly relations had declined between their own group and Anglo-Celts in Sydney over the past year. Perhaps as a reflection of their limited personal contacts with people of Lebanese and Turkish backgrounds, the third-generation group were less likely to view relations as 'friendly' with these groups. Indeed, many said that they were 'indifferent' to the nature of the relationship with the Lebanese or Turkish groups.

Although not necessarily sharing the same friendship groups, all the groups had quite similar types of involvement with formal organisations over the previous year. Two-thirds had been involved with organisations and in many cases this brought them into contact with others from different ethnic backgrounds. The most popular organisations were those involved in sport (particularly among the young men), followed by artistic, musical and cultural organisations and then those with a religious focus which were more popular with the young women. The involvement with religious organisations was most likely to involve mixing within the young people's own ethnic community (59 per cent) whereas involvements in cultural (32 per cent) and sporting (28 per cent) organisations was more likely to involve mixing outside their ethnic community.

When describing the ethnic composition of their local neighbourhood there was evidence that the third generation was more likely to be isolated from those of NESB background; this was reinforced as 25 per cent said they lived in suburbs where almost nobody in the area was NESB. Even so, 10 per cent described their suburb as one where almost everyone was NESB. In itself, this is a reflection of the diversity of Australian suburbs. It may also reflect the gentrification of inner-city working class suburbs which have become popular with young professionals from Anglo-Celtic backgrounds. Of all the groups, the Muslim Lebanese (32 per cent) were most likely to live in neighbourhoods consisting entirely of people from NESB backgrounds.

One issue which potentially affects the young people's attitudes to society concerns their responses to socio-cultural diversity. More than two-thirds of all interviewees felt that living together with people of different origins was enriching, rather than threatening, for their own culture. The group expressing less certainty about this were the Muslim Lebanese women, only one-third of whom saw the experience as enriching. When individuals were given the opportunity to actually implement this positive evaluation by indicating their preferred residential area the findings were a little different. More than half of the third generation and of the Turks said it made no difference to them. The figure was slightly lower for the Lebanese although there was some indication that the Christian Lebanese in Sydney would prefer to live in a neighbourhood where almost nobody was of NESB origin. In contrast, 20 per cent of the Sydney Muslim Lebanese, who of all the groups in this study have been the object of greatest negative media and public scrutiny, indicated a preference for living in a neighbourhood where the majority of the population were of NESB background, perhaps because they felt this would involve less hostility and threats. However, this was still less than the one-third who actually lived in such neighbourhoods. And a similar disjuncture between preference and reality was also noted amongst the Sydney Turks

These findings, which indicate that the second generation are more likely to have close social contacts with those of Anglo-Celtic background than vice versa, are similar to those reported in Butcher and Thomas' study of youth culture. They noted that the young people of non-Anglo Australian background were actually more 'multicultural' in their range of social contacts and activities than were those from Anglo-Australian backgrounds[39].

Social incorporation is, however, a two-way process involving minority and the majority groups. Despite evidence of friendship patterns and participation in social and community activities, the existence of negative stereotypes, prejudice and discrimination can constitute barriers to the acceptance and participation of minority groups in the wider society. Since, in Australia, Muslims, and those of Lebanese background, have been particular targets of hostility from the media and other sections of the community we asked them whether they had experienced hostility or unfair treatment because of their origins or background. Somewhat surprisingly some 40 per cent of all the second-generation groups, compared with three-quarters of the third generation, said they had never had such experiences. Women were less likely to report such experiences than men. This raises the questions as to whether this is because they are less likely to venture outside their own circle of friends than are the young men. Certainly our interviewees rarely reported experiencing hostility or unfairness in their local neighbourhood. This was in contrast to when they went out for entertainment or to restaurants where they also were more likely to report hostility or unfair

---

39   Butcher, M and Thomas, M (2003). *Op cit*: 15.

treatment than in encounters with the police. Of all the groups, the Muslim Lebanese young men were most likely to report negative experiences in their socialising and in their contacts with the police.

Muslim Lebanese men were the group least likely to report they had 'never' been the victims of discriminatory experiences, yet even 39 per cent of them reported the absence of such discrimination. It appears that within this group there is an important divergence of experience since 17 per cent also reported that they regularly or frequently experienced hostility or unfair treatment from the police. This was a far higher rate than for the other second-generation groups of Turkish (8 per cent) and Christian Lebanese (6 per cent). Even so, 57 per cent of the Muslim Lebanese reported they had never had such experiences with the police, a figure comparable to that for the Christian Lebanese and Turkish but still well below the figure of 90 per cent among the third generation.

The two main explanations for experiencing hostility were ethnic origin or background and religion. The latter reason was most likely to be mentioned by Muslim Lebanese and Turks and, in particular, the young women from these groups. Among the women who wore headscarves 71 per cent of the Muslim Lebanese and 67 per cent of the Turks mentioned religious discrimination. This was almost double the rate for explanations in terms of ethnic origin or background (43 per cent and 33 per cent respectively).

Two other locations where discrimination is often mentioned are schools and the labour market. Secondary school was the most likely location for all reported experiences of hostility and unfair treatment. Half of the Turkish and Lebanese groups and one-quarter of the third-generation group reported that they had experienced such treatment in their secondary schooling. Among those who were employed, workplace-related experiences were lower. The highest rates of hostility and unfair treatment were reported by those from Muslim Lebanese backgrounds, only 39 per cent of whom reported never experiencing work-related discrimination compared with 11 per cent of the third generation, 21 per cent of Turkish and 33 per cent of Christian Lebanese.

Assessment of the social dimensions of incorporation of Australian ethnic groups is more complex than their socio-economic incorporation. Even when examining second-generation groups such as the Lebanese and Turks on a restricted range of social indicators, it is apparent that these groups, which are particularly likely to be the targets of hostility and discrimination, actually are incorporated in a manner characterised by participation in the wider Australian society. That said, they are more likely to have contacts with NESB minority background groups than with the dominant Anglo-Celtic majority. Even so, it appears they are actually less 'isolated' in the range and diversity of their social contacts than are members of the predominantly Anglo-Celtic third-generation majority whose friends and residential areas are more homogeneous and less likely to include those from non-English-speaking backgrounds.

Identity and belonging

Citizenship is often cited as a measure of attachment or belonging to a society. However, given the instrumental benefits which are attached to citizenship, both domestically and when travelling internationally, legal citizenship is, at best, a proxy for other ways of assessing attachment or identification[40]. Second-generation Australians automatically have Australian citizenship and, in some instances, also the citizenship of their families' country of origin. First generation migrants however need to take active steps to gain Australian citizenship. Although it does not provide information on the eligibility of the first generation to acquire Australian citizenship, data from the 2006 census does indicate the variation between first-generation ancestry groups in the extent to which they have acquired Australian citizenship (Figure 9).

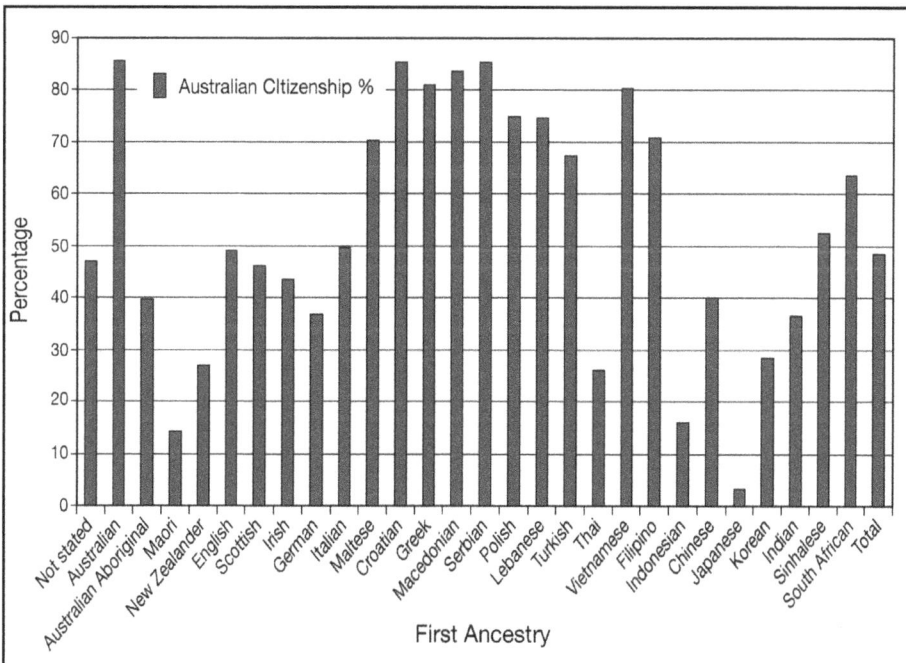

Figure 9 Overseas born with Australian citizenship, 2006

---

40 Ip, D F, Inglis, C and Wu, C-T (1997). Concepts of Citizenship and Identity Among Recent Asian Immigrants in Australia. *Asian and Pacific Migration Journal*, 6 (3-4): 363-384.

A better indicator of attachment or belonging than citizenship is how an individual identifies themselves in various social situations. Important though inequality and disadvantage are in affecting inter-ethnic relations, the incorporation of minority groups into societies also involves a variety of other, often more subtle, factors including perceptions of acceptance and discrimination. Jeff Reitz and Rupa Banerjee have highlighted the importance of these dimensions in their analysis of Canadian data which shows that, although as in Australia important steps have been made towards overcoming social and economic disadvantage, many groups still perceive themselves as lacking acceptance and being socially marginalised. This, in turn, has affected their sense of identity and belonging within the larger society and has the potential to negatively affect inter-ethnic relations and social cohesion[41]. Much of the literature on Australian ethnic minority youth, especially young Lebanese men, has highlighted their desire for respect and acceptance[42].

When asked about their identification with a religious identity it was apparent that many of the Muslim Lebanese and Turks identified strongly or quite strongly as Muslim. This was in contrast to the predominantly Christian third generation and, to a lesser extent, the Christian Lebanese who are more likely to strongly identify as Christians than the third generation. The Lebanese commitment to a Christian or Muslim identity hence needs to be seen as framed not only by Australian but, also, Lebanese society where confessional differences are embedded in the country's constitution and much of daily social life.

Despite the negative experiences reported by the Lebanese and Turkish young people in the present study, a majority of both the second-generation and the third-generation groups stated that they strongly or very strongly identify as 'Australian'. The strength of this identification is only slightly below their far less problematic identification with the city where they live, whether it is Sydney or Melbourne. Especially in the context of the recent tendency to 'demonise' Islam in many sections of Australian public discourse, the strength of their identification with Australia is surprising, especially as it also is found among those who strongly identify with their Muslim background as well as

41   Reitz, J and Banerjee, R (2007). Racial Inequality, Social Cohesion, and Policy Issues in Canada. Belonging? Diversity, Recognition and Shared Citizenship in Canada. In K Banting, T J Courchene and F L Seidle (eds), *Belonging? Diversity, Recognition and Shared Citizenship in Canada*, Montreal Institute for Research on Public Policy, Montreal: 489-545.

42   Butcher, M and Thomas, M (2006). Ingenious: Emerging hybrid youth cultures in western Sydney, in P Nilan and C Feixa (eds) (2006), *Op cit*: 53-71; Butcher, M and Thomas, M (2003). *Op cit*; Dunn, K M, Forrest, J, Burnley, I and McDonald, A (2004). Constructing racism in Australia. *Australian Journal of Social Issues, 39* (4): 409-430; Noble, G (2007). *Op cit*; Noble, G, et al (1999a), *Op cit*; Noble, G, et al (1999b). *Op cit*; Noble, G, Poynting, S and Tabar, P (1999b). Youth, Ethnicity and the Mapping of Identities: Strategic essentialism and strategic hybridity among male Arabic-speaking youth in South-western Sydney. *Communal/Plural, 7,* 1: 29-44.

their 'Turkish' or 'Lebanese' identity. This finding was in marked contrast to those reported from the parallel studies in many of the European countries such as the Netherlands, Germany, Austria, Sweden, France, Belgium and Switzerland[43].

These findings cannot be explained by differences in the way the Australian and European studies asked about religious, ethnic or national identities since the same questions were used. What is different is that the official discourse on Australia as a multicultural society comprising individuals from many diverse backgrounds provides a 'space' which accepts and includes those who are not from the majority Anglo-Celtic background. This is so even if, in colloquial usage, it is not uncommon for individuals from other backgrounds to distinguish themselves from 'the Australians' or 'Aussies', especially when referring to patterns of behaviour or cultural practices and beliefs, such as those concerning the strength of family ties, where they consider their own to be superior.

Although globalisation and transnationalism have frequently been invoked as processes which may distance young adults from a sense of belonging and identification with their country of residence, this does not appear to be the case among the second-generation Lebanese and Turkish youth. Almost all these young people use the internet which gives them the opportunity to explore and establish overseas contacts. More than half of them have also had at least one visit to their parents' homeland in the last five years, usually for a holiday and/or family reasons. A quarter of the Turks and Christian Lebanese also have sent money back as have 40 per cent of the Muslim Lebanese. Yet, these activities co-exist with a strong Australian identity. Nor was their any indication that they were associated with plans to spend more than a year in the parents' homeland, as a majority have no such plans. A definitive 'certainly not' response was most likely to be given by the Christian Lebanese (76 per cent), followed by the Muslim Lebanese (67 per cent) and the Turkish (56 per cent). In fact, only between 2 per cent and 6 per cent had definite plans to spend more than a year in their parents' homeland. Again it appears that among the young second-generation interviewees, the transnational ties co-exist with a continuing intention to see Australia as their home, consistent with their strong identity as 'Australian'.

---

43   See the papers presented at the TIES conference in Amsterdam, December 2008. Inglis, C (2008). *Op cit.*

Conclusion

The diversity of the ethnic backgrounds and experiences of migration among young Australians is typical of the multicultural nature of the whole society. It also makes a general assessment of their incorporation or integration into Australian society more complex. Changing immigration policies, source countries and global changes all affect how they are incorporated. Neither ethnic group, generation, length of residence nor migration status can alone explain the patterns found, although there is greater uniformity in the experiences of the Australian-born than there is among the overseas-born. One effect of the adoption of multicultural policies is that they have shifted attention to the response by Australian institutions and society towards minority groups as being important in individuals' integration into the society. These policies have not managed to eliminate discrimination nor prejudice. They have the potential to result in a problematic form of incorporation in which, while individuals live in Australian society, their ability to participate and feel included differs in quality and extent from the majority population. Certainly, much of the recent youth research has been couched in terms of the problems confronting young people from ethnic minority backgrounds and implies that their incorporation into Australian society is highly problematic. The absence of research on 'non-problematic' young people has resulted in a lack of alternative perspectives from which to evaluate their experiences and assess the extent of their incorporation into Australian society.

While only able to explore selected dimensions of incorporation in this chapter, the shift in focus towards a broader cross-section of young people gives no basis for concluding that multiculturalism has undermined their level of incorporation and integration or led to threats to social harmony. In terms of the socio-economic dimensions of integration, the findings suggest that inequality is far less among ethnic groups in Australia than in most other comparable countries. Although the data used to assess the social integration of young people is more limited, it is consistent with other research that shows those from ethnic minority backgrounds are actually more likely to be involved in ethnically diverse social networks than those from third-generation, majority backgrounds. Regrettably, discrimination and prejudice are part of the experiences of many young people. Despite this, and despite their maintenance of a variety of transnational linkages overseas, there is evidence from Australian-born young people, whose origins are in Lebanon and Turkey, that their identification with Australia coexists with their distinctive ethnic and religious identities. Since both groups are often identified as having a problematic experience of incorporation this is a positive outcome.

Apart from specific policy initiatives, multiculturalism's inclusive construction of Australian society appears to have contributed to integration, which in turn has expanded the boundaries of multicultural Australian society. However, it also is important to acknowledge the extent to which they have approached and overcome a variety of difficulties and barriers to achieving such a level of integration. Whether similar findings about the ability of multiculturalism to contribute to integration can be sustained in studies which include a more detailed examination of the dimensions of incorporation, and groups from a wider range of diverse ethnic origins, is still to be determined.

Chapter 10: Dynamics of the Integration/Multicultural Connection[1]

Reg Appleyard

The demographic objective of Australia's post war immigration policy – to achieve numbers equal to one per cent of the population each year – initially gave top priority to persons from the United Kingdom. This was supplemented by immigrants, mainly northern Europeans, under specific programs with countries such as the Netherlands, and also under the IRO (International Refugee Organization). When the pool of so-called displaced persons dried up, the government turned to countries in southern Europe to achieve its policy target. Initial reluctance to give southern Europeans a central place in the immigration program had been based mainly on the view that they would neither 'assimilate' nor learn English as readily as northern Europeans. However, by the early 1950s, the government saw value in bringing single male workers from southern Europe to help resolve the high, unfilled demand for unskilled labour in Australia's manufacturing, extractive and transport industries[2]. The program included Greek males who worked as labourers in those industries and other Greeks nominated by relatives who had settled in Australia prior to World War II.[3]

The personally nominated males generally came from the same villages/towns as their nominators; those sponsored by the government came from many parts of Greece. Their prospects for marriage in Australia were not good: not only was there a dearth of single Greek females of marriageable ages, but, the newcomers were unable to communicate easily with Australian females. Some sponsored fiancées in Greece; others married by proxy girls unknown and unseen, a practice neither readily accepted nor understood by the Australian community. Newspaper images of Greek girls peering over a ship's rail, photograph in hand

---

1   Based on results from a longitudinal study of female Greek emigrants interviewed in Greece prior to their departure for Australia in 1964, and in Australia (and in Greece with those who returned) in 1965, 1976, 1990/91 and 2007/8. Co-researchers for the project were Anna Amera (Athens) and Elsa Demetriou (Melbourne).

2   Between 1950 and 1955, 19,193 males arrived from Greece compared with 9,225 females. Appleyard, R (1991). 'The Greeks of Australia: A new diasporic Hellenism', in S Vryonis Jnr. (ed), *Greece on the Road to Democracy. From the Junta to Pasok, 1974-1986*, Aristide D Caratzas: 365.

3   Appleyard, R and Amera, A (1986). 'Post-war immigration of Greek women to Australia: A longitudinal study', in R J Simon and C B Brettell (eds), *International Migration. The Female Experience*, Rowman and Allanheld, New Jersey: 216-217.

of the proxy groom on the Melbourne wharf below, holding a bunch of flowers, were accompanied by editorials criticising the proxy practice as unfair to women and un-Australian.

The government's response was to introduce a new program under which single Greek females would arrive in Australia unattached and, in due course, hopefully meet and marry a Greek with whom they had fallen in love, not a proxy who they had never met[4]. As in the male worker program, single females aged 17 to 23 years could either be sponsored by the Australian government or nominated by relatives in Australia. The former, living mainly in rural towns and villages, were interviewed on behalf of the Australian government by officials from the Intergovernmental Committee for European Migration (ICEM, now IOM). Pre-selected applicants were then taken to training schools at Kiffisia (Athens) or Thessaloniki where they enrolled in a ten-week course. Although titled 'Language Training', the course essentially introduced the women to aspects of modern urban domestic life and provided information on economic and social conditions in Australia. On completing the course, the women were flown to Sydney or Melbourne. Personally nominated applicants were not required to enrol at the training schools. Once their applications had been approved they too were flown to Sydney or Melbourne.

The survey of single Greek female emigrants

In 1964, two years after the program began, the author was on study leave in Geneva, working on a research project with ICEM. His suggestion to ICEM officials that they support a sample survey of workers under both the government-sponsored and personally nominated programs was accepted. Interviews conducted with the women prior to their departure for Australia, and then again up to one year later, were directed not only to establishing whether or not policy objectives had been achieved, but also to obtaining information on the respondents' socio-economic backgrounds, decision-making processes and expectations of Australia.

Interviews were conducted in Greek by co-researcher Anna Amera with fifty-one government-sponsored women at the Kiffisia and Thessaloniki schools. She also interviewed twenty-eight nominated dependents in their villages/towns prior to their departure for Australia where they were met by their nominators and drawn into a protective family circle where only Greek was spoken, introduced to Greeks known by their nominators and found employment generally in nearby factories.

---

4   Between 1962 and 1966, more Greek females (36,640) than males (34,469) entered Australia for settlement. Appleyard, R (1991). *Op cit.*

Seventy per cent of the government-sponsored women were aged under 20, all were unmarried, 54 per cent had left school before age 12, and 43 per cent were not gainfully employed. About one-half had been born in villages or small towns that they had never left, and a further one-third had grown up in villages but later moved to towns in Greece. Hardship of village life, inadequate spending money, and especially their parents' inability to provide a dowry large enough to attract a suitable groom, were their main reasons for deciding to emigrate. Many had thought about emigrating since childhood, but until the Australian government's offer, never had the opportunity to do so. Even so, their decisions to accept the offer took a great deal of courage. Few had ever ventured outside their village hinterland, and since leaving school their time had been divided between shepherding goats and digging in the fields in summer, and helping their mothers with domestic and cottage-industry chores during the winter. As first links in migration chains, they carried a heavy responsibility to succeed. Parents clearly saw the opportunities that their presence in Australia would create for other siblings, especially a brother who would be nominated by the respondent as soon as possible. Many girls realised that the prospects for marriage in Australia were excellent; others had fiancés in the village who they intended to nominate. During their time at the Kiffisia/Thessaloniki schools, government-sponsored women formed social sub-groups which were retained in Australia and had a significant influence on their adaptation.

Because hardship of village life, and in particular dearth of income, was the government-sponsored worker's main reason for emigrating, they were delighted to learn before they left Greece that employment had already been arranged in Australia at a fruit-canning factory at Berri, South Australia. However, their employment, despite 'unbelievably high wages', was not a pleasant experience. Itinerant male workers (many were Greek) in the same town harassed them in ways they had never experienced. In their villages, and in the mountains where they shepherded goats, they had been well protected from male harassment by an unwritten code that meted severe punishment on transgressors. Furthermore, at Berri they found it difficult to cope with the pace set by machinery in the canning factory. Most of them left Berri within two weeks to seek the 'relative protection' they anticipated would be provided by Greek communities in Melbourne and Sydney.

Retaining the village/community groupings they had established at Kiffisia and Thessaloniki, the government-sponsored workers either boarded in inner-city hostels or rented dwellings occupied by other Greeks. When re-interviewed in 1965, all of the thirty respondents were sharing bedrooms, and had saved the equivalent of 'thirteen weeks pay'. All but three had already sent remittances to Greece; but purchase of consumer durables and vehicles had been negligible. Twenty-three had obtained repetitive-type factory jobs found for them by Greek neighbours, many of whom worked in the same factories. Employers resolved the workers' inability to speak English by grouping them into units where only Greek was spoken. However, in many respects they were left to fend for themselves, official services being insufficiently flexible to cope with the unusual group. For example, if a worker sought information from the employment office on an available job, the name and address of a potential employer would be written in English on a piece of paper and so the worker had no idea where to go when she left the office.

Only eighteen of the thirty government-sponsored respondents had enrolled in official evening classes in English language and three of these had withdrawn after four weeks and a further four after two months. Only one stayed the full one-year course. Workers seldom found it necessary to use more than a few words in English. They worked in factories with other Greeks, lived in houses inhabited only by Greeks and socialised almost exclusively with other Greeks who, like themselves, had been in Australia for only a year or two.

The groupings of kinfolk/friends from similar villages and communities in Greece that had been formed at the Kiffisia/Thessaloniki schools soon became formalised as associations that provided opportunities to meet single Greek males. While those who had fiancés in their villages saved hard to cover the cost of his airline ticket to Australia, others readily saw that the good prospects for marriage suggested prior to their departure proved to be accurate. Eight of the 30 respondents were already married and a further seven were engaged, including those who had fiancés in Greece. Others found it difficult to deviate from village precepts regarding courtship. Their responses to the attentions of Greek men (not all of whom were interested in marriage) was to move from mixed to solely female companionship. Many respondents told us that their greatest need during the first year in Australia was the companionship of a brother or other close relative who could guide, advise and protect them.

While they anticipated that the established Greek communities in Melbourne and Sydney, organised and led by Greeks who had emigrated to Australia during the inter-war years, would embrace and protect them, this did not occur. Indeed, the only contact many had made with Greeks outside their own associations was during attendance at Orthodox Church services and celebrations. Their associations were, in many respects, minority groups within the wider Greek communities in Melbourne and Sydney.

Second follow-up interviews were conducted in 1976 with both the government-sponsored and personally nominated female workers in Australia, and in Greece with those who had returned. The economic achievements of the Australia-domiciled respondents were impressive. All but one respondent had married (within two years) a Greek of similar social class and migration vintage, courtship having 'proceeded in ways and circumstances almost unthinkable at home'[5]. Ninety per cent were owner-occupiers of their homes; one half had paid off their mortgages; one half owned or were buying independent businesses; 18 per cent owned second houses; 14 per cent had investments in Greece; and ownership of consumer durables was almost at 'saturation'. High propensity to save from incomes earned by both partners was the foundation of these achievements. Sixty per cent of respondents still lived in the inner suburbs, although 25 per cent had already moved to the outer suburbs of Melbourne and Sydney[6].

Their English comprehension, described as 'uniformly poor', had improved little during the first decade and their social contact with non-Greece-born Australians was confined mainly to workmates, tradesmen and, for those who had purchased shops, customers. There is no doubt that the village/town associations played important roles in their early adaptation. Indeed, Mistilis has observed, regarding Greeks in Sydney, that strong identification with culture, combined with fondness for organisation, enabled Greeks to develop communities no matter how little help they received either from the government of Greece or their adopted country[7]. However, by 1976, the importance of village associations for our groups had already declined, many having been disbanded and those still in existence being held together by recollection and sentiment.

Neither the Australian government nor existing established Greek communities had been able to provide adequate services to facilitate the adaptation of respondents in this sample. The Greek community was really too small, and too limited in resources, to meet the cost of a comprehensive adaptation service. At the end of a decade in Australia respondents still retained only desultory contact with the Greek Orthodox Church, attending celebrations such as at Easter and the christening of their children. The Church's capacity to assist new arrivals had also been reduced by serious political divisions within the organisation[8]. Personally nominated respondents had access to the established community through their nominators, but government-sponsored workers' contact was only occasional. Nor did the Good Neighbour Council, the official body established to assist newcomers 'assimilate', have either the resources or expertise (or perhaps the will) to resolve the issues faced by Greek migrants and thousands of others arriving in Australia during the 1970s.

---

5   Appleyard, R T and Amera, A (1986). *Op cit:* 223.
6   Appleyard, R T, Amera, A and Demetriou, E (1991). *Education and Social Mobility of Second-Generation Greeks in Australia. Results of a Survey*, mimeo: 13.
7   Mistilis, N (1988). 'Greek community life in Sydney', *Encyclopedia of the Australian People*, Sydney.
8   Appleyard, R T (1988). 'Issues of socio-cultural adaptation and conflict", in C Stahl (ed), *International Migration Today; Volume 2, Emerging Issues*, UNESCO, Paris, and The Centre for Migration and Development Studies, University of Western Australia: 142.

The 1990/91 follow-up interviews revealed that, although respondents and their families still lived in Melbourne or Sydney, they had moved from inner to outer suburbs where they had acquired comfortable homes. As noted above, this mobility was already underway in 1976 when we discovered that one-quarter of respondents had made the move. Lack of formal skills reduced respondents' opportunities for higher levels of employment, but almost all remained in the workforce until the 1990s, leaving it only for short periods before and after childbirth. Investment in property and in business, initiated during the first decade in Australia, increased significantly after the 1970s. Many families had also acquired properties in Greece, generally located in their home village or a nearby town. While some respondents (and their adult children) deem these properties 'holiday houses' which they visit frequently, others spend several years there, retaining, of course, their properties in Australia. At any one time members of the family (including their 40+ year-old children) are accommodated in both the Australian and Greece-owned properties.

For example, a respondent from a village in the Peloponnese acquired a property there after having bought a large home in Mascot, New South Wales. Her husband owns a ready-made clothing business. Plans to sell the Mascot property and return to live in the village house came to nought because their children refused to leave Australia. One son was enrolled in an electrical engineering course at the University of NSW. However, the respondent and her husband return to the village house 'quite frequently … we take it in turns'. Another respondent and her husband returned to Greece in 1972 intending permanent stay but returned to Australia after a short time, then returned to their Greece property again in 1981. Another respondent, Anna (who lives in Malvern, Victoria and is employed as an office cleaner), and her husband, have also made many visits to Greece, mainly to keep in touch with their ageing parents. Interviews conducted with respondents in 2007/08 also show that others have returned permanently to Greece, including one who returned in 1985 when her husband acquired a machinery shop from savings they had accumulated in Australia where, she said, they had done well. These examples typify the nature and reasons for respondents' inter-country mobility during the last decade in particular.

Second generation

Our second follow-up interviews in 1976 revealed that of the 122 children born to respondents, 72 were already in primary schools. Because they had grown up in homes where only Greek was spoken, and played mainly with other Greek children in the neighbourhood, the eldest child entered primary school knowing little or no English. Eva Isaacs' study of Greek children in Sydney, conducted about the same time as our second follow-up interviews, concluded that,

The Greek child grows up in Australia in a home environment where parents and relatives are determined to hand on units of traditional behaviour without modification. The world they wish to preserve is the one they knew in Greece. Their social norms developed out of constant interaction between family and community where there were few strangers and everybody knew everybody else[9].

Inner-city schools in Melbourne and Sydney had been criticised in a government report published in 1975 for not resolving difficulties associated with trying to teach English to classes of high migrant density[10]. The respondents' first child experienced these difficulties when he/she entered primary classes unable to speak or understand English. Their placement in withdrawal classes where they received special instruction in English eventually facilitated progress in general classes, although parents argued that the withdrawal classes did not entirely overcome their handicap[11]. By the time the second child began primary school he/she had been exposed at home to English spoken by the first child. And many respondents noted that the third child often spoke in English to the older children. The more proficient in English the children became, the further they slipped from parental influence and control. Indeed, parents relied increasingly upon their children to 'explain' in situations where only English was spoken.

While it is not surprising that all respondents insisted that their children 'learn to read and write Greek and speak it properly', the only medium for achieving this objective was a Greek ethnic school. In 1974 there were 350 Greek ethnic schools in Australia, over 300 of which were associated with the Greek Orthodox Church. Others were run by independent Greek communities and by persons offering private services[12]. Respondents were uniformly critical of the quality of language teaching provided by all these schools. Many argued that Greek should be offered as a second language at primary and secondary levels in government schools. Nor did many of the respondents' children enjoy ethnic school classes, partly because they encroached on their leisure time and partly because class discipline was severe, corporal punishment being not uncommon.

Our third follow-up interviews conducted in 1990/91 focused on the adaptation and achievements of the respondents' children. Interviews conducted with 64 children living in Australia (many others had returned to Greece with their parents) showed that 79 per cent of those aged 17 to 24 years had remained at school to Year 12/HSC or its equivalent. Twenty-eight per cent had then

---

9   Isaacs, E (1975). *Greek Children in Sydney*, Australian Department of Education. Inquiry into Schools of High Migrant Density, Canberra.
10   Appleyard, R T, et al (1991). *Op cit:* 17.
11   Appleyard, R T and Amera, A (1978). 'The education of Greek migrant children in Australia: A parent view', *International Migration*: 16, 3/4: 105-121
12   Tsounis, M P (1974). *Greek Ethnic Schools in Australia*, Australian Immigration Monograph Series No. 1, Department of Demography, Australian National University, Canberra.

proceeded to further training through TAFE/Technical School/Apprenticeship, and a surprising 42 per cent went on to universities and Colleges of Advanced Education.

By 1991, 93 per cent of the children had attended ethnic schools, entering at primary school ages. Parental determination that they learn 'proper Greek' had not waned over the years, although the children were not so positive about the experience; 43 per cent claiming it was 'not worth much'. One daughter of a respondent said that she had wanted to learn Greek at an early age, went on to complete HSC level and expressed pride in having done so. 'It's my heritage,' she said, and was critical of the 'kitchen Greek' spoken by children in many Greek homes. At the 1990/91 interviews, 48 per cent of children said they still communicated in Greek with their parents. A further 38 per cent communicated in either English or Greek.

Most of the respondents who had lived in the inner suburbs of Melbourne and Sydney during their first decade in Australia had, by 1990/91, moved to the outer suburbs of those cities. This had provided opportunities for the second generation to make new social contacts in schools populated by a higher proportion of Anglo-Australian children than in inner-city schools. However, if their secondary school classes included other Greeks (and the outer suburbs had seen significant 'new Greek' populations after the 1980s) there was a 'natural tendency', as one child put it, for friendships to be formed between them. One second-generation respondent said that she preferred Greek friends because she could 'relate to them more … tell them her secrets. We had more in common. We all had strict parents you see, and we operated on the same wave length'.

Regarding their social networks in general (not simply school contacts), almost one-half of those aged 17 to 24 years comprised 'mostly Greeks', compared with 33 per cent for those aged 10 to 16 years. This may be partly explained by the latter group beginning schools in the outer suburbs where the proportion of Greek children in schools and in the community was much lower than in the inner suburban schools attended by their older brothers and sisters.

On no issue was discussion more profound than on aspects of ethnic identity. The large majority of second-generation respondents argued that Greek values, ideals and family unity outweighed such Australian inputs as workforce and location. Australia, they argued, did not exert a strong influence as a cultural base. The most satisfying aspect of living in Australia was the ability to still have a Greek way of life and close family relationships.

Ability to communicate in Greek was related closely to their preferences concerning the ethnicity of marriage partners. Forty-eight per cent indicated that they would definitely prefer to marry a Greek; a further 6 per cent had already done so[13]. There was also consensus that the older they became the more they began to 'appreciate Greek culture', whereas when younger they had rejected quite strongly what they described as their parents' 'old fashioned views'. Forty-seven per cent of second-generation respondents had already visited Greece, either with their parents when younger or alone or with friends when older. A further 48 per cent were interested in visiting or planning to visit Greece. But while these figures clearly convey an increasing interest in Greek culture, only four respondents said that they may one day settle there.

Although data obtained from interviews with respondents and their children at the fourth follow-up survey in 2007/8 have not yet been analysed and integrated into the longitudinal network, we can report that the majority of second-generation respondents have married persons of Greek ancestry and most of those who were still unmarried expressed the intention of marrying a Greek. The son of a government-sponsored worker spoke for many when he said that his marriage to a Greek woman would facilitate his strongly held intention to pass on Greek language and traditions to his children. And the daughter of another respondent told us that she will 'insist that their children attend a Greek language school'.

There was also general consensus that it had been their parents' insistence that they remain at high school that had provided the foundation for their achievements. The son of another government-sponsored respondent, and his brother, had attained university degrees. 'Our parents,' he said, 'had high expectations, especially our getting to university. We know that education was important for them.'

Integration/multiculturalism

Integration is an ongoing experience for the migrant. Our research confirms that critical issues were different at each stage of the resettlement process[14]. Socio-cultural adaptation occurs within the changing political and socio-economic background of the receiving country. Although migrants are eligible, indeed encouraged, to become naturalised many have neither done so, nor thereafter participated in political processes. Sestito[15] argued in 1982 that it was political parties that initiated the migrants' interest in politics rather than the migrants themselves demanding greater participation and benefits. Greeks, however, have tended to become involved in internal (at the expense of Australian) politics, a

---

13   The 28 per cent who gave no response were aged 10 to 16 years.
14   Appleyard, R T and Amera, A (1978). *Op cit.*
15   Sestito, R (1982). *The Policies of Multiculturalism*, Centre for Independent Studies, Sydney.

situation which, Sestito claims, changed after the mid-1970s, partly because the non-British communities in Australia were more aware and confident of their political power, and partly because of the encouragement provided by changing government policies concerning adaptation/integration. Jayasuriya[16] concluded that after the mid-1960s governments supported a milder form of adaptation which signalled greater tolerance of cultural differences and diversity of lifestyles. Then with the election of a Labor government in the early 1970s, migrants were encouraged to cultivate their cultural differences in order to restore their self-esteem. This led quickly to the adoption of the new policy of multiculturalism. It was the sheer magnitude of votes at stake, argues Sestito, that led both parties to bargain with the promise of special benefits. Multiculturalism, he concludes, was the creation of political parties.

Changing government policies regarding integration reflect not only changing attitudes, but also recognition that the nation's ethnic mix, and the stage reached by each constituent group in the adaptation process, requires new and different approaches. It is well to be reminded of Charles Price's view that in the long term Australia will be less a multicultural and more a mixed cultural society, one in which people inherit in themselves many different cultures. This process will be facilitated by second-generation migrants marrying outside their communities, although such a process had not been adopted by the second-generation Greeks in our study.

Jayasuriya also argues that in its normative-prescriptive usage, multiculturalism is predicated on the existence (or desired existence) of mutual tolerance and respect for cultural differences. Distinction between life-style and life-chances is central to an understanding of the meaning and significance of multiculturalism as a philosophy of migrant resettlement. Life-chances, he declares, revolve around the question of overcoming structural inequalities, and have to do with competition, power and conflict rather than consensus.

The double disadvantage of ethnicity and class deprivation was clearly manifested in the early adaptation of the Greek migrants discussed in this chapter. Even so, the study has revealed that language, community structure and the determination of the migrants themselves, were significant variables in the process of socio-cultural adaptation.

---

16 Jayasuriya, L (1983). 'Multiculturalism: Fact, policy or rhetoric?' *The Nation is People*, The Extension Service, The University of Western Australia, Nedlands.

Implication of survey findings for the integration/multicultural process

Selected findings relating to a longitudinal-type survey of Greek women migrants (and their Australia-born children), interviewed on five occasions over a 45 year period, have confirmed and explained the dynamic nature of their integration. The single Greek women were participants in a program adopted by the Australian government to resolve difficulties associated with the gender differential of Greece-born persons in Australia. Many of the government-sponsored women, while attending language-training classes in Greece prior to their departure, formed social groups comprising fellow students from the same village or region. These groups were retained during their early years in the inner suburbs of Melbourne and Sydney. Identified informally as 'associations', they were essentially minority groups operating within the wider Greek communities. Their role and influence in the integration process was central during the first decade, but, as the women married and became increasingly involved in activities associated with the wider Greek communities, their role and influence declined.

During June 2008, Michael Clyne suggested to the authors of chapters in this volume that they give consideration to specific aspects of the integration/multicultural process, which, he argued, would not only give some 'unity' to the chapters but also provide 'collective impetus'. The aspects that he suggested be addressed include the extent of marriage within two generations, linguistic indicators of integration and socio-economic mobility. He also encouraged authors to cover, as far as available data made possible, the contribution of second-generation migrants in the integration and multicultural process.

As noted above, a primary objective of the government's single Greek female program was to balance the gender differential of single adult Greeks in Australia. Within one year of their arrival, eight of the 30 government-sponsored respondents had married an Australia-domiciled Greek or a fiancé from Greece. And within two years all but one respondent had married a Greek of social class and migration vintage similar to themselves.

Inability to communicate in English had greatly restricted their contact with non-Greek Australians, which, of course, largely explains their marriage to Greek men. The 1965 interviews showed that only 18 of the 30 government-sponsored respondents had enrolled in English language classes and all but one had withdrawn from the one-year course within a few months. Their English comprehension remained 'uniformly poor' over the survey period and outside their homes they struggled to communicate with Australian workmates, tradesmen and customers.

Regarding their mobility, both socio-economic and geographical: by 1976 they had accumulated substantial assets, mainly because both partners were employed full time and exercised a high propensity to save. By 1991 most of the couples had moved from inner to outer suburbs of Melbourne and Sydney where they acquired comfortable homes. The 2007/2008 interviews also showed that many families had acquired properties in Greece, generally in their home villages or nearby towns. While some of these properties were used as 'holiday houses', more typical was their use as 'second properties' where they (now aged in their sixties) and their Australia-born children (many in their forties) spent periods of up to two years.

Interviews conducted with the respondents' children in 1990/91 and 2007/8 indicated that although the first child entered inner-city primary school knowing little or no English, and was placed in a 'withdrawal class' where he/she received special instruction in English, younger brothers and sisters entered the same schools with 'limited English'. Parental insistence that their children 'learn Greek properly' led to almost all being enrolled in Greek language schools. Parents also placed strong emphasis on the importance of education despite, but perhaps because of, their own limited education. Almost 80 per cent of the children remained at school to Year 12/HSC. A surprising, but nonetheless encouraging, finding was that 42 per cent of the children aged 17 to 24 years at the 1990/91 interviews, had completed degrees at universities and Colleges of Advanced Education.

A large majority of the children indicated that, for them, Greek ideals, values and family unity outweighed such Australian inputs as workforce and location. The most satisfactory aspect of living in Australia was, in addition to a high living standard, the ability to still have a Greek way of life and close family relationships. When seen in 1990/91, 47 per cent had already visited Greece, and 48 per cent said they would definitely marry a Greek, 6 per cent having already done so. The 2007/8 interviews, yet to be analysed, indicate that a large majority had already married or intend marrying a person of Greek ancestry[17].

---

17   Appleyard, Amera and Demetriou are presently writing an overview volume on the project's findings.

Epilogue: A Multicultural Future

Michael Clyne and James Jupp

Unfriendly critics were arguing by 2005 that 'multiculturalism was dead in Australia'. This was based on the approach of the Howard Coalition government, which had gradually run down multicultural programmes and finally eliminated the term from the once again renamed Department of Immigration and Citizenship (DIAC). Emphasis on 'integration', citizenship and values had become official Commonwealth policy, inspired partly by developments in Britain and the European Union that were responding to increased concern at Islamist militancy and refugee intakes[1]. Elections in Canada and New Zealand brought in governments less sympathetic to multiculturalism than their predecessors. The election of two British National Party candidates to the parliament of the European Union caused the British government and opposition to emphasise the same concerns as their Australian counterparts. Even many supporters of multiculturalism began to feel that the 'strict limits' promised in the Galbally report of 1978 ought to be defined and implemented. In 1978 the problem of Islamic fundamentalism had not been considered, but thirty years later it dominated and distorted public and official discussion.

A premature death

This obituary was premature and unduly pessimistic. In Australia the Labor-controlled states and territories continued actively to pursue multicultural policies. While control changed in Western Australia, this still left seven of the eight committed to multiculturalism. Much of the support for 'cultural' activity rests at the state level, with the Commonwealth more concerned with migrant settlement. The constitution does not specifically allocate multicultural functions, as these were unknown in 1901. Constitutional power over aliens (51xix) and immigration (51xxvii) justified Commonwealth domination of multicultural policy and its allocation to the Immigration Department for all but a few years.

The election of a Labor government in 2007 did not immediately change matters. Much remained in place, including tests for citizenship and an extended waiting period. The Rudd government committed itself to developing multicultural policies and began a still unfinished national consultation. The multicultural

---

1   Vertovec, S and Wessendorf, S (eds) (2010). *The Multiculturalism Backlash*, Routledge, London.

reality of Australia does not change simply because governments want it to. Governments may alter the sources of immigration but cannot dictate cultural variety in the sense of using languages, forming associations, creating new media, retaining links with the homeland and with relatives elsewhere, and practising religions. The latter is specifically protected by s.116 of the Commonwealth constitution. Other multicultural manifestations might be better protected by a Bill of Rights, as in most other democracies. However that has yet to be developed and has been strongly opposed by several religious denominations. Lifestyles and beliefs have been criticised but not interfered with by the states. Political common sense suggests that the normal and harmless activities of several million voters are best left alone.

Assimilation and diversity

The 2006 Census, issued just as these controversies were gaining force, showed clearly that political imperatives would prevent any sudden and drastic return to the assimilationism of the 1950s. The loss of John Howard's own electorate of Bennelong, with its large and varied ethnic minority population, underlined this in 2007[2]. The census showed that one quarter of the Australian population was overseas-born, that over 40 per cent had one or both parents born overseas, that one in six normally used a language other than English (LOTE) at home, that (apart from Jews and Catholics) over one million identified with religions from Asia, the Middle East and Africa, and that less than two-thirds claimed to be Christians. This was a very mixed population, but still with a majority core of British or Irish descended Anglophone Christian Australians. No other ethnicity threatens this core, but it no longer has a monopoly. The large-scale additions to the population after 2006 included an exceptionally large proportion of temporary workers and overseas students who may not intend to remain in Australia, although many do.

Not all immigrants favour multiculturalism and not all third-generation Australians oppose it, as Andrew Markus makes plain. Not all immigrants are naturalised citizens and hence voters, but the great majority are, with citizenship levels at 96 per cent for Greek and Macedonian Orthodox and Baha'i, at 77 per cent for Muslims (of whom one third were born in Australia) and 76 per cent for Buddhists. However the figures are presented, the 'multicultural constituency' is too large to ignore, even if it is disunited, ambivalent or not identified consistently with one or other of the major parties. For many years Federal election data showed quite clearly that the electorates in which non-English-speaking (NESB/CALD) migrants are concentrated almost invariably return ALP

---

2 Jupp, J (2009b). 'Immigration and Ethnicity', *Australian Cultural History*, vol.27, 2: 157-166.

candidates. In 2007, of thirty electorates with one quarter or more speaking a LOTE at home (20 per cent of the total) all but two (Menzies and Melbourne) were won by the ALP. The state-level political parties seem more sensitive to these realities than the national organisations centred on Canberra.

The inevitability of acculturation

The current size and complexity of the 'ethnic minority' population is, then, too important to be ignored. A further argument has been that while the minorities created by immigration are undoubtedly there they will fade away over the generations. The evidence for this rests heavily on the Europeans who came under the White Australia policy between 1947 and 1973. Census analysis, referred to in this book, gives some credence to this view[3]. There are marked shifts away from the use of LOTEs over three generations[4]. There are rising numbers of cross-ethnic marriages and hence of children from 'two cultures' who are attracted to the 'third' ('Australian'). Acculturation does happen and is inevitable but is not the same as total assimilation, as officially urged before the 1970s. Essentially acculturation refers to language shift and identification with the country of residence rather than of origin, while assimilation means total elimination of any characteristics which differ from those of the majority. With a continuing immigration programme, acculturation is competing with newly arrived ethnicities.

One of the features of multicultural advocacy among the 'communities' has been to ignore or belittle the natural process of acculturation. Irish Australians were pioneers in this denial, claiming Irish origins long after they had lost the Irish language or forgotten where the migrants of five or six generations ago came from. This is marked in the United States where every president (including Obama) spends time and effort finding an Irish ancestor. On this kind of calculation, 60 per cent of the Irish in the world are Americans. The diaspora has been very important in Irish and American politics and is also significant for several Australian communities such as Tamils, Greeks and Jews.

Yet the argument that assimilation is always inevitable and that multiculturalism is, therefore, a declining phenomenon, needs serious appraisal. Even today organisations and services based on the post-war Displaced Persons generation survive and even thrive, despite their original constituents having an average age of more than seventy and despite the collapse of the Communist system which had severed their links with their homelands for over forty years. Total assimilation can be a very long process even when the original overseas source

---

3 See Khoo (chapter 6) and Inglis (chapter 9), this volume.
4 See Clyne (chapter 4), this volume.

has dried up, as it has for most southern and eastern Europeans. Moreover many of the ethnic organisations change their emphasis and services to cater for the elderly, with appropriate funding from state agencies other than the Department of Immigration (DIAC

Languages, organisations, media, loyalties and even religions decline and die in isolation. Yet Australia is no longer isolated as it was a century ago. Australians of all origins are now in direct, sometimes instant, communication with their homelands and their relatives. Flights, the internet, mobile phones, electronic media, the whole apparatus of the global village, have dissolved the tyranny of distance. Most immigrant communities in Australia are part of international diasporas, with which they often maintain regular links. Their homeland governments encourage this, especially since the collapse of restrictive Communism. The Greek government has a ministry for overseas Greeks and some Italian provincial governments have similar arrangements for their compatriots. The Indian government has created a category of overseas Indians with a view to attracting their investment and possible return. Diasporas are often as important as homeland influences, particularly those located in Europe and North America. They help to modify the impact of the receiving majority culture in many countries of immigration.

Thus, while a degree of acculturation of individuals over one or more generations will undoubtedly happen, it will not necessarily invalidate the multicultural arrangements in a diverse society. Religious change is likely to be slow. Religions are more likely to inhibit out-marriage than secular allegiances or even language. Studies, such as that of Siew-Ean Khoo (this volume), show quite different levels of intermarriage between birthplace groups. These are not necessarily related only to length of Australian residence. Recruitment has moved out of Europe and towards Asia and the Middle East and arranged and cross-cousin marriages are likely to reinforce the inheritance of ethnicity through generations. As the Canadian category of 'visible' ethnicity acknowledges, many arrivals since the 1970s will continue to look different in the eyes of the majority. Whether they are treated with suspicion will be a major concern of multicultural policies into the distant future, as will measurable inequalities between those of different ancestries.

'Integration' as an alternative

The tendency to declare multiculturalism 'dead' or 'past its use by date' revived the term 'integration', which was fashionable in Australia for a brief period between 1966 and 1973. With three governments (Whitlam, Fraser and Hawke) dominating Federal politics for two decades (1972-1992) and committed to multiculturalism, this alternative faded away. In fact it represented, and may still represent, just another variant of multiculturalism with a less challenging name. 'Integration' accepts that ethnic allegiances will remain and be organised, but argues that they are not the basic building blocks of nation building. These are: acceptance of a set of universally acceptable values; individual access to social and economic improvement; mastery of the official language as the key to education and employment; acceptance of the local citizenship and its benefits and obligations; rejection of violent and revolutionary strategies; making a 'contribution' to society; mixing freely with other citizens of varied origins; being proud of and well informed about the nation's history and achievements. No emphasis is placed on minority cultural or linguistic maintenance, which are seen as private concerns but not divisive.

In practice the state can no more impose integration than it can multiculturalism. Attempts to do so by the Howard government included: setting tests of local knowledge for intending citizens; evading the UN Convention relating to asylum seekers; resisting rights-based legislation; tightening laws against terror; encouraging 'moderate Muslims' to take the lead in Muslim structures; reassertion of national myths such as Gallipoli, the bush and mateship; upholding the role of the monarchy; strengthening the role of religion in education, charity and welfare; favouring private initiative over state control. Most of these assume integration into existing society, rather than major modification to that society to accommodate diversity.

This is a rather motley collection of policies, reflecting the mixed inheritance of the elements that make up the Liberal-National alliance. It contains some contradictions, for example the expectation that migrants should adhere to Australian values and loyalties even when only present on temporary visas (the number of which has greatly increased). Values are difficult to define, being either 'motherhood statements' on the 'do as you would be done by' principle, or high expectations of integrity and honesty which many in business or politics would find preposterous. Regular references to the Judeo-Christian ethic, while excluding Muslims and other religions, ignore the fact that Muslims at least also subscribe to the 'Judeo' ethics laid down in the Old Testament. In practice Australian laws are no longer specifically based on Christian principles but may unconsciously embody them.

Essentially adherence to the rule of law, peaceful resolution of personal or collective conflicts, choice of government through the ballot box, equality of men and women, payment of taxes and other lawful charges, respect for property, control of private prejudices, acceptance of legal obligations such as school attendance or voting, and similar desirable attributes of a dutiful citizen, are very widely spread through Australian society, regardless of ethnic background.

They are also acceptable in most established democracies. Once the argument attempts to define specifically 'Australian' values, knowledge and practices it comes up against the reality that Australia is a multicultural society, drawing in people from a variety of backgrounds and circumstances over different periods of time. Recognition of this caused changes in the citizenship test away from the 1950s suburban dream of the former prime minister.

Concrete and measurable integration

As the various analyses in this book show, there is a great deal of effective integration taking place in Australian society. Ability to speak English, willingness to become citizens and thus voters, obedience to the law, second-generation acculturation, relocation to outer suburbia, rejection of political extremes, active interest in sport, religious adherence, regular employment, second-generation educational success, home ownership and many other attributes have all been measured over the past thirty years and found to support the claim that migrants have settled into Australian society very well.

There have been no recorded instances of successful terrorism in Australia, only trials for advocating or plotting terrorism under new laws. There are pockets of disadvantage and criminality in the major cities, but these are not exclusive to migrants in general or to particular ethnic groups. Small minorities have adopted criminal or extremist behaviour, but their backgrounds are very varied. There is no ethnic group which comes anywhere near the complex of social problems characteristic of Indigenous Australians, nor any one with such a consistent history of discrimination, cultural destruction, alienation or rejection.

The studies here suggest that while adaptation and acculturation are difficult and complex social processes, they have largely been achieved in a multicultural public policy environment and a carefully planned immigration intake. Prejudice and xenophobia remain and occasionally burst forth. Politicians sometimes 'play the race card' especially when asylum seekers appear on the horizon. But the studies here suggest that integration, social cohesion and equity have been the overall consequence of the multicultural policies pursued in the past thirty-five years. These approaches lay the foundation for policies which will need to be pursued into the foreseeable future.

Problems and the future

Where multiculturalism has failed is mainly due to political timidity or conservatism. As elsewhere public opinion and political reactions have failed to cope with the alleged threat from the Islamic revival. Media and partisan influences have stressed the extreme aspects of Islam elsewhere, without asking how significant these might be in Australia. Issues like the *burqua* have been blown out of all proportion. This has provoked a defensive reaction from many who do not adopt this form of dress but believe that their religious sisters have a right to use it if they choose. The actual numbers involved are quite tiny, many of them recent converts. The call to recreate the long dead Caliphate is as powerless as traditional appeals for the socialist revolution. Neither is likely to occur. Above all, the advent of very small numbers of asylum seekers arriving by boat, most of them in recent years from war zones in Afghanistan, Sri Lanka and Iraq, has served the conservatives well, with their 2010 election slogan 'stop the boats'. With characteristic timidity the ALP did nothing to effectively counter the picture created by its political opponents. This was left to organisations and individuals largely outside the centres of power, such as the Greens, welfare and religious groups. Ethnic and multicultural organisations were also reluctant to swim against the stream of an indignant public opinion.

For the future it might be desirable to separate multiculturalism from immigration, as the Hawke/Keating governments did by locating the policy within the Department of Prime Minister and Cabinet or as most state governments did by locating it within the powers of the Premiers. Otherwise multiculturalism remains a limited policy, being largely a form of migrant settlement. It becomes mixed up with issues such as the current hostility to a 'larger Australia', asylum seekers and migrant selection. Yet ethnic and religious institutions and practices continue to exist and even flourish several generations away from the original arrival of their founders. Some organisations of Scottish, Cornish, Welsh, German, Chinese, Greek and Italian orientation have survived for well over a century. Experience here and elsewhere has been that ethnic and religious prejudices and loyalties do not die easily. A truly multicultural society does not disappear with the first generation, but our present arrangements assume that it will. Canada recognises this reality more effectively than Australia.

Basic issues at present include the degree of tolerance appropriate for practices which are either currently illegal or undesirable in a liberal, secular democracy. These include the role of women in certain religions (and not just Islam); the extent to which some races (and especially Aborigines) are disadvantaged over the long term; the persistence of ethnic and religious prejudices and discrimination; the role of the media and the education systems in dealing with multicultural issues and realities; the participation of hitherto excluded minorities from the highest political, bureaucratic and social levels; the redefinition of 'Australian' values, practices and traditions to expand their scope away from British and Irish origins; and the public discussion of population and immigration issues free from their use for political advantage. Multiculturalism is a form of nation building and not just aimed at immigrant settlement or combating prejudice.

Bibliography

Altman, D (2006). *51st State?* Scribe, Carlton.

Anderson, B (1983). *Imagined Communities: Reflections on the Origin and Spread of Nationalism*, Verso, London.

Ang, I, Brand, J E, Noble, G and Wilding, D (2002). *Living Diversity. Australia's Multicultural Future*, Special Broadcasting Corporation, Artarmon, viewed 8 April, 2009, http://www20.sbs.com.au/sbscorporate/index.php?id=547.

Ano, K (2002). Relationship between fluency and accuracy in spoken English of High School Learners, *Step Bulletin* 14: 39-49.

Appleyard, R (1964). *British Emigration to Australia,* ANU Press, Canberra.

Appleyard, R (1988). 'Issues of socio-cultural adaptation and conflict", in C Stahl (ed), *International Migration Today; Volume 2, Emerging Issues*, UNESCO, Paris, and The Centre for Migration and Development Studies, University of Western Australia.

Appleyard, R (1991). 'The Greeks of Australia: A new diasporic Hellenism', in S Vryonis Jnr (ed), *Greece on the Road to Democracy. From the Junta to Pasok, 1974-1986*, Aristide D Caratzas: 363-384.

Appleyard, R and Amera, A (1978). 'The education of Greek migrant children in Australia: A parent view', *International Migration*: 16, 3/4: 105-121.

Appleyard, R and Amera, A (1986). 'Post-war immigration of Greek women to Australia: A longitudinal study', in R J Simon and C B Brettell (eds), *International Migration. The Female Experience*, Rowman and Allanheld, New Jersey: 215-228.

Appleyard, R, Amera, A and Demetriou, E (1991). *Education and Social Mobility of Second-Generation Greeks in Australia. Results of a Survey*, mimeo, 46pp.

Australian Bureau of Statistics (2006). *Census Dictionary: Australia 2006 (Reissue),* Catalogue No. 2901.0, ABS, Canberra.

Australian Bureau of Statistics (2007). *Australian Demographic Statistics, December Quarter*, Catalogue No. 3101.0, ABS, Canberra.

Australian Government (2009). *Social Inclusion Principles for Australia*, viewed 21 August, 2009.

Australian Mosaic (2009). 23 October, Federation of Ethnic Communities Councils of Australia, Canberra.

Australian Survey of Social Attitudes, viewed 8 April, 2009, http://aussa.anu.edu.au/questionnaires.php.

Banting, K and Kymlicka, W (eds) (2006). *Multiculturallism and the Welfare State*, Oxford University Press, Oxford.

Barker, E (1915). *Political Thought in England from Herbert Spencer to the Present Day*, Henry Holt, New York.

Barker, E (1927). *National Character and the Factors in its Formation*, Harper and Brothers, New York.

Batrouney, A and Batrouney, T (1985). *The Lebanese in Australia,* AE Press, Melbourne.

Bauer, O (2000) [1907]. *The Question of Nationalities and Social Democracy*, University of Minnesota Press, Minneapolis.

Bean, F and Stevens, G (2003). *America's Newcomers and the Dynamics of Diversity*, Russell Sage Foundation, New York.

Bell, M (1992). *Internal Migration in Australia 1981-1986*, AGPS, Canberra.

Benjamin, R (1998). *'A Serious Influx of Jews'*, Allen and Unwin, Sydney.

Bentley, A F (1908). *The Process of Government*, Principia Press, Bloomington, Indiana.

Berlin, I (1969). *Four Essays on Liberty,* Oxford University Press, Oxford and New York.

Bettoni, C and Gibbons, J (1988). 'Linguistic purism and language shift: A guise-voiced study of the Italian community in Sydney', *International Journal of the Sociology of Language*, vol. 72: 37-50.

Bettoni, C and Rubino, A (1996). *Emigrazione e compartamento linguistico. Un' indagine sul trilinguismo dei siciliani e dei veneti in Australia*, Congedo.

Betts, K (1999). *The Great Divide: Immigration Politics in Australia*, Duffy and Snellgrove, Sydney.

Birrell, R, Hawthorne, L and Richardson, S (2006). *Evaluation of the General Skilled Migration Categories*, AGPS, Canberra.

Blainey, G (1984). *All for Australia*, Methuen Haynes, North Ryde.

Blainey, G (1993). 'A Critique of Indo-Chinese in Australia: The Issues of Unemployment and Residential Concentration', *BIPR Bulletin*: 9, July: 42-45.

Blainey, G (1994). 'Melting Pot on the Boil', *The Bulletin,* 30 August: 22-27.

Borrie, W D (1954). *Italians and Germans in Australia: a Study of Assimilation,* F W Cheshire, Melbourne.

Bouchard, G and Taylor, C (2008). *Building the Future. A Time for Reconciliation. Abridged Report.* Commission de consultation sur les practique l'accommodement reliées aux differences culturelles, Montréal.

Bourne, R (1916). 'Trans-National America', *Atlantic Monthly*, vol. 118: 86-97.

Brotherhood of St Laurence (1971). *Two Worlds: School and the Migrant Family,* Stockland Holdings, Melbourne.

Brubaker, R (2001). 'The return of assimilation? Changing perspectives on immigration and its sequels in France, Germany, and the United States', *Ethnic and Racial Studies*, vol. 24, 4: 531-548.

Bujalka, H (2006). A Quantitative Assessment of the Development of Fluency in English/Italian and Italian/English. Unpublished Thesis, University of Western Australia, School of Psychology.

Burnley, I H (1989). 'Settlement Dimensions of the Viet Nam-born Population in Sydney', *Australian GeographicalStudies*, 27, 2: 129-154.

Burnley, I H (1996). *Atlas of the Australian People-1991 Census of New South Wales,* AGPS, Canberra.

Burnley, I H (1999). 'Levels of Immigrant Residential Concentration in Sydney and their Relationship with Disadvantage, *Urban Studies,* 36, 8: 1295-1315.

Burnley, I H (2004). Migration Processes and Geographies of Population Diversity in Sydney, Australia: A 2001 Census Evaluation. Presentation to Conference of New Zealand Geographical Society, Auckland.

Burrow, J W (1988). *Whigs and Liberals: Continuity and Change in English Political Thought,* Clarendon Press, Oxford.

Butcher, M and Thomas, M (2006). 'Ingenious: Emerging hybrid youth cultures in western Sydney', in P Nilan and C Feixa (eds), *Global Youth? Hybrid identities, plural worlds*, Routledge, London: 53-71.

Butcher, M and Thomas, M (eds) (2003). *Ingenious: Emerging youth cultures in urban Australia*, Pluto Press, Melbourne.

Cahill, D, Bouma, G, Dellal, H and Leahy, M (2004). *Religion, Cultural Diversity and Safeguarding Australia*, Australian Multicultural Foundation, Melbourne.

Canovan, M (1996). *Nationhood and Political Theory,* Edward Elgar, Cheltenham.

Castles, S (2001). 'Multiculturalism in Australia', in J Jupp (ed), *The Australian People: An Encyclopedia of the Nation, Its People and Their Origins*, Cambridge University Press, Cambridge.

Castles, S, Kalantzis, M, Cope, B and Morrissey, M (1992). *Mistaken Identity: Multiculturalism and the Demise of Nationalism in Australia,* Pluto Press, Sydney.

Chomsky, N (1965). *Aspects of the Theory of Syntax*, MIT Press, Cambridge (Mass.).

Clark, J L D and Clifford, R (1988). 'The PSI/ILR/ACTFL proficiency scales and testing techniques: Development, current status and needed research'. *Studies in Second Language Acquisition*, 10: 129-147.

Clyne, M (1970). 'Migrant English in Australia', in W S Ransom (ed), *English Transported,* ANU, Canberra.

Clyne, M (1977). ''Nieuw-Hollands' or Double-Dutch?' *Dutch Studies*, vol. 1: 1-30.

Clyne, M (1991). *Community Languages: The Australian Experience,* Cambridge University Press, Cambridge.

Clyne, M (2003). *Dynamics of Language Contact*, Cambridge University Press, Cambridge.

Clyne, M (2005). 'The use of exclusionary language to manipulate opinion: John Howard, asylum seekers and the re-emergence of political incorrectness in Australia'. *Journal of Language and Politics*, vol. 4.

Clyne, M (2006). *Tiles in a multicultural mosaic*, Pacific Linguistics, Melbourne.

Clyne, M, Eisikovits, E and Tollfree, L (2002). 'Ethnolects as in-group markers', in A Duszak (ed), *Us and Others*, Benjamin, Amsterdam: 133-157.

Clyne, M, Eisikovits E and Tollfree, L (2004). 'Ethnic varieties of English', in *English in Australia.*

Clyne, M and Fernandez, S (2007). *Community Language Learning in Australia,* Springer, Berlin.

Clyne, M, Fernandez, S, Chen, I and Summo-O'Connell, R (1997). *Background Speakers,* Language Australia, Canberra.

Clyne, M, Grey, F and Kipp, S (2004). 'Matching policy implementation with demography', *Language Policy*, vol. 3: 241-270.

Clyne, M, Hajek, J and Kipp, S (2008). 'Tale of two multilingual cities in a multilingual continent', *People and Place*, vol. 6, 3: 1-8.

Clyne, M and Kipp, S (1995). 'The extent of community language maintenance in Australia', *People and Place*, vol. 3, no. 4: 4-8.

Clyne, M and Kipp, S (1997). *Pluricentric Languages in an Immigrant Context,* Mouton de Gruyter, Berlin: 463.

Clyne, M and Kipp, S (1999). *Pluricentric Languages in an Immigrant Context: Spanish, Arabic and Chinese*, Mouton de Gruyter, Berlin.

Clyne, M and Kipp, S (2006). *Tiles in a Multilingual Mosaic: Macedonian, Somali and Filipino in Melbourne*, Pacific Linguistics, Canberra.

Collins, J, Noble, G, Poynting, S and Tabar, P (2000). *Kebabs, Kids, Cops and Crime: Youth, Ethnicity and Crime*, Pluto Press, Annandale.

Commonwealth of Australia (1999). *A New Agenda for Multicultural Australia*, AGPS, Canberra.

Commonwealth of Australia (2003). *Multicultural Australia: United in Diversity*, AGPS, Canberra.

Dahl, R A (1967). *Pluralist democracy in the United States: Conflict and consent*, Rand McNally, Chicago.

Davidson, A (1997). *From Subject to Citizen,* Cambridge University Press, Melbourne.

Dawkins, J (1991). *Australia's Language: The Australian Language and Literacy Policy*, AGPS, Canberra.

de Bot, K and Clyne, M (1989). 'Language reversion revisited', *Studies in Second Language Acquisition*, vol. 9: 167-177.

de Bot, K and Clyne, M (1994). 'A 16-Year Longitudinal Study of Language Attrition in Dutch Immigrants in Australia', *Journal of Multilingual and Multicultural Development*, vol. 15, 1: 17-28.

Deen, H (2008). *The Jihad Seminar,* University of Western Australia Press, Perth.

Department of Education, Employment and Workplace Relations (2010). *National Asian Languages and Studies in Schools Program – Overview*, DEEWR, Canberra.

Department of Immigration and Citizenship (2008). *Community Projects* 2007-2008, http://www.immi.gov.au/media/publications/multicultural/pdf_doc/Community.

Department of Immigration and Citizenship (2009). *Immigration Update: July to December 2008*, Belconnen, ACT.

Department of Immigration and Citizenship (2009a). 'Community Information Summary: Hong Kong-born Community,' http://www.immi.gov.au/media/publications/statistics/comm-summ/summary.htm.

Department of Immigration and Citizenship (2009b). 'Community Information Summary: Malaysia-born Community,' http://www.immi.gov.au/media/publications/statistics/comm-summ/summary.htm.

Department of Immigration and Multicultural Affairs (2006). *The Evolution of Australia's Multicultural Policies, Fact Sheet No. 6.*

Department of Immigration and Multicultural Affairs. *Population Flows: Immigration Aspects*, various issues, AGPS, Canberra.

Drachsler, J (1920). *Democracy and Assimilation: The Blending of Immigrant Heritages in America*, the Macmillan Company, New York.

Dryzek, J, Honig, B and Phillips, A (eds) (2006). *The Oxford Handbook of Political Theory*, Oxford University Press, Oxford.

Dunn, K (2003). 'Racism in Australia: Findings of a survey on racist attitudes and experiences of racism', paper presented to conferences at the University of Sydney and Victoria University of Wellington, New Zealand, viewed 8 April, 2009, http://www.uws.edu.au/social_sciences/soss/research/challenging_racism/ publications.

Dunn, K (2005). 'A paradigm of trans-nationalism for migration studies', *New Zealand Population Review*, vol. 31, 2: 15-31.

Dunn, K M, Forrest, J, Burnley, I and McDonald, A (2004). 'Constructing racism in Australia', *Australian Journal of Social Issues*, vol. 39, 4: 409-430.

Dworkin, R (1985). *A Matter of Principle*, Harvard University Press, Cambridge, Mass.

Easteal, P (2009). *Voices of the Survivors*, Spinifex Press, Melbourne.

Ethnic Communities Council of Victoria (2008). Media Release, 5 February 2008, *Monash University Study on Migration not representative of Victoria*, viewed 8 April, 2009, http://eccv.org.au/doc/MEDIARELEASE08.pdf.

European Commission (2005). *Communication from the Commission to the Council, the European Parliament, the European Economic and Social Committee and the Committee of the Regions: A common agenda for integration-framework for the integration of third-country nationals in the European Union.*

Ewart, J (2009). *Haneef: A Question of Character,* Halstead Press, Canberra.

Fergusson, D (2004). *Church, State and Civil Society,* Cambridge University Press, Melbourne.

Fishman, J A (1968). *Readings in the Sociology of Language,* Mouton, The Hague.

FitzGerald, S (chair) (1988). *Immigration: A Commitment to Australia,* AGPS, Canberra.

Forrest, J and Dunn, K M (2007). 'Constructing racism in Sydney, Australia's largest EthniCity', *Urban Studies*, vol. 44, 4: 699-721.

Galbally, F (chair) (1978). *Migrant Services and Programs,* AGPS, Canberra.

Galligan, B and Roberts, W (2004). *Australian Citizenship*, Melbourne University Press, Melbourne.

Galligan, B and Roberts, W (2008). 'Multiculturalism, national identity and pluralist democracy: The Australian variant', in G B Levey (ed), *Political Theory and Australian Multiculturalism*, Berghahn Books, New York and Oxford.

Gilbert, H, Khoo, T and Lo, J (eds) (2000). *Diaspora: Negotiating Asian-Australia*, University of Queensland Press, St Lucia.

Giorgas, D and Jones, F L (2002). 'Intermarriage patterns and social cohesion among first, second and later generation Australians', *Journal of Population Research*, vol. 19, 1: 47-64.

Glazer, N and Moynihan, D P (1963). *Beyond the Melting Pot: The Negroes, Puerto Ricans, Jews, Italians, and Irish of New York City*, MIT Press and Harvard University Press, Cambridge, Mass.

Goldman-Eisler, F (1968). *Psycholinguistics: Experiments in spontaneous speech,* Academic Press, New York.

Goot, M (1999). 'Migrant numbers, Asian immigration and multiculturalism: Trends in the polls, 1943-1998', Australian Multiculturalism for a New Century: Towards inclusiveness, statistical appendix part 2, National Multicultural Advisory Council, Canberra, viewed 8 April, 2009, http://www.immi.gov.au/media/publications/multicultural/nmac/statistics.pdf.

Goot, M and Watson, I (2005). 'Immigration, multiculturalism and national identity', in S Wilson, G Meagher, R Gibson, D Denemark and M Western (eds) Australian Social Attitudes. The First Report, UNSW Press, Sydney.

Gordon, M M (1964). Assimilation in American Life: The Role of Race, Religion, and National Origins, Oxford University Press, New York.

Government of South Australia (2004a). Prosperity through People: a Population Policy for South Australia, Government of South Australia, Adelaide.

Government of South Australia (2004b). South Australia's Strategic Plan, Government of South Australia, Adelaide.

Government of Victoria (2004). Beyond Five Million: The Victorian Government's Population Policy, State of Victoria, Melbourne.

Green, T H (1911). Lectures on the Principles of Political Obligation, Longmans, London and New York.

Guerra, C and White, R (eds) (1995). Ethnic Minority Youth in Australia: Challenges and Myths, National Clearing House for Youth Studies, Hobart.

Gunnell, J G (2004). Imagining the American Polity: Political Science and the Discourses of Democracy, Pennsylvania State University Press, University Park (USA).

Hage, G (1998). White Nation: Fantasies of White Supremacy in a Multicultural Society, Pluto Press, Sydney.

Hammar, T (1993). 'The 'Sweden-wide Strategy' of Refugee Dispersal' In R Black and V Robinson (eds), Geographyand Refugees, Belhaven, London.

Handlin, O (1951). The Uprooted: The Epic Story of the Great Migrations that Made the American People, Grosset and Dunlap, New York.

Harding, G and Webster, E (2002). The Working Holiday Maker Scheme and the Australian Labour Market, Melbourne Institute of Applied Economic and Social Research, University of Melbourne.

Hassan, R (2008). Inside Muslim Minds, Melbourne University Press, Melbourne.

Hawthorne, L (2005). 'Picking Winners': The Recent Transformation of Australia's Skilled Migration Policy, *International Migration Review*, XXXIX, 3: 663-696.

Healy, E and Birrell, B (2003). 'Metropolis Divided: The Political Dynamic of Spatial Inequality and Migrant Settlement in Sydney', *People and Place*, 11,2: 65-87.

Heath, A and Cheung, S Y (eds) (2007). *Unequal Chances: Ethnic minorities in western labour markets*, Oxford University Press for the British Academy, Oxford.

Herberg, W (1955). *Protestant–Catholic–Jew: An Essay in American Religious Sociology*, Doubleday, Garden City, NY.

Higham, J (1955). *Strangers in the Land: Patterns of American Nativism, 1860-1925*, Rutgers University Press, New Brunswick, NJ.

Hirst, J (2001). 'Aborigines and migrants: Diversity and unity in multicultural Australia', *Australian Book Review* No. 228: 30–35.

Hirst, P (ed) (1989). *The Pluralist Theory of the State: Selected Writings of G D H Cole, J N Figgis and H J Laski*, Routledge, London.

Hogan, M (1987). *The Sectarian Strand*, Penguin, Ringwood, Victoria.

Horne, D (1994). *The Public Culture: An argument with the future*, Pluto Press, London

Horne, D (1997). *The Avenue of the Fair Go: A Group Tour of Australian Political Thought*, Harper Collins, Pymble, NSW.

Hugo, G J (1993). The Changing Spatial Distribution of Major Ethnic Groups in Australia 1961-1986. (revised version of a report prepared for the Office of Multicultural Affairs, April.

Hugo, G J (1994). 'The Turnaround in Australia. Some observations from the 1991 Census', *Australian Geographer,* 25, 1: 1-17.

Hugo, G J (1999a). A New Paradigm of International Migration in Australia', *New Zealand Population Review*, 25, 1-2: 1-39.

Hugo, G J (1999b). *Regional Development through Immigration? The Reality behind the Rhetoric*, Department of the Parliamentary Library Research Paper No.9 1999-2000, Department of the Parliamentary Library, Canberra.

Hugo, G J (2001). International Migration and Agricultural Labour in Australia. Paper presented at Changing Face Workshop, Imperial Valley, California, 16-18 January.

Hugo, G J (2002). From Compassion to Compliance? Trends in Refugee and Humanitarian Migration in Australia, *GeoJournal*, 56: 27-37.

Hugo, G J (2003). Changing Patterns of Population Distribution. In S E Khoo and P McDonald (eds), *The Transformation of Australia's Population 1970-2030*, University of New South Wales Press, Sydney.

Hugo, G J (2004). *Australia's most recent immigrants*, Australian Census Analytic Program, Cat. No. 2053.0, Australian Bureau of Statistics, Canberra.

Hugo, G J (2005). Migration Policies in Australia and their Impact on Development in Countries of Origin, in

International Migration and the Millenium Development Goals, UNFPA Expert Group Meeting, United Nations Population Fund, New York.

Hugo, G J (2007). 'Space, Place, Population and Census Analysis in Australia'. *Australian Geographer*. 38, 3: 335-357.

Hugo, G J (2008a). 'Immigrant Settlement Outside of Australia's Capital Cities', in *Population, Space and Place*, 14, 6: 553-571.

Hugo, G J (2008b). 'Sydney: The Globalization of an Established Immigrant Gateway', in M Price and L Benton-Short (eds), *Migrants in the Metropolis - the Rise of Immigrants Gateway Cities*, Syracuse University Press: 68-96.

Hugo, G J and Moren, R (2008). Immigrant Settlement in non Metropolitan Areas of OECD Countries; Editorial Introduction, *Population, Space and Place*, 14, 6: 473-477.

Huntington, S P (1996). *The Clash of Civilizations and the Remaking of World Order*, Simon and Schuster, New York.

Industry Commission (1995). *Charitable Organisations in Australia Report No.45*, Industry Commission, Canberra.

Inglis, C (2000). 'The 'rediscovery' of ethnicity: Theorising and analysis at the end of the twentieth century', in S Quah and A Sales (eds), *The International Handbook of Sociology*, Sage, London: 151-170.

Inglis, C (2007). 'Transnationalism in an uncertain environment: Relationship between migration, policy and theory', *IJMS: International Journal on Multicultural Societies*, vol. 9, 2: 185-204.

Inglis, C (2008). *The Integration of the Australian Second Generation*, paper presented at the TIES Academic Conference, http://www.tiesproject.eu/component/option,com_docman/task,cat_view/gid,131/Itemid, 142/.

Inglis, C and Model, S (2007). 'Diversity and mobility in Australia', in A Heath and SY Cheung (eds), *Unequal Chances: Ethnic minorities in western labour markets*, Oxford University Press for the British Academy, Oxford.

Interim Committee for the Australian Schools Commission (1973). *Schools in Australia: Report of the Interim Committee for the Australian Schools Commission, May 1973, [the Karmel Report]*, AGPS, Canberra.

Ip, D F, Inglis, C and Wu, C T (1997). 'Concepts of citizenship and identity among recent Asian immigrants in Australia', *Asian and Pacific Migration Journal*, vol. 6, 3-4: 363-384.

Isaacs, E (1975). *Greek Children in Sydney*, Australian Department of Education. Inquiry into Schools of High Migrant Density, Canberra.

Jakubowicz, A (1985). *Education and Ethnic Minorities - Issues of Participation and Equity*, National Advisory and Coordinating Committee on Multicultural Education, Canberra.

Jayasuriya, L (1983). 'Multiculturalism: Fact, policy or rhetoric?', *The Nation is People*, The Extension Service, The University of Western Australia, Nedlands.

Jayasuriya, L (2005). 'Australian multiculturalism and the politics of a new pluralism', *Dialogue*, vol. 24, 1: 75–84.

Jones, F L (1994). 'Multiculturalism and ethnic intermarriage: Melting pot or nation of tribes?', paper presented at the Seventh National Conference of the Australian Population Association, Canberra, 22 September.

Jones, F L and Luijkx, R (1996). 'Postwar patterns of intermarriage in Australia: The Mediterranean experience', *European Sociological Review*, vol. 12, 1: 67-86.

Jupp, J (1966). *Arrivals and Departures*, Cheshire-Lansdowne, Melbourne.

Jupp, J (1993). 'Ethnic Concentrations: A Reply to Bob Birrell, *People and Place*, 4, 4: 51-52.

Jupp, J (1998). *Immigration*, Oxford University Press, Sydney.

Jupp, J (2002). *From White Australia to Woomera*, Cambridge University Press, Melbourne.

Jupp, J (2004). *How Well Does Australian Democracy Serve Immigrant Australians?* Democratic Audit of Australia, Canberra.

Jupp, J (ed) (2009a). *The Encyclopedia of Religion in Australia*, Cambridge University Press, Melbourne.

Jupp, J (2009b). 'Immigration and Ethnicity', *Australian Cultural History,* vol.27, 2: 157-166.

Jupp, J (2011a). 'Politics, public policy and multiculturalism' (This vol.)

Jupp, J (2011b). 'Religion and integration in a multifaith society' (This vol.)

Jupp, J, Nieuwenhuysen, J and Dawson, E (eds) (2007). *Social Cohesion in Australia*, Cambridge University Press, Melbourne.

Kalantzis, M (2000). 'Multicultural citizenship, in W Hudson & J Kane (eds), *Rethinking Australian Citizenship*, Cambridge University Press, Cambridge.

Kallen, H M (1924). *Democracy and Culture in the United States*, Boni and Liveright, New York.

Kalmijn, M and Flap, H (2001). 'Assortative Meeting and Mating: Unintended Consequences of Organized Settings for Partner Choices.' *Social Forces,* 79: 1289-1312.

Katsikis, M (1993). *Language attitudes, ethnicity and language maintenance: The case of second generation Greek-Australians*, BA (Hons) thesis, Dept of Linguistics, Monash University.

Katsikis, M (1997). *The generation gap: Insights into the language and cultural maintenance of third generation Greek-Australians.* MA thesis, Dept of Linguistics, Monash University.

Kaya, A (2009). *Islam, Migration and Integration: The Age of Securitization*, Palgrave Macmillan, Basingstoke.

Khoo, S E (1991). 'Consistency of ancestry reporting between parents and children in the 1986 census', *Journal of the Australian PopulationAssociation*, vol. 8, 2: 129-139.

Khoo, S E (1995). 'Language maintenance amongst the second generation', *People and Place*, vol. 3, 4: 9-12.

Khoo, S E (2001). 'The context of spouse migration to Australia', *International Migration*, vol. 39, 1: 111-132.

Khoo, S E (2004). 'Intermarriage in Australia: Patterns by ancestry, gender and generation', *People and Place*, vol. 12, 2: 35-44.

Khoo, S E (2009). 'Migrant youth and social connectedness', in F Mansouri (ed), *Youth identity and migration: Culture, values and social connectedness*, Common Ground Publishing, Melbourne: 165-177.

Khoo, S E (2011) 'Intermarriage, integration and multiculturalism: A demographic perspective', (This vol.)

Khoo, S E, Birrell, B and Heard, G (2009). 'Intermarriage by birthplace and ancestry in Australia', *People and Place*, vol. 17, 1: 15-27.

Khoo, S E and Lucas, D (2004). *Australians' Ancestries, 2001. Australian Census Analytic Program*, Australian Bureau of Statistics, Canberra.

Khoo, S E and Temple, J (2008). 'Immigrants' social and community participation in Australia', Paper presented at the Australian Population Association Biennial National Conference, Alice Springs, 2008.

Khoo, S E, Voigt-Graf, C, Hugo, G and McDonald, P (2003). 'Temporary Skilled Migration to Australia: The 457 Visa Sub-Class, *People and Place,* 11, 4: 27-40.

Kirsner, K, Dunn, J and Hird, K (2005). Language Production: A complex dynamic system with a chronometric footprint. *Proceedings of the 7th International Conference on Cognitive Systems,* New Delhi (India).

Kirsner, K, Dunn, J, Hird, K and Hennesy, N (2003). Temporal co-ordination; the lynch-pin of language production, in Palethorpe, S and Tabian, M (eds), *Proceedings of the 6th International Seminar on SpeechProductio*n, Macquarie University, CD-ROM: 19-24.

Kirsner, K, Dunn, J, Hird, K, Parkin, T and Clark, C (2002). 'Time for a Pause...', 9th International Conference on Speech Science, Melbourne

Knopfelmacher, F (1982). 'The case against multi-culturalism', in R Manne (ed), *The New Conservatism in Australia*, Oxford University Press, Oxford.

Koleth, E (2010). 'Multiculturalism: A review of Australian policy statements and recent debates in Australia and Overseas', Canberra, Parliamentary Library Research Paper No.6.

Kukathas, C (1992). 'Are there any cultural rights?', *Political Theory*, vol. 20, 1: 105–39.

Kukathas, C (1993a). 'The idea of a multicultural society', in C Kukathas (ed), *Multicultural Citizens: The Philosophy and Politics of Identity*, Centre for Independent Studies, Sydney.

Kukathas, C (1993b). 'Multiculturalism and the idea of an Australian identity', in C Kukathas (ed), *Multicultural Citizens: The Philosophy and Politics of Identity*, Centre for Independent Studies, Sydney.

Kukathas, C (2003). *The Liberal Archipelago: A Theory of Diversity and Freedom*, Clarendon Press, Oxford.

Kunz, E F (1988). *Displaced Persons: Calwell's New Australians*, Australian National University Press, Sydney.

Kymlicka, W (1989). *Liberalism, Community, and Culture*, Clarendon Press, Oxford.

Kymlicka, W (1995). *Multicultural Citizenship: A Liberal Theory of Minority Rights*, Clarendon Press, Oxford.

Kymlicka, W (2001). 'Western political theory and ethnic relations in Eastern Europe', in W Kymlicka and M Opalski (eds), *Can Liberal Pluralism be Exported?*, Oxford University Press, Oxford.

Kymlicka, W (2005). *Multicultural Odysseys; Navigating the new international politics of diversity*, Oxford University Press

Latham, M (2004). *A Big Country: Australia's National Identity*, ALP press release, 20 April.

Le, H V (2009). 'Multicultural South Australia', *Multicultural SA Newsletter*, February 2009, viewed 8 April, 2009, http://www.multicultural.sa.gov.au/documents/MulticulturalSANewsletterFeb2009.pdf.

Leach, M, Stokes, G, and Ward, I (2000). *The Rise and Fall of One Nation*, University of Queensland Press, St Lucia (Qld).

Lennon, P (1990). Investigating Fluency in EFL: A quantitative approach, *Language Learning*, 40, 387-417.

Levey, G B (2001). 'The political theories of Australian multiculturalism', *The University of New South Wales Law Journal*, vol. 24, 3: 869–81.

Levey, G B (2005). 'National-cultural autonomy and liberal nationalism', in E Nimni (ed), *National-Cultural Autonomy and Its Contemporary Critics*, Routledge, London.

Levey, G B (2008). 'Multicultural political thought in Australian perspective', in G B Levey (ed), *Political Theory and Australian Multiculturalism*, Berghahn Books, New York and Oxford.

Levey, G B (2010). 'Liberal multiculturalism', in D Ivison (ed), *The Ashgate Research Companion to Multiculturalism*, Ashgate, Aldershot.

Levey, G B (2011). 'Multicultural Integration in Political Theory', (This vol.)

Lo Bianco, J (1987). *National Policy on Languages*, AGPS, Canberra.

Lo Bianco, J (2001). 'Language Policy and Education in Australia', in J Lo Bianco amd R Wickert (eds), *Australian policy activism in language and literacy*, Language Australia, Canberra: 11-44.

Lohrey, A (2006). Voting for Jesus, *Quarterly Essay*, Melbourne.

Lopez, M (2000). *The Origins of Multiculturalism in Australian Politics 1945–75*, Melbourne University Press, Melbourne.

Lounsbury, F G (1954). Transitional probability, linguistic structures, in C Osgood and T A Sebeock (eds), *Psycholinguistics: A survey of theory and research problems*, Waverley Press, Baltimore (MD): 93-101.

Maddox, M (2005). *God Under Howard; the Rise of the Religious Right in Australian Politics*, Allen and Unwin, Sydney.

Magiste, E (1979). The competing language systems of the multilingual: A developmental study of decoding and encoding processes. *Journal of Verbal Learning and Verbal Behaviour*, 18, 1: 78-89.

Mares, P (2001). *Borderline*, University of NSW Press, Sydney.

Markus, A (1993). `Racism and the recession', *People and Place*, vol. 1, 2: 35-39.

Markus, A (1999). 'Attitudes towards immigration and national identity: A re-awakening of xenophobia?', *People and Place*, vol. 7, 3: 39-51.

Markus, A (2001). *Race: John Howard and the Remaking of Australia*, Allen and Unwin, Sydney.

Markus, A and Dharmalingham, A (2007). 'Attitudinal divergence in a Melbourne region of high immigrant concentration: A case study', *People and Place*, vol. 15, 4: 38-48.

Markus, A and Dharmalingham, A (2008). *Mapping Social Cohesion*, Institute for the Study of Global Movements, Monash University, viewed 8 April, 2009, http://www.globalmovements.monash.edu.au/.

Markus, A and Kirpitchenko, L (2007). 'Conceptualising social cohesion', in J Jupp, J Nieuwenhuysen and E Dawson (eds), *Social Cohesion in Australia*, Cambridge University Press, Melbourne: 21-32.

Markus, A, Jupp, J and McDonald, P (2009). *Australia's Immigration Revolution*, Allen and Unwin, Sydney.

Martin, J (1965). *Refugee Settlers*, ANU Press, Canberra.

Martin, J (1978). *The Migrant Presence*, Allen and Unwin, Sydney.

Martin, J (1981). *The Ethnic Dimension: Papers on Ethnicity and Pluralism*, by Jean Martin, (ed) S Encel, George Allen and Unwin, Sydney.

McAllister, I and Moore, R (1989). *Ethnic Prejudice in Australian Society: Patterns, intensity and explanations*, Office of Multicultural Affairs, Canberra.

McLachlan, G and Peel, D (2000). *Finite Mixture Models*, Wiley, New York.

Mill, J S (1972) [1859]. *Utilitarianism, On Liberty, and Considerations on Representative Government*, H B Acton (ed), J M Dent and Sons, London.

Miller, D (1995). *On Nationality,* Clarendon Press, Oxford.

Miller, D, Coleman, J, Connolly, W, Ryan, A (eds) (1991). *Blackwell Encyclopedia of Political Thought*, Basil Blackwell, Oxford.

Mistilis, N (1988). 'Greek community life in Sydney', in J Jupp (ed) *Encyclopedia of the Australian People*, Angus and Robertson, Sydney.

Mol, H (1985). *The Faith of Australians*, George Allen and Unwin, Sydney.

Moore, H (2005). *Identifying 'The Target Population': A genealogy of policy making for English as a Second Language (ESL) in Australian schools (1947-1997)*, PhD thesis, Ontario Institute for Studies in Education, University of Toronto.

Mulcock, J (2002). *Searching for our Indigenous Selves: Belonging and Spirituality in Anglo-Celtic Australia*. PhD Thesis, University of Western Australia.

National Multicultural Advisory Council (1999). *Australian Multiculturalism for a New Century: Towards Inclusiveness*, AGPS, Canberra.

Nicholas, L E and Brookshire, R H (1993). A system for quantifying the informativeness and efficiency of the connected speech of adults with aphasia. *Journal of Speech and Hearing Research*, 36: 338-350.

Nilan, P and Feixa, C (eds) (2006). *Global Youth? Hybrid identities, plural worlds*, Routledge, London.

Noble, G (2007). 'Respect and respectability amongst second-generation Arab and Muslim Australian men', *Journal of Intercultural Studies*, vol. 28: 331-344.

Noble, G, Poynting, S and Tabar, P (1999a). 'Lebanese youth and social identity', in R White (ed) *Australian Youth Subcultures: On the margins and in the mainstream*, Australian Clearing House for Youth Studies, Hobart: 130-137.

Noble, G, Poynting, S and Tabar, P (1999b). 'Youth, ethnicity and the mapping of identities: Strategic essentialism and strategic hybridity among male Arabic-speaking youth in south-western Sydney, *Communal/Plural*, vol. 7, 1: 29-44.

O'Farrell, P (1992). *The Catholic Church and the Community*, University of New South Wales Press, Sydney.

Office of Multicultural Affairs (1989). *National Agenda for a Multicultural Australia*, AGPS, Canberra.

Orton, J (2008). *Chinese language education in Australian schools*, University of Melbourne, Victoria.

Ozolins, U (1993). *The Politics of Language in Australia*, Cambridge University Press, Cambridge.

Parekh, Lord B (2006). *Rethinking Multiculturalism*, Palgrave Macmillan, Basingstoke (UK).

Pauwels, A (1986). *Dialects and Language Maintenance,* Foris, Dordrecht.

Pauwels, A (1990). 'Dutch in Australia: Perception of and attitudes towards transference and other language contact phenomena', in S Romaine (ed), *Language in Australia*, Cambridge University Press, Cambridge: 228-240.

Pauwels, A (1995). 'Linguistic practices and language maintenance among bilingual women and men in Australia', *Nordlyn*, vol. 11: 21-50.

Penny, J and Khoo, S E (1996). *Intermarriage: A Study of Migration and Integration*, AGPS, Canberra.

Pe-Pua, R (1999). 'Youth and ethnicity: Images and constructions', in R White (ed), *Australian Youth Subcultures: On the margins and in the mainstream*, Australian Clearing House for Youth Studies, Hobart: 130-137.

Pike, D (1957). *Paradise of Dissent*, Melbourne University Press, Melbourne.

Poole, M E (1981). 'Educational opportunities for minority groups: Australian research reviewed', in J Megarry (ed), *Education of Minorities: World Yearbook of Education*, Kogan Page, London.

Plane, D A and Rogerson, P A (1994). *The Geographical Analysis of Population: With Applications to Planning and Business*, John Wiley, New York.

Poulsen, M, Johnston, R and Forrest, J (2002). 'Is Sydney a Divided City Ethnically?', *Australian GeographicalReview*, 41, 3: 356-377.

Poulsen, M, Johnston, R and Forrest, J (2004). 'Plural Cities and Ethnic Enclaves: Introducing a Measurement Procedure for Comparative Study', *International Journal of Urban and Regional Research*, 2: 229-243.

Portes, A and Rumbaut, R (2001). *Legacies: The Story of the Immigrant Second Generation*, University of California Press, Berkeley.

Poynting, S (2000). 'Ethnicising criminality and criminalising ethnicity', in J Collins and S Poynting (eds), *The Other Sydney: Communities, Identities and Inequalities in Western Sydney*, Common Ground Publishing, Altona: 63-78.

Poynting, S and Morgan, G (eds) (2007). *Outrageous! Moral panics in Australia*, Australian Clearing House for Youth Studies Publishing, Hobart.

Poynting, S, Noble, G and Tabar, P (1998). "If anyone called me a wog, they wouldn't be speaking to me alone': protest masculinity and Lebanese youth in Western Sydney', *Journal of Interdisciplinary Gender Studies*, vol. 3, 2: 76-94.

Poynting, S, Noble, G, Taylor, C and Collins, J (2004). *Bin Laden in the suburbs: Criminalising the Arab other*, Institute of Criminology, Sydney.

Price, C A (1963). *Southern Europeans in Australia*, Oxford University Press, Melbourne.

Price, C A (1981). *Australian Immigration: A Digest*, ANU, Canberra.

Price, C A (1982). *The Fertility and Marriage Patterns of Australia's Ethnic Groups*, Department of Demography, ANU, Canberra.

Price, C A (1989). *Ethnic Groups in Australia*, Office of Multicultural Affairs, Canberra.

Price, C A (1993). 'Ethnic intermixture in Australia', *People and Place*, vol. 1, 1: 6-8.

Price, C A (1994). 'Ethnic intermixture in Australia,' *People and Place*, vol. 2, 4: 8-11.

Price, C A and Zubrzycki, J (1962a). 'The use of intermarriage statistics as an index of assimilation', *Population Studies*, vol. 16, 1: 58-69.

Price, C A and Zubrzycki, J (1962b). 'Intermarriage patterns in Australia', *Population Studies*, vol. 16, 2: 123-133.

Quinting, G (1971). *Hesitation phenomena in adult aphasic and normal speech*, Mouton, The Hague.

Raikovski, P (1987). *In the Tracks of the Camel Men*, Angus and Robertson, Sydney.

Rawls, J (1971). *A Theory of Justice*, Harvard University Press, Cambridge, Mass.

Read, P (2000). *Belonging: Australians, Place and Aboriginal Ownership*, Cambridge University Press, Cambridge.

Reitz, J and Banerjee, R (2007). 'Racial inequality, social cohesion, and policy issues in Canada', in K Banting, T J Courchene and F L Seidle (eds), *Belonging? Diversity, Recognition and Shared Citizenship in Canada*, Institute for Research on Public Policy, Montreal: 489-545.

Richardson, A (1974). *British Immigrants and Australia*, ANU Press, Canberra.

Roberts, T S and McInnerney, J M (2007). Seven problems of online group learning (and their solutions). *Educational Technology and Society*, 10, 4: 257-268.

Robinson, V (1993). 'North and South: Resettling Vietnamese Refugees in Australia and the UK', in Black, R and Robinson, V (eds), *Geography and Refugees*, Belhaven, London.

Robinson, V and Hale, S (1989). *The Geography of Vietnamese Secondary Migration in the UK*, Warwick University Centre for Research in Ethnic Relations, Coventry (UK).

Sandel, M J (1982). *Liberalism and the Limits of Justice*, University of Cambridge Press, Cambridge.

Schattschneider, E E (1960). *The Semi-Sovereign People*, Holt, Rinehart and Winston, New York.

Schmidt, R (1992). Psychological mechanisms underlying second language fluency. *Studies inSecond LanguageAcquisition*, 14: 357-385.

Seebus, I (2008). *Dinkum Dutch - Aussies language and identity among elderly Dutch-Australians*, PhD thesis, University of Melbourne.

Senate Standing Committee on Employment, Workforce Relations and Workforce Participation (2006). *Perspectives on theFuture of the Harvest Labour Force*, Department of the Senate, Canberra.

Sestito, R (1982). *The Politics of Multiculturalism*, Centre for Independent Studies, Sydney.

Sherington, G (1995). 'Youth policy and ethnic youth: A history', in C Guerra and R White (eds), *Ethnic Minority Youth in Australia: Challenges and myths*, National Clearinghouse for Youth Studies, Hobart: 25-34.

Slaughter, Y (2007). *The study of Asian languages in two Australian states: Considerations for language-in-education policy and planning*, PhD thesis, University of Melbourne.

Smolicz, J J (1981). 'Core values and ethnic identity', *Ethnic and Racial Studies*, vol. 4: 75-90.

Smolicz, J J (2001). in M Secombe (ed) *Education and Culture*, J Nicholas, Melbourne.

Smolicz, J J and Secombe, M (1988). 'Types of language activation and evaluation in an ethnically plural society', in U Ammon (ed) *Status and Function of Languages and Language varieties*, De Gruyter, Berlin: 478-511.

Speelman, C and Kirsner, K (2005). *Beyond the learning curve: The construction of mind*, Oxford University Press.

Svensson, F (1979). 'Liberal democracy and group rights: The legacy of individualism and its impact on American tribes', *Political Studies*: 27: 421-39.

Sydney Morning Herald (2006). 'A glue that keeps Australian society together', 16 December.

Tamir, Y (1993). *Liberal Nationalism*, Princeton University Press, Princeton, NJ.

Tamis, A (1986). *The state of Modern Greek as spoken in Victoria*, PhD thesis, University of Melbourne.

Tan, Y, Richardson, S, Lester, L, Bai, T and Sun, L (2009). *Evaluation of Australia's Working Holiday Maker Program*, National Institute of Labour Studies, Flinders University, Adelaide.

Tavan, G (2005). *The Long, Slow Death of White Australia*, Scribe, Melbourne.

Taylor, C (1985). 'Atomism', in *Philosophical Papers*, vol. 2, *Philosophy and the Human Sciences*, Cambridge University Press, Cambridge.

Taylor, C (1992). *Multiculturalismand the 'Politics of Recognition': An Essay*, Amy Gutmann, (ed) Princeton University Press, Princeton, NJ.

Theophanous, A (1995). *Understanding Multiculturalism and Australian Identity*, Elikia Books, Melbourne.

Thomas, W and Collier, V (1997). *School effectiveness for language minority students*. NCBE Resource Collection Series Number 9, Washington DC.

Trigger, D (2008,). 'Place, belonging and nativeness in Australia', in F Vanclay, M Higgins and A Blackshaw (eds), *Making Sense of Place*, National Museum of Australia, Canberra.

Truman, D B (1951). *The Governmental Process*, Knopf, New York.

Truman, T (1959). *Catholic Action and Politics,* Georgian House, Melbourne.

Tsokalidou, R (1994). Cracking the code. An insight into code switching and gender in second generation Greek Australians, unpublished PhD thesis, Monash University.

Tsolidis, G (1986). *Educating Voula: A report on non-English-speaking background girls and education*, Ministerial Advisory Committee on Multicultural and Migrant Education, Melbourne.

Tsounis, M P (1974). *Greek Ethnic Schools in Australia,* Australian Immigration Monograph Series No. 1, Department of Demography, Australian National University, Canberra.

Van Dyke, V (1977). 'The individual, the state, and ethnic communities in political theory', *World Politics*, vol. 29: 343-69.

Van Dyke, V (1982). 'Collective entities and moral rights: problems in liberal-democratic thought', *Journal of Politics*, vol. 44: 21-40.

Vertovec, S and Wessendorf, S (eds) (2010). *The Multiculturalism Backlash,* Routledge, London.

Viviani, N, Coughlan, J and Rowland, T (1993). *Indo-Chinese in Australia: The Issues of Unemployment and Residential Concentration*, AGPS, Canberra.

Walzer, M (1980). 'Pluralism: A political perspective', in S A Thernstrom (ed), *The Harvard Encyclopedia of American Ethnic Groups*, Harvard University Press, Cambridge, Mass.

Ward, R (1958). *The Australian Legend*, Oxford University Press, Melbourne.

White, R (1999a). 'Youth gangs', in R White (ed), *Australian Youth Subcultures: On the margins and in the mainstream*, Australian Clearinghouse for Youth Studies, Hobart: 36-46.

White, R (ed) (1999b). *Australian Youth Subcultures: On the margins and in the mainstream*, Australian Clearinghouse for Youth Studies, Hobart.

White, R, Perrone, S, Guerra, C and Lampugnani, R (1999). *Ethnic Youth Gangs in Australia: Do they exist? Overview Report*, Australian Multicultural Foundation, Melbourne.

Whitlam, E G (1985). *The Whitlam Government 1972-1975*, Penguin Books, Ringwood (Vic.)

Wieviorka, M (1998). 'Is multiculturalism the solution?', *Ethnic and Racial Studies*, vol. 21, 5: 880-910.

Windschuttle, K (2004). *The White Australia Policy*, Macleay Press, Sydney.

Windschuttle, K (2005). 'It's not a race war, it's a clash of cultures.' *The Australian*, 16 December.

Wingo, A (2003). *Veil Politics in Liberal Democratic States*, Cambridge University Press, Cambridge.

Winter, J and Pauwels, A (2000). 'Gender and Language Contact Research in the Australian Context', *Journal of Multilingual and Multicultural Development*, vol. 21, 6: 508-522.

Woods, A (2004). *Language and faith in ethnic churches*, Multilingual Matters, Clevedon.

Wright, S (2008). 'Citizenship tests in Europe – editorial introduction', *IJMS: International Journal on Multicultural Societies*, vol 10, 1: 109.

Zangwill, I (1909). *The Melting-Pot: Drama in Four Acts*, Macmillan, New York

Zimmern, A E (1918). *Nationality and Government*, Robert M McBride and Co., New York.

Zubrzycki, J (1996). 'Cynics woo the ethnic vote.' *The Australian*, 15 October.

Index

www.ingramcontent.com/pod-product-compliance
Lightning Source LLC
Chambersburg PA
CBHW061240270326

41927CB00035B/3445